Nigel Cawthorne has written over a hundred books including *A Brief History of Robin Hood*, *A Brief Guide to James Bond* and *A Brief Guide to Sherlock Holmes*.

His writing has appeared in over 150 newspapers, magazines and partworks – from the *Sun* to the *Financial Times*, and from *Flatbush Life* to *The New York Tribune*. He lives in London.

Highlights from the series

A BRIEF GUIDE TO J. R. R. TOLKIEN

The Unauthorized Guide to the Author of *The Hobbit* and *The Lord of the Rings*

NIGEL CAWTHORNE

RUNNING PRESS
PHILADELPHIA · LONDON

ROBINSON

Constable & Robinson Ltd
55–56 Russell Square
London WC1B 4HP
www.constablerobinson.com

First published in the UK by Robinson,
an imprint of Constable & Robinson Ltd, 2012

A copy of the British Library Cataloguing in
Publication data is available from the British Library

UK ISBN 978-1-78033-859-0

13 5 7 9 10 8 6 4 2

First published in the United States in 2011 by Running Press Book Publishers,
A Member of the Perseus Books Group

US ISBN 978-0-7624-4741-1
US Library of Congress Control Number: 2012931368

9 8 7 6 5 4 3 2 1
Digit on the right indicates the number of this printing

Running Press Book Publishers
2300 Chestnut Street
Philadelphia, PA 19103-4371

Visit us on the web!
www.runningpress.com

Typeset by TW Typesetting, Plymouth, Devon

Printed and bound in the UK

CONTENTS

INTRODUCTION: THE MAN AND THE MYTH

The Lord of the Rings was the must-read trilogy of 1960s' counterculture that has now reached a vast new audience through the cinema. But it was written by a middle-aged Oxford don, a veteran of the First World War – very much a pillar of the establishment. An authority on Anglo-Saxon, Middle English and Chaucer, John Ronald Reuel Tolkien was a gentle, blue-eyed man who dressed in tweeds, smoked a pipe, liked to take walks and rode an old bicycle. He could hardly be more different from his readers.

Tolkien did not come from Middle-earth but, rather, Middle England, though he was, in fact, born in South Africa. Returning to England at the age of four, he settled in the Midlands. His mother then died when he was twelve. The ward of a Catholic priest, he went up to Oxford to study Classics, but switched his course to English Language and Literature After graduating with first-class honours, he joined the Lancashire Fusiliers and saw action in the First Battle of the Somme in 1916, an experience that coloured the huge battles that take place in Middle-earth. He developed a secret code to get around military censorship to communicate with his wife. By 1918, most of his friends were dead.

After the war, he went to work at the *Oxford English Dictionary*, researching the history and etymology of words of Germanic origin beginning with the letter W. As Professor of English at Leeds University, he produced *A Middle English Vocabulary* and a definitive edition of *Sir Gawain and the Green Knight* with fellow philologist E. V. Gordon, both works becoming academic standards. He also translated the Middle-English poems *Sir Gawain*, *Pearl* and *Sir Orfeo*. In 1925, he returned to Oxford as Professor of Anglo-Saxon at Pembroke College, where he came to academic prominence for his lecture on the epic poem *Beowulf*, which has been widely reprinted. In 1945, he moved to Merton College to become Professor of English Language and Literature.

He began to write *The Hobbit* in the late 1920s to relieve the boredom of marking exam papers, telling the story to his four children. Fellow don and author C.S. Lewis suggested that he submit it for publication to Allen & Unwin. It was accepted and published in 1937, with the American edition winning the *New York Herald Tribune* prize as best children's book the following year.

In 1938, Tolkien began *The Lord of the Rings* to illustrate a lecture on fairy tales. It took fourteen years to complete and is filled with verbal jokes, strange alphabets, names from the Norse, Anglo-Saxon and Welsh. For its story, it calls on the legend of *The Ring of the Nibelung* and the early Scandinavian classic *The Elder Edda*, among other works of folklore. When *The Lord of the Rings* was published in the fifties, it was damned by the critics. The London *Observer* called it 'sheer escapist literature ... dull, ill-written and whimsical' and expressed the wish that Tolkien's work would soon pass into 'merciful oblivion'.

Tolkien did not see what was wrong with escapism in a world full of factories, bombs and machine-guns. He said: 'Fantasy is escapist, and that is its glory. If a soldier is imprisoned by the enemy, don't we consider it his duty to escape? . . . If we value the freedom of mind and soul, if we're partisans of liberty, then it's our plain duty to escape, and to take as many people with us as we can!'

Other prisoners of reality seized the opportunity. In the United States, *The Lord of the Rings* trilogy in hardback was a Book-of-the-Month Club Selection and the paperback sold a quarter of a million copies in ten months. By the late sixties, fan clubs were sprouting up all over America and members of the cult – many of them students – decorated their walls with the maps of Middle-earth. Now, courtesy of the movies, these hippies and other baby boomers are introducing *The Lord of the Rings* and *The Hobbit* to their grandchildren.

After retiring from academia in 1959, Tolkien resumed writing *The Silmarillion*, which he had begun years before and underpinned his other work. His aim, he said, was to create a mythology for England, though he scored his greatest success in the US. Indeed, *The Lord of the Rings* has been translated into at least thirty-eight languages.

The Silmarillion was published after his death in 1973. Since then Tolkien's son Christopher has mined his father's papers for other work showing the staggering scope of his father's imagination. Professor Tolkien had spent his life creating an alternative reality where every element has its own history and chronology, words and names have their own etymology, and mythology and reality live side-by-side.

The Lord of the Rings and *The Hobbit* are the third and fourth bestselling novels of all time, after Charles Dickens's *A Tale of Two Cities* and Antoine de Saint-Exupéry's *The Little Prince*. In a 1999 poll of amazon.com customers, *The Lord of the Rings* was judged to be their 'book of the century'. A survey conducted in Britain by the BBC in 2003 found that *The Lord of the Rings* was the nation's best-loved book. The following year the same was found to be the case in both Germany and Australia. In 2008, *The Times* ranked Tolkien sixth on its list of 'The fifty greatest British writers since 1945'. Meanwhile *The Lord of the Rings* movies broke box-office records in the US, despite the irony of the last and biggest grossing of the trilogy being called *The Return of the King*. As a result, in 2009, *Forbes* magazine listed J.R.R. Tolkien as their fifth highest-earning dead celebrity, immediately behind Elvis Presley and Michael Jackson. With the new *Hobbit* movies coming out, Tolkien shows no sign of slipping down the rankings any time soon.

Nigel Cawthorne
Bloomsbury, May 2012
www.nigel-cawthorne.com

I

PORTRAIT OF AN ARTIST AS A YOUNG HOBBIT

There is nothing remotely remarkable about the background of John Ronald Reuel Tolkien. His father, Arthur, was a bank clerk from Birmingham who went out to the Orange Free State, South Africa, to manage a branch in the capital Bloemfontein. His mother, Mabel Suffield, was the daughter of a family of shopkeepers in Birmingham. Arthur was thirteen years her senior. When he proposed to the eighteen-year-old Mabel, her parents did not approve. Arthur went out to South Africa on his own; Mabel followed when she was twenty-one.

The couple married in Cape Town Cathedral, before moving up to Bloemfontein, then little more than a shanty town of a few hundred ramshackle buildings. Life was tough. The English immigrants were shunned by the Afrikaners, descendants of earlier Dutch settlers. The Boer War was just eight years away. Nine months after the wedding, the couple's first son, John, was born on 3 January 1892. His father wanted to maintain the family tradition and give him the biblical name Reuel. His mother favoured the more prosaic middle name Ronald. So he got both. However, in his family, he was always called Ronald.

In his first summer, the infant Tolkien underwent an experience that had a resonance in his fiction. He was bitten by a tarantula, but his quick-witted African nanny found the bite and sucked out the venom. Menacing spiders appear both in *The Hobbit*, *The Two Towers*, the second volume of *The Lord of the Rings* and *The Silmarillion*. Ronald recovered, but he remained a sickly child, suffering from a chest condition and skin complaint made worse by the heat and dust.

Ronald soon had a younger brother, Hilary. His mother took the two boys on a vacation to Cape Town, then went back to England for a visit. The Boers' leader Paul Kruger was now threatening rebellion against the British and she was advised not to return. But back in Bloemfontein Arthur fell ill with rheumatic fever. Mabel quickly made plans to return to South Africa with the boys to nurse him. Although he was just four, Ronald dictated a letter to his father, telling him how much he missed him. It was never sent. A telegram arrived saying that his father had suffered a severe haemorrhage. The next day he was dead.

Arthur Tolkien had invested his money in a mining company. Dividends gave Mabel thirty shillings a week – £1.50, worth less than £90 ($144) today. This was scarcely enough to live on, but her brother-in-law helped out. Mabel and the boys moved out of the grimy industrial city of

Birmingham into a small cottage in the hamlet of Sarehole, in Warwickshire, which was surrounded by woods and fields. For the children, it was idyllic. Free to roam the countryside, it became their own fantasy land. A local farmer became an evil wizard; a miller the 'White Ogre' because he was always covered in flour – and he later became Sandyman, the miller in Hobbiton.

With his mother's encouragement, Ronald became an avid reader. Among his influential early reading was *The Red Fairy Book* by Andrew Lang, a Scottish academic who collected fairy tales. He was particularly taken with 'The Story of Sigurd' and Fafnir, the son of a dwarf-king who is turned into a dragon, which was originally written in Old Norse. Meanwhile Ronald's mother taught him French and the rudiments of Latin, though there was nothing she could do to make him take any interest in music.

Ronald was nine when they moved back into Birmingham. He had won a place at the prestigious King Edward's School. At the same time, the widowed Mabel sought consolation in the Catholic Church, causing a rift with her staunchly Protestant family. Her brother-in-law cut off her allowance and they were forced to move to a dark, pokey house that was due for demolition. Later they moved to a house by a railway line a few streets from Mabel's parents. But the boys could not visit their grandparents if they were accompanied by their mother. Their Auntie Jane had to take them instead.

They moved again, this time so that Mabel could be near Birmingham Oratory, which had been founded in 1849 by the famous Catholic convert John Henry Newman. They grew close to the family priest, the pipe-smoking Father Francis Xavier Morgan. However, the house was in a dangerous area and the boys were not allowed out once it grew dark. The boys went to an overcrowded local school while their mother worked on getting them scholarships so they could attend King Edward's. But then she was hospitalized with diabetes, at that time an untreatable condition. Hilary moved in with his grandparents, while Ronald was sent to Hove on the south coast to live with Auntie Jane and her husband.

When Mabel's condition alleviated slightly, the family were reunited in the two rooms of a tiny cottage, lodgings Father Francis had found for them. Owned by Oratory, the cottage was back out in the Worcestershire countryside at Rednal. There, with their young cousins Mary and Marjorie Incledon, the two Tolkien boys retuned to their rural fantasy land, making up words in a language they called 'Animalic'. Later Ronald and Mary invented a more sophisticated language they called 'Nevosh', or the 'New Nonsense', even chanting limericks in it.

The boys had another blissful bucolic summer before, that autumn, their mother died. She was thirty-four. Tolkien blamed her family. He believed that their rejection of her because of her conversion to Catholicism had contributed to her decline. From that time on, he was a devout Catholic. The experience also left him a life-long depressive.

The two boys moved in with their Aunt Beatrice. She had a large house in the Edgbaston district of Birmingham but, recently widowed, she was emotionally cold. She barely spoke to the boys and Ronald was shocked to find her burning their mother's papers. However, there was always Father Francis to turn to. Mabel had appointed him their guardian shortly before she died. In the mornings, they would serve as altar boys at mass and breakfast with him afterwards.

Ronald was doing well at school. Now eleven, he excelled at languages. As well as learning modern French and German, he began learning classical Greek and, through Chaucer, Middle English, later starting on ancient Finnish and Norse. Then, with his close friend Christopher Wiseman, he moved on to the study of Anglo-Saxon and *Beowulf*. Books were already central to his life. Together they rummaged around in the remoter corners of the school library and a Cornish bookshop nearby. Ronald spent what money he could scrape together buying German books on philology – broadly, the love of words. The word alone had him enamoured. This would have led him to the etymology of his own rather unusual surname. His father's family traced their origins to Lower Saxony, the original home of the Anglo-Saxons, and the name Tolkien is thought to derive from the German world *tollkühn*, meaning daredevil or, more pejoratively, reckless or foolhardy. However, a German writer has suggested that it is more likely that the name derives from the village of Tolkynen in East Prussia, now Tolkiny, Poland. The name of the village comes from Old Prussian.

The study rarely stopped. Most of the school holidays were spent revising for exams, though Ronald and Hilary would spend Easter at the Oratory and Father Francis would take them on a short holiday each summer, usually to Lyme Regis in Dorset (now Devon). More books were to be found in Father Francis's room, many in Spanish, and Ronald began work on a new made-up language, 'Naffarin'

As they were not happy with the forbidding Aunt Beatrice, Father Francis rented them a room in the home of a local wine merchant whose wife threw musical evenings for the Oratory fathers once a week. The couple had another lodger, nineteen-year-old Edith Bratt. She too had lost her mother; illegitimate, she had never known her father. Together Edith and Ronald would cycle out into the countryside and while away the time talking in the shade of an oak tree. This went on, clandestinely, for nearly three years. But then Father Francis discovered what was happening and put his foot down. The Oxbridge entrance exams were looming. Ronald must concentrate on his books. He must have no more contact with Edith until he was of age, some three years away. She was sent to other lodgings forty miles away in Cheltenham. Not only did Tolkien lose the girl he loved, he then failed the entrance exam.

After a miserable Christmas, Ronald managed to meet up with Edith secretly out in the countryside. After exchanging gifts, they promised to be true. Father Francis heard of it and, in future, forbade them even to exchange letters. Otherwise, he would not fund Ronald through college.

. Tolkien now had no alternative but to throw himself into his schoolwork. His social life, such as it was, was confined to other boys from school. Tolkien and three friends – Wiseman, Robert Gilson and Geoffrey Bache Smith – formed the T.C.B.S. This stood for Tea Club, Barrovian Society, after Barrow's Stores where they often took their afternoon tea. Over a cup they would read *Beowulf* or *Sir Gawain and the Green Knight*, and discuss mythology and ancient languages.

Sitting the Oxbridge entrance exam again in 1910, Tolkien passed this time. Though he failed to win a scholarship, he was awarded an exhibition, which gave him just £60 a year – worth £3,500 ($5,600) today. With a small bursary from King Edward's School and an allowance from Father Francis, Tolkien had just enough to survive for three years studying

Classics at Exeter College, Oxford. Overjoyed, he broke his word to Father Francis and sent a telegram to Edith, telling her the news.

At Oxford, he threw himself into student life, drinking beer, smoking a pipe and neglecting his studies. A clubbable fellow, he was known as 'Tollers'. By the end of his first year, he had run up debts. However, he had also taken advantage of the intellectual opportunities afforded him. He joined the Dialectical Society and the Essay Society, and enjoyed debating. He was also under the tutelage of an inspiring teacher, Dr Joseph Wright. From a small town in Yorkshire, Wright was largely self-taught, but had risen to become Deputy Professor of Comparative Philology, mastering numerous languages, both ancient and modern, along the way. Tolkien had read his *Primer of the Gothic Language* at school. From Dr Wright, Tolkien learnt of the connection been various languages, despite their separation in culture and time.

On this twenty-first birthday, Tolkien wrote to Edith, his hopes high. She wrote back with the crushing news that she was engaged. Nevertheless, he took a train to see her. She met him at the station. They talked long into the night and Edith broke off her engagement. This gave him a new distraction. When he should have been cramming for his exams, he was visiting Edith. And instead of attending lectures on Greek and Latin, he was spending time inventing a new language of his own – 'Elvish'. After his first set of exams, he was awarded only a second. However, his paper on Comparative Philology was outstanding, so it was recommended that he switch courses from Classics to English Language and Literature. This was a relief for Tolkien. He had little interest in Greek and Roman literature. He was more interested in Norse and Icelandic legends. Though studying English was not perfect, it was nearer the mark. He had little time for Shakespeare – indeed, any writer after the fourteenth century. His passion was the study of language.

His relationship with Edith did not go smoothly. If they were to marry, he insisted that she convert to Catholicism. As she was living in a staunchly Protestant household, she had to move again. While he was now set on an academic path, she had yet to find a life of her own. Then in the summer of 1913, they were to be parted. Tolkien took a job chaperoning three Mexican boys and two of their aunts on a tour of France. Though he had mastered ancient Norse, his Spanish was rudimentary and his academic knowledge of French did not help him with the waiters of Paris. In Brittany, one of the aunts was hit by a car and died.

Returning to England, he threw himself back into university life with renewed vigour, becoming president of a debating society, joining a dining club, drinking expensive wine and brandy, and winning the Skeat Prize for English. His prize was £5 plus a leather-bound copy of *The House of the Wolflings*, a fantasy novel by William Morris, founder of the Arts and Crafts movement. It is set among Germanic Gothic tribes in the forest of Mirkwood, an ancient wood that also inhabits Middle-earth. Meanwhile Edith was living in Warwick with her crippled cousin Jennie and being instructed in the Catholic faith by Father Murphy. Early in 1914, she was accepted into the Roman Catholic Church and their betrothal was blessed by Father Murphy. It was only then that Tolkien told his friends about Edith.

That August Britain declared war on Germany. Unlike so many young men of his generation, Tolkien did not join up.

In autumn, he returned to a deserted Oxford to finish his degree. However, he did join the Officers' Training Corps and learnt to drill. He also spent his spare time writing poetry – notably 'The Voyage of Earendel the Evening Star', concerning a character borrowed from the Anglo-Saxon poet Cynewulf; 'Sea Chant of an Elder Day,' a more realistic work; the humorous 'Goblin Feet'; 'The Man in the Moon Came Down Too Soon', which was later published in *The Adventures of Tom Bombadil* (1962); and some verse in Finnish. 'Goblin Feet' was accepted by Blackwell's for their annual book of *Oxford Poetry*. Encouraged by this, Tolkien sent a sheaf of poems to the publishers Sidgwick & Jackson. They were rejected.

That summer Tolkien took his final examinations and gained a first. Then he took up a commission as a second lieutenant in the Lancashire Fusiliers, alongside his school friend Geoffrey Smith. As a result, he swapped the comfort of an Oxford college for a narrow bunk, smelly latrine and inedible food in the barracks of a training camp. He managed to see Edith occasionally. Otherwise, to stave off the boredom of the camp, he began work on 'The Book of Lost Tales', which would eventually become *The Silmarillion*.

After six months of basic training, Tolkien opted to become a signaller. Knowing that he was soon to be posted abroad – and his life would probably be short – he and Edith decided to marry in March 1916. Finally, he got round to telling Father Francis, who was, against all expectations, delighted. Although he offered to marry them at the Oratory, Father Murphy conducted the service back in Warwick.

Now a full lieutenant, Tolkien landed in France on 6 June 1916. He spent three weeks in a camp at Étaples before orders came to move up. Next he was billeted in the shattered village of Bouzincourt while, with over half a million men, they awaited the order to counter-attack. It came on 1 July. That day, the first day of the First Battle of the Somme, the British lost twenty thousand dead, another forty thousand wounded. It was the worst single-day loss in the history of the British Army. Among the dead was Tolkien's friend Robert Gilson who was serving with the Suffolk Regiment.

Tolkien's battalion was kept in reserve. Geoffrey Smith, who had been at the front, arrived to meet him. They watched as other companies went up to the front and returned with half their number missing. Then, eight days after the beginning of the battle, it was Tolkien's turn. His company attacked a village occupied by a large German force. In fierce fighting, many of his comrades fell to machine-gun fire. After forty-eight hours, Tolkien emerged miraculously unscathed. It was only when he returned to camp that he learnt of the death of Gilson.

As the murderous battle dragged on, Tolkien returned to the front again and again, each time emerging, against the odds, unharmed. As autumn approached, the rains came. The trenches filled with water, filth and rats. After five months, Tolkien came down with trench fever, a bacterial infection spread by lice. A few days before the battle ended on 13 November, Tolkien was back in Birmingham, in a hospital where Edith soon visited him. There were no antibiotics in those days, so little could be done. Many men died from trench fever, but Tolkien survived. After six weeks he was discharged. He went to stay with Edith and her cousin Jennie, now living in Great Haywood, Staffordshire, to convalesce.

Due to the war, there was little food and fuel, but the break was restful. However, there was still the possibility that he would be returned to France. News from the front was bad. Geoffrey Smith had died from shrapnel wounds and gangrene. That Christmas, there was no end to the war in sight and the slaughter seemed particularly senseless. But there were walks in the countryside to be enjoyed and Edith fell pregnant – though it was hardly a propitious time to bring new life into the world.

Tolkien suffered a relapse, but when he recovered he was sent to Yorkshire to retrain, ready to be returned to the war. Edith and Jennie followed him north. They found lodgings on the dreary coastal town of Hornsea. During training, Tolkien fell ill repeatedly. Heavily pregnant, there was little Edith could do to help him, so she went back to Cheltenham to have their first child, a son, John Francis Reuel Tolkien. She then returned north with the child, staying in the village of Roos near the camp. Again they could enjoy walks in the countryside and Edith danced for him in the woods. In Tolkien's favourite tale in *The Silmarillion*, the mortal man Beren comes across the immortal elven-maid Lúthien Tinúviel dancing in the woods of Neldoreth. Tolkien had the name 'Lúthien' inscribed on Edith's gravestone, telling his son Christopher that he had conceived the scene in the woods at Roos.

There was some cause to be optimistic then. America had joined the war. Though the Russians, now under the leadership of the Bolsheviks, were suing for peace, victory for the Allies in the west seemed assured. In the spring of 1918, Tolkien was posted to Staffordshire, while the last of his battalion still serving in France were killed or taken prisoner.

2

JOURNEY TO MIDDLE-EARTH

On 12 November 1918, the day after the war ended, Tolkien wrote to his commanding officer, asking for a posting to Oxford so he could continue his education while he was waiting to be demobbed. In fact, he had something else in mind. From his study of ancient languages and cultures he had realized that, unlike the countries of Scandinavia or Central Europe, England had no set of legends that made up a coherent mythology. He decided that it was his job to create one. He owed it to his fallen friends. After Gilson had died, Smith had written that those of the T.C.B.S. who survived had to represent them all. But in the meantime, he had a wife and child to support.

His request to return to Oxford was granted. He got a job working on a new edition of *The New English Dictionary*, which eventually became the *Oxford English Dictionary*.

Tolkien was assigned a few words of Germanic origin beginning with the letter W. He had to tease out their etymology, then write a report, only a fraction of which would appear in the final volume. A single word would take him a week to research. He supplemented his salary taking on private tuition. This allowed his growing family to move from a small apartment to a house. A good teacher, he was soon able to give up working on the dictionary.

With Edith pregnant with their second child, Tolkien applied for the post of Reader in English Language at the University of Leeds and got the position. Post-war Leeds was a depressing place. He was also offered a lucrative professorship in Cape Town, but Edith had just given birth to their second child and he passed on it. Soon he began to enjoy his tenure at Leeds. He worked alongside Eric Gordon, who shared his interest in ancient languages. Together they produced a definitive edition of *Sir Gawain and the Green Knight*, which was published by the Clarendon Press in Oxford in 1925. They also started the Viking Club. Though ostensibly dedicated to the celebration of the Norse language and customs, members drank beer and revelled in bawdy verse. In his spare time, Tolkien began writing long narrative poems. One was 'Túrin Túrambar', the story of a dragon slayer; the other 'The Gest of Beren and Lúthien', his romantic tale of a mortal man who falls in love with an elven maid and, for her sake, goes on a terrible quest. He sent parts of the two poems to a retired schoolmaster who had once taught him. The response was not good. Criticism stung Tolkien and he did not show his work to other people for several years.

He was awarded the chair of the English Department at Leeds. The extra money was useful as Edith was pregnant again. But then he was offered the position of Professor of Anglo-Saxon at Oxford. The appointment came as a surprise. He was just thirty-three and there were several more qualified candidates. Without hesitation, he took it. He found a large house with big garden at 22 Northmoor Road and moved in with his family. Four years later, they moved next door to number 20, buying the house from the publisher Basil Blackwell.

In the morning he would cycle to college where he was expected to deliver a series of lectures each year. But these were much the same as those he had given in Leeds and the high-ceilinged lecture halls provided the perfect backdrop for lectures on medieval literature. It was particularly apt when he declaimed the opening verses of *Beowulf*. Having acted at school and as an undergraduate, he enjoyed his role at the lectern and played up to his audience.

He would also teach specialized subjects to smaller groups, though in tutorials he was known to stray into tales about elves and goblins, half-mumbling to himself. Even when he was still a relatively young man, with his sports jacket, corduroy trousers and pipe, he looked every inch an Oxford don. At a fancy-dress party, he would happily arrive as an axe-toting Viking on his bike. When, briefly, he owned a car, he was a similarly eccentric driver.

The downside of his new position was the administrative work, which he loathed. Then there was the departmental politics to deal with. It took him six years to get the curriculum altered so that students in their final year could drop Middle and Old English if they wanted to concentrate on modern texts, leaving a dedicated group who, like him, were fascinated by medieval, especially pre-Chaucerian, work.

Then there was the mundane business of supporting a family. An Oxford professor earned kudos and social standing, but little money. He would take on private tuition, teaching first thing in the morning before going to college. For twenty years, he marked School Certificate examination papers every summer to make ends meet. Meanwhile, he produced work for academic journals and the Clarendon Press. This left little time for his private writing. But after a long day's work, he would pick up his pen at 10 p.m. and head for Middle-earth, writing until one or two o'clock in the morning. Then after a few hours' sleep, he would start his daily routine all over again. Nor did he deny his four children affection. Not only were there kisses and cuddles, but he also wrote them an enormous number of letters. The most highly prized were his annual 'letter from Father Christmas'. These were collected and published as *The Father Christmas Letters* in 1976. An expanded version appeared in 1999 as *Letters from Father Christmas*. Along with the regular characters such as polar bears and seals, there were, of course, Snow-elves. He wrote other stories purely to amuse his children, illustrating some with water colours. His favourite subject was dragons. In these tales written solely for his children, Tom Bomdadil, his wife Goldberry, Old Man Willow and the Barrow-wights, who all appear in *The Lord of the Rings*, made their first appearance.

As early as 1924, while they were still in Leeds, Tolkien's eldest son John remembered his father telling him a story when he could not get to sleep. He later wrote it down. Called 'The Orgog', it is the convoluted tale of a strange creature travelling through a fantastic landscape. In 1925, he began telling his second son Michael another tale when he lost his favourite toy, a lead dog. This was written down around Christmas 1927 and went on to become the novella *Roverandom*, published in 1998. It featured an irritable wizard who turns a dog into a toy, then back again.

Michael's diary records that his father began *Mr Bliss* in the summer of 1928. An illustrated children's book, the story is based on Tolkien's own mishaps when he first owned a car. The earliest surviving manuscript is dated 1930 and a facsimile edition was published in 1982.

Around 1928, Tolkien wrote a series of six poems, collected under the title 'Tales and Songs of Bimble Bay'. Three of them appear in explanatory footnotes in *The Annotated Hobbit* (2003). One is about a slimy creature called Glip, who seems to be a forerunner of Gollum. Tolkien seems to have started his medieval fable *Farmer Giles of Ham* as a family game in the countryside around that time. Expanded in 1938, it was published in 1949.

There were other tales that Tolkien did not write down. There was the story of the red-headed boy named Carrots who had strange adventures inside a cuckoo clock. Then there was the villain Bill Stickers – taken from the then ubiquitous notice 'Bill stickers will be prosecuted' – and his nemesis Major Road Ahead, after another sign. As none of these stories was intended for publication, Tolkien could experiment freely with the narrative.

No one is very sure when Tolkien began writing *The Hobbit*. Tolkien recalled that it was on a summer's day and he was sitting by the window in the study of his home in Northmoor Road, marking School Certificate papers. Other evidence suggests it was somewhere between 1928 and 1930. Tolkien himself thought it was 1930. He recalled: 'One of the candidates had mercifully left one of the pages with no writing on it (which is the best thing that can possibly happen to an examiner) and I wrote on it: 'In a hole in the ground there lived a hobbit.'

This is indeed the first sentence of *The Hobbit*.

'Names always generated a story in my mind,' he said. 'Eventually I thought I'd better find out what hobbits were like. But that's only the beginning.'

Tolkien's youngest son Christopher thought this happened earlier than his father recalled. Shortly after *The Hobbit* was published in 1937, he recorded in his letter to Father Christmas that his father had written the book 'ages ago' and had read it to him and his two siblings, John and Michael, one winter in the evenings after tea.

'The ending chapters were rather roughly done,' he said, 'and not typed out at all; he finished it about a year ago.'

This spurred Tolkien to recall that his eldest boy John was thirteen at the time he started reading to them. It did not appeal to the younger children until they were a little older. John was thirteen in 1930. However, Tolkien's second son Michael kept some of his own compositions which he believes were from 1929. They ape his father's work, not in its early stages but nearing completion. A typescript, minus the last few chapters, was certainly in existence in 1932 when he showed it to his friend and colleague, the writer C.S. Lewis. Tolkien himself told publisher George Unwin that the book had taken him two or three years to write because he wrote very slowly.

According to Tolkien the name 'hobbit' appeared spontaneously in his mind. In January 1938, shortly after *The Hobbit* was published, an anonymous correspondent wrote to the *Observer* newspaper suggesting that a fairy story called 'The Hobbit' had appeared in a collection published in 1904. Tolkien wrote back saying that he had no knowledge of it. Then in 1970, when the *Oxford English Dictionary* were planning to include the word 'hobbit', they researched the word's origins and found no earlier use. Tolkien was given as the originator. Folklorists now claim to have found an earlier usage, but the *OED* has yet to change its citation.

When Tolkien set about the task of finding out what hobbits were like, he only had to look in the mirror.

'I am in fact a hobbit,' he wrote, 'in all but size. I like gardens, trees, and unmechanized farmlands; I smoke a pipe and like good plain food (unrefrigerated), but detest French cooking; I like, and even dare to wear in these dull days, ornamental waistcoats. I am fond of mushrooms (out of a field); have a very simple sense of humour (which even my appreciative critics find tiresome); I go to bed late and get up late (when possible). I do not travel much.'

Others have spotted deeper similarities. Bilbo Baggins lived in earlier, simpler times. Certainly Tolkien wanted no part of the twentieth century. As far as he was concerned, science and technology had brought nothing worthwhile to mankind. He only owned a car, briefly, because Edith wanted him to have one, and he got rid of it as soon as he could. He never owned a television and rarely listened to the radio. He had no time for modern literature, theatre or music, and had no interest in contemporary politics. Indeed, he disliked the modern world and would have been far happier living in Middle-earth – which is what he did most of the time, in his head.

Auntie Jane's farm in Worchestershire where Tolkien and his brother had once stayed was called 'Bag End' by the locals. And Birmingham was surrounded by shires – Staffordshire, Shropshire, Worcestershire, Warwickshire.

On another occasion, Tolkien said that hobbits 'were just rustic English people, made small in size because it reflects the generally small reach of their imagination – not the reach of their courage or power.'

This perception came from his experience of combat in the First World War.

'I've always been impressed,' he said, 'that we are here, surviving, because of the indomitable courage of quite small people against impossible odds.'

There are other origins that Tolkien identified. He once said that *The Hobbit* sprang from 'previously digested' legends and stories that he had been studying for years. In a letter to the poet W.H. Auden in 1955, he said that the 1927 children's book *The Marvellous Snergs* by E.A. Wyke-Smith was 'probably an unconscious sourcebook for the Hobbits, not of anything else'. Like hobbits, Smergs were small – 'only slightly taller than the average table but broad in the shoulders and of great strength'. Both Smergs and hobbits like feasting and one main character in *The Marvellous Snergs* is called Gorbo.

After writing the first line introducing the idea of a hobbit, it was some months before Tolkien returned to the story.

'I thought it was too good to leave just on the back of an examination,' he said. 'I wrote the first chapter first – then I forgot about it, then I wrote another part. I myself can still see the gaps. There is a very big gap after they reach the eyrie of the Eagles. After that I really did not know how to go on.'

But go on he did, in a gloriously haphazard fashion.

'I just spun a yarn out of any elements in my head,' he said. 'I don't remember organizing the thing at all.'

The earliest version now existing is six hand-written pages from Chapter One. Gandalf appears, but he is the head dwarf. The wizard's name is Bladorthin and the dragon is named Pryftan. The draft consists of twelve typed pages, followed by another 154 handwritten pages, covering roughly Chapters One to Twelve, plus Chapter Fourteen, of the finished work. The name of the dragon has been hand corrected from Pryftan to Smaug. Beorn, the hairy man who turns into a bear, is called Medwed throughout. The wizard does not produce the key to the back door of Lonely Mountain. Instead a key found in a troll's hoard is used to open Durin's Door. And in the last thirty-five pages, the head dwarf is named Thorin and Gandalf becomes the wizard.

The next draft is a typescript. In it, Medwed becomes Beorn. This is thought to be the typescript that Tolkien eventually showed his friend C.S. Lewis as it still had no ending beyond an outline. It was produced on a special Hammond typewriter that had two sets of keys, so the songs could be rendered in italic. Then there are handwritten versions of Chapters Thirteen and Fifteen to Nineteen. These are inserted in the next typescript. There is another typed draft, which does not seem to have been used. These last three stages are thought to have been undertaken in 1936, when the manuscript was finally being completed for publication. After that the book appears in proof form.

Tolkien kept a beautifully typed 'home manuscript' which he passed around to friends. One of the people who read it was a pupil of Tolkien's named Elaine Griffiths. She had a friend named Susan Dagnall who had gone to work at the publishers Allen & Unwin. Susan returned to Oxford in the late spring of 1936 to discuss work on a translation of *Beowulf* Tolkien had recommended Elaine for, and Elaine suggested that she read the manuscript of *The Hobbit*. She did and urged Tolkien to finish it. So he got back down to work. After labouring throughout the summer, he delivered the completed work on 3 October 1936.

Stanley Unwin and his reader liked it. Then he handed it to his ten-year-old son, Rayner, who said that he thought children between five and nine would enjoy the story. *The Hobbit* was accepted for publication and contracts were signed that December. Tolkien also supplied copy for Allen & Unwin's catalogue which was used on the jacket as well.

The book was published with ten of Tolkien's illustrations in black and white, plus two maps. Other colour illustrations have been added in subsequent editions. Drawings and jacket designs went back and forth, along with thirty-one letters from Allen & Unwin and twenty-six from Tolkien – some up to five pages long – all detailed, fluent and precise. At one point, he questions the use of the word 'dwarves', pointing out that the proper English spelling for the plural of dwarf is 'dwarfs', though philologically it should be 'dwarrows'. Nevertheless, throughout Tolkien's published works the plural 'dwarves' is used. (It should be pointed out that 'dwarves' is permitted in American English, though not in British English.)

Tolkien made heavy corrections to the proofs, rewriting whole sections, exasperating his publishers and the printers with his attention to detail. Knowing little of the processes of publishing, Tolkien naïvely suggested that the map of Middle-earth be printed in invisible ink, so that it would only reveal itself when opened to the light.

The publishers tried to dissuade him from making extensive corrections, reminding him that resetting the text was expensive and he would have to bear the cost himself. Undeterred, Tolkien went ahead, but went to great lengths to tailor new sentences so that they would exactly fill the space of those he had taken out.

During the process, he decided that he did not like the numerous asides where the author directly addresses the reader – though forty-five remained after he had finished. At proof stages, he also came across inconsistencies in the chronology and geography of the story, all of which had to be corrected. The process took two months. Despite this, Tolkien wanted the book to be published in June, rather than September to catch the Christmas market, as planned. The reason was that Tolkien was supposed to have been getting on with his academic work and he did not want to be accused of squandering his time on a children's book when he was being paid to produce something more high-minded. The publishers got their way and Tolkien's colleagues hardly noticed the publication until a review appeared in *The Times*. Their reaction was, he said, '(as I foresaw) not unmixed with surprise and pity'. Nevertheless, R.M. Dawkins, Professor of Byzantine Greek and a member of Tolkien's Icelandic reading group, the Coalbiters Club, bought a copy 'because first editions of *Alice* are now very valuable'.

Proofs were sent to Houghton Mifflin in Boston. They were unenthusiastic but decided to go ahead anyway. They wanted to add colour illustrations, produced by their own artists. Tolkien agreed to this provided he could veto 'anything from or influenced by the Disney studios (for all whose works I have a heartfelt loathing)'. He then sent them some samples of his own colour work, before sending five colour paintings that he had produced specifically for *The Hobbit* executed during the first weeks of the summer vacation in July 1937. Houghton Mifflin took four of them and paid him $100. Allen & Unwin agreed to include the colour illustrations if they reprinted the book. They also gave Tolkien a £25 advance on publication which he spent on another second-hand car.

Allen & Unwin then took the rare step of putting a full-page advertisement in the *Publisher's Circular* and *The Publisher & Bookseller*, calling *The Hobbit* 'the children's book of the year' in advance of publication on 21 September. The publisher's jacket blurb read: 'J.R.R. Tolkien . . . has four children and *The Hobbit* . . . was read aloud to them in nursery days . . . The manuscript . . . was lent to friends in Oxford and read to their children . . . The birth of *The Hobbit* recalls very strongly that of *Alice in Wonderland*. Here again a professor of an abstruse subject is at play.'

Tolkien even objected to this innocent description, concerned that the inaccuracies might be exaggerated into falsehoods. The book had not been read to his children in their nursery years. They did not have a nursery and John was thirteen when he first heard the story. He had not 'lent' the manuscript to anyone. Rather it was forced on people. Those who had seen it had certainly not read it to their children. He objected to *The Hobbit* being compared to *Alice in Wonderland*, though everyone did it. Anglo-Saxon was not an abstruse subject. Nor, for that matter, was Charles Dodgson, aka Lewis Carroll, a professor, but a mere college lecturer.

Allen & Unwin put another full-page advertisement in the *Publisher's Circular* and *The Publisher & Bookseller* in November, carrying a selection of comments from the critics. Naturally, they were favourable. The first print-run sold well and a second edition was prepared with the colour illustrations returned from the US. However, for the colour edition, the publishers held the price at the original 7s 6d – 27½p, about £14 ($22) at today's prices.

Reviewing the book for *The Times Literary Supplement*, C.S. Lewis also compared *The Hobbit* to *Alice in Wonderland* as well as to *The Wind in the Willows*. In another anonymous review in *The Times* itself Lewis said: 'The truth is that in this book a number of good things, never before united, have come together; a fund of humour, an understanding of children, and a happy fusion of the scholar's with the poet's grasp of mythology. On the edge of a valley one of Professor Tolkien's characters can pause and say: "It smells like elves." It may be years before we produce another author with such a nose for an elf. The Professor has the air of inventing nothing. He has studied trolls and dragons at first hand and describes them with that fidelity which is worth oceans of glib "originality".'

The US edition was published on 2 March 1938, where he would get more disinterested reviews. May Lamberton Becker in the *New York Herald Tribune* said: 'At the time of writing, still under the spell of the story, I cannot bend my mind to ask myself whether our American children will like it. My impulse is to say if they don't so much the worst for them.' She also compared Tolkien to Lewis Carroll. 'Into these pages a world is packed, an odyssey compressed, as adventures on the road to the dragon's ill-got treasure thickens. I do not know how our children will like a story so close-packed, one of whose chapters would make a book elsewhere; they may think they are getting too much for their money. But dwarves have come this year into fashion in America . . .' The movies *Snow White and the Seven Dwarves* had been released in 1937. Indeed, Sophia L. Goldsmith wrote in the *New York Post*: 'This book . . . has immense charm, genuine wit, and dwarves which put Snow White's boy friends completely in the shade.'

The Hobbit won the $250 prize as the best book for younger children at the *New York Herald Tribune*'s second annual Children's Festival in May. By June it had sold nearly three thousand copies in the US and Houghton Mifflin had shuffled it to the top of their children's list. Reprinted at the end of 1938, sales of the US edition topped five thousand copies.

Back in Britain, *The Hobbit* sold three thousand copies in its first year in the bookshops, but sales were hurt by the outbreak of the Second World War. Print runs were hit by paper rationing which was introduced in April 1940. Then Allen & Unwin's warehouse was bombed with the loss of over a million books. Sales picked up once more when *Farmer Giles of Ham* was published in 1949, and again in the 1950s in anticipation of the publication of *The Lord of the Rings*.

Within weeks of *The Hobbit*'s publication, Stanley Unwin was talking to Tolkien about a sequel. When they met for lunch in November 1937, Tolkien took with him a bundle of incomplete and unconnected stories that would one day appear as *The Silmarillion*, his unfinished poem 'The Gest of Beren and Lúthien', the Father Christmas letters and a mixed bag of children's stories. He had already shown *Mr Bliss* to his editor, but it did not seem an appropriate follow-up to *The Hobbit*. None of the other material he had presented seemed suitable either. But then, on 19 December, he wrote to Allen & Unwin, telling them he had just written 'A Long-Expected Party', the first chapter of a new book about hobbits – indeed, that is the title of the first chapter of *The Lord of the Rings*. This version began with Bilbo Baggins giving a party to celebrate his seventieth birthday, not yet his eleventy-first. Tolkien had the Christmas holiday ahead of him with no marking to do, so he spent his time polishing it. In February 1938, he sent his fourth draft to Stanley Unwin, saying he should get his young son Rayner, who had proved such a reliable critic with *The Hobbit*, to read it.

'I have no confidence in it,' Tolkien wrote, 'but if he thought it a promising beginning, could add it to the tale that is brewing.'

The typescript he sent was little different from the final version of Chapter One, except that Bilbo's adopted cousin is called Bingo Bolger-Baggins, not Frodo, and had appeared in an earlier draft as his son. Rayner was delighted. Tolkien sat down for three weeks and wrote another two chapters, though 'The Shadow of the Past' – Chapter Two in the final version, which explains much of the background – was not inserted until sometime later. By February or March 1938, the main themes of the story became clear. The central element was the ring. The hobbits would again be on a quest. Ranged against them would be the Dark Lord, Sauron, who was alluded to as the Necromancer in *The Hobbit*.

In July and August, Tolkien had another imaginative rush and worked out the main structure of the story, adding 'The Shadow of the Past'. During a family holiday to Sidmouth in Devon, he got up to Chapter Ten, though Frodo was still called Bingo and has been joined by a 'Ranger' hobbit called Trotter.

The Hobbit, though plainly successful, had yet to yield much cash. Tolkien was short of money and was still marking exams to make ends meet. He knew that the new hobbit book Unwin wanted from him might be the solution. But it was getting, he said, 'out of hand'. He already realized that the book he was writing was no bedtime story. It was altogether more adult – his own children were telling him so, though John, who was now in his twenties, liked it. He held back his new work and sent Allen & Unwin the short story *Farmer Giles of Ham* instead. This was eventually accepted for publication, though paper rationing during the war meant that it was not printed until 1949.

In late 1938, Tolkien began to work on a lecture that he was to give at the University of St Andrews in March the following year. It was to be about fairy stories. A subject close to Tolkien's heart, he maintained that fairy stories drew on a well-spring of tradition and he began to look at his work in a new way. He then realized that Middle-earth was a much bigger place than he had realized in *The Hobbit* – and so was the story he was trying to tell.

By the beginning of February 1939, he was already calling the new book *The Lord of the Rings*. He had written twelve chapters, running to three hundred pages, which he had rewritten several times. It would need another two hundred pages to finish it and he wrote to his publishers asking for the latest date they would need the completed manuscript. Tolkien himself was convinced that *The Lord of the Rings* was better than *The Hobbit*, though he said he was worried that 'it many not prove a very fit sequel'. Nevertheless, he promised to deliver the manuscript by 15 June.

But Tolkien was not the kind of a writer who could work to a deadline. In the early 1930s, he had been working on translations of the three poems *Sir Gawain and the Green Knight*, *Pearl* and *Sir Orfeo*, which were to be published in one volume. Thirty years later, he had completed the task. All that remained was for him to write a preface. For the next ten years, the publishers tried every way they could think of to get it out of him, including using his friends as intermediaries to cajole him. Nothing worked. When he died, it was still unwritten. The book was published posthumously with a preface written by his son Christopher. Friends thought that *The Lord of the Rings* would go the same way.

By September 1939, the hobbits had reached Rivendell where the fellowship of the ring was founded. But then, just twenty years since the end of the Great War, Britain was at war again. However, Oxford was not a bad place to be during the Second World War. There was an informal agreement that the Germans would not bomb Oxford and Cambridge, provided the British did not bomb Heidelberg or Göttingen. So Tolkien, who made his contribution to the war effort as a member of the Air Raid Protection service, had little to do.

Before the war had broken out, Tolkien had been asked whether, in a national emergency, he would work in the cryptographic department of the Foreign Office. In March 1939, he took a four-day course in cryptography. In the event, he was not called on to work as a cryptographer.

There were, of course, shortages – not least of paper. Tolkien began to write on the back of old exam papers and other scraps he could find. The war also brought evacuees who were billeted in the Tolkiens' large house on North-moor Road. By then only Christopher and Tolkien's young daughter Priscilla still lived there. John had been studying for the priesthood in Rome before being repatriated, while Michael was at Trinity College, before serving as an anti-aircraft gunner.

In December 1939, Tolkien wrote to Stanley Unwin, saying that he had 'never quite ceased to work' on *The Lord of the Rings* and was now up to Chapter Sixteen – Chapter Four of Book Two in the finished version. He returned to work on it in August 1940. By then, Bingo had become

Frodo. Tolkien's notes show that he started a new plot and he produced the third version (of fifteen) of the poem Bilbo recites at Rivendell.

Tolkien's son Michael was seriously wounded in January 1941 and for the rest of the year little more work was done on the manuscript. But by the beginning of 1942, Tolkien had finished what would be Book Two and had completed the first four chapters of Book Three by the end of January. In December 1942, he wrote to Stanley Unwin asking, given the wartime restrictions, whether there was any point – 'other than private and family amusement' – in continuing. He had, however, reached Chapter Thirty-one (Book Three, Chapter Nine in the finished version). He figured he was now just six chapters from the end. He did no more work on it until the spring of 1943, believing that he could then tie up the loose ends. However, it proved impossible to truncate the plot that way.

Up until this point, Tolkien had been using *The Silmarillion* as his subtext. Now he dipped in again to find what new treasures he could find. By now *The Lord of the Rings* had become as important to him as *The Silmarillion* had always been. The idea that this was a sequel to *The Hobbit* was long forgotten.

In the autumn and winter of 1943, Tolkien stopped work on the book completely. It was then that he went back to an old story of his, *Leaf by Niggle*. It is the tale of an artist who is painting a tree, but becomes so obsessed with every detail that he can never finish it. This could be taken as an allegory of Tolkien's situation. However, he finished the tale. It was published in the *Dublin Review* in 1945 and he went back to *The Lord of the Rings*. By the summer of 1944, he had reached the end of Book Four, the end of the second volume, *The Two Towers*, in published form.

That autumn he ground to a halt again. This time he did no work on the book for a year. By then the Second World War was over. Christopher had returned from a posting in South Africa and was now back at college again. In the summer of 1945, Tolkien was appointed Professor of Language and Literature at Merton College. With his new post came a small pay rise.

Now his children – and the evacuees – had left Northmoor Road, Tolkien moved to a smaller house he rented from the college at 99 Holywell Street, nearer the centre of town. This made financial sense, but he was robbed of his spacious study and now had to work in a small attic room.

By 1947, Rayner Unwin was an undergraduate at Oxford and Tolkien showed him Book One. He was impressed. In the reader's report he sent to his father, he conceded that *The Lord of the Rings* was not really a children's book, but he felt that, if adults could be encouraged to read it, they would get something out of it. His conclusion was that Allen & Unwin should publish it.

Tolkien was heartened by Rayner's assessment, but he still had to finish the book. By the end of 1947, he had reached the end. But he could not let the book go. For another two years, he revised, polished and rewrote it. Eventually, in the autumn of 1949, he forced himself to stop. He retyped the entire manuscript one last time and gave it to C.S. Lewis for his appraisal, which was positive. It was, Tolkien told Stanley Unwin, 'written with my life-blood, such as that is, thick or thin; and I can do no other'.

However, he had had something of a falling out with Unwin. Tolkien was by no means pleased with the production of *Farmer Giles of Ham*. He disliked the cover artwork and had insisted on a new illustrator. Hoping, still, to trade on the continuing success of *The Hobbit*, Allen & Unwin had printed five thousand copies. By the spring of 1950, only two thousand had been sold. Tolkien blamed Unwin for not promoting the book sufficiently. He was also less than pleased with the post-war edition of *The Hobbit* that appeared without the colour plates that had graced the second edition in 1938. In the era of austerity, colour printing was simply too expensive. The financial considerations were of no concern to Tolkien.

He had also presented Unwin with what he considered to be his masterwork, *The Silmarillion*, several times. Plainly, Unwin was not keen to publish it and Tolkien feared that *The Lord of the Rings* was not comprehensible without it. The two were a single entity, he insisted, and must be published together.

In the meantime, Tolkien had met an editor at the London publishing house Collins. Named Milton Waldman, he had heard about his epic work through Gervase Matthews, a friend of Tolkien's through the informal readers' group known as the Inklings. But instead of sending Waldman *The Lord of the Rings*, Tolkien sent him *The Silmarillion*. Waldman was captivated and, when he told Tolkien that he would recommend that Collins publish it, Tolkien sent him *The Lord of the Rings* too. Waldman was impressed by this as well, but Collins had a hidden agenda. They wanted to get their hands on the rights to *The Hobbit* which had already proved successful. So Waldman told Tolkien that, as Collins were stationers and printers as well as publishers, they would have no problem getting their hands on the paper needed to publish his epic – something that would still be a problem for Allen & Unwin.

Waldman now wanted to know whether there would be

any contractual problems if Tolkien moved to Collins. In his contract for *The Hobbit*, there was a clause obliging him to give Allen & Unwin first refusal on any sequel. Tolkien had offered them *The Silmarillion* repeatedly and they had published *Farmer Giles of Ham*, so he considered that he had fulfilled his contractual obligation to Allen & Unwin.

However, Stanley Unwin might not see it that way. So Tolkien wrote to him, trying to put him off *The Lord of the Rings*.

'I have produced a monster,' he wrote to Unwin, 'an immensely long, complex, rather bitter, and very terrifying romance quite unfit for children (if fit for anybody) . . .'

It was not a sequel to *The Hobbit*, but to *The Silmarillion*. Again he insisted that, for *The Lord of the Rings* to be intelligible, *The Silmarillion* would have to be published alongside it, making over a million words in all, he said. In fact, he was overestimating by several hundred thousand words. He could not contemplate any drastic rewriting or compression, nor would he allow *The Lord of the Rings* to be split into several volumes. However, he was prepared to offer Unwin a sequel to *Farmer Giles of Ham*, called *Little Kingdom of Wormings*, and other short stories.

Tolkien told Waldman that he would soon be free of Allen & Unwin. However, Rayner Unwin had seen *The Lord of the Rings* in early draft and reassured his father that it did not have to be published alongside *The Silmarillion*. Some material from *The Silmarillion* might augment it, but an editor working alongside Tolkien could extract that material. Then, in due course, they could drop *The Silmarillion*.

Rayner Unwin did not expect any of this to get back to Tolkien, but his father included a few of his remarks in a letter to Tolkien a few days later. Tolkien was furious. Now he insisted that they take both books or neither. Unwin was adamant that he did not want *The Silmarillion*, so Tolkien was now free to make a deal with Collins.

Waldman had seen both *The Lord of the Rings* and *The Silmarillion*. The first was around half a million words; the second 125,000. Where had Tolkien's figure of a million words come from? Then Tolkien dropped his bombshell. *The Silmarillion* was far from finished. He expected to produce another 375,000 words for it. This was doubly shocking as Waldman wanted Tolkien to make substantial cuts to *The Lord of the Rings*. Tolkien was taken aback. In Waldman, he thought he had found a sympathetic publisher. In working out his mythology, he saw no limits. A book had to be as long as it needed to be, not limited merely by such banal considerations as the cost of paper and ink. In response, Tolkien sent Waldman new sections he had written for *The Silmarillion* with no indication of where they would go. Waldman had left for his summer holiday in Italy. Those delegated to deal with his affairs at Collins while he was away were puzzled and relations with Tolkien grew frosty.

Waldman's return was delayed by ill health. Meanwhile, he tried to keep Tolkien on board by writing to him. Tolkien replied with a forty-one-page letter containing over ten thousand words, explaining his whole mythology and seeking to convince him that *The Lord of the Rings* and *The Silmarillion* were indivisible and interdependent. Even if Waldman had been convinced, it would have made no difference. Tolkien was out of luck. The price of paper soared in 1951, making the publication of two books of the length he envisaged uneconomical.

Tolkien had to backtrack rapidly. In June 1952, he wrote

to Rayner Unwin asking: 'Can anything be done ... to unlock the gate I slammed myself?'

Rayner replied, asking to see a copy of the completed manuscript of *The Lord of the Rings*. As ever, Tolkien was not quite ready and retreated to his son Michael's house in nearby Woodcote to make further revisions to the typescript.

That September, Rayner picked up the manuscript of *The Lord of the Rings* from Tolkien's home in Oxford. There was now no question of publishing *The Silmarillion* as companion volume. *The Lord of the Rings* would be published in three volumes over a period of over twelve months, each costing twenty-one shillings – £1.05, worth £20 ($32) today.

The prospects for publication were not good. The enthusiasm for Middle-earth that had existed after the publication of *The Hobbit* was long gone. *The Lord of the Rings* was an altogether darker, heavier work. Nor did it fit into any existing genre. The market was small. Rayner had now received a quote on the print costs and wrote to his father who was on business in the Far East, saying that he reckoned publishing *The Lord of the Rings* would lose them a thousand pounds. On the other hand, it was a work of genius and would bring the publishing house a certain kudos.

Stanley Unwin cabled back: 'If you believe it is a work of genius, then you may lose a thousand pounds.'

Given the financial outlook, Stanley Unwin offered Tolkien what he imagined was a tough deal. There would be no advance and no royalty. After the costs of production, printing, distribution and advertising were taken into consideration, they would split any profits fifty–fifty. Not expecting any money, Tolkien signed. He just wanted to see *The Lord of the Rings* in print. Under the contract, the manuscript had to be ready for the printer by 25 March 1953 and Tolkien had to deliver a brief description of the work for publicity purposes of no more than a hundred words.

Meanwhile the Tolkiens were on the move again. Although 99 Holywell Street was just a short walk from Merton College, heavy traffic sped past day and night. Instead, they moved to 76 Sandfield Road, a quiet street in Headington, then a separate town to the east of Oxford. While the move was in hand, Tolkien also had to perform his academic duties as well as make final amendments to the manuscript.

The manuscript had to be split into three volumes. This was relatively easy as Tolkien had already divided the work into six books, so it was simply a matter of printing and binding them in pairs. Or so Allen & Unwin thought. The day before the manuscript was due to be delivered Tolkien was still worried about this. Books Three and Four were not really related, he pointed out. He also wanted to use the book titles as subtitles on the volumes: Volume One, *The Ring Sets Out* and *The Ring Goes South*; Volume Two, *The Treason of Isengard* and *The Ring Goes East*; Volume Three, *The War of the Ring* and *The End of the Third Age*. If they could not do that, he would prefer to call the three volumes *The Shadow Grows*, *The Ring in the Shadow* and *The War of the Ring* or *The Return of the King*.

In the galley proofs, there are other book titles which were ultimately abandoned: Book One, *The First Journey*; Book Two, *The Journey of the Nine Companions*; Book Three, *The Treason of Isengard*; Book Four, *The Journey of the Ring-bearers*; Book Five, *The War of the Ring*; Book Six, *The End of the Third Age*.

On 11 April 1953, Tolkien wrote to Rayner Unwin, saying that he had completed the revision of the manuscript for the press – 'I hope to the last comma' – of Part One: *The Return of the Shadow*. But he had missed the post that day. He also supplied a foreword, but was still debating what to include in the appendices that would follow the short Book Six. He also wanted to include a facsimile of the burnt pages of the *Book of Mazarbul*, which features in Book Two, Chapter Five, 'The Bridge of Khazad-Dûm'. But Allen & Unwin could hardly afford expensive halftones on top of the other costs. Economies were made on the illustration of Moria Gate in Book Two, Chapter Two, 'The Council of Elrond', and on the three maps Tolkien thought were necessary. The costs of production were already prohibitive, so only blocks deemed absolutely necessary were included.

Tolkien then thought that *The Lord of the Rings* should apply only to Volume One, but did not propose an overall title. By 17 August 1953, Tolkien conceded that *The Lord of the Rings* should be the overall title and gave the volume titles as: Volume One, *The Fellowship of the Ring*; Volume Two, *The Two Towers*; and Volume Three, *The War of the Ring* or, if Rayner preferred it, *The Return of the King*. Tolkien preferred *The War of the Ring* because it got the ring in again and it gave less away about the story. He had picked obscure chapter titles for that very reason. However, Unwin preferred *The Return of the King*.

The Two Towers would do for Volume Two, he thought, because it was suitably ambiguous for two books that did not really belong together. But which two towers were they: Isengard and Barad-dûr; Mina Tirith and Barad-dûr; or Isengard and Cirith Ungol? He could not make up his mind. In a later letter to Rayner Unwin, he decided they were 'Orhanc and the Tower of Cirith Ungol'. However, on his original design for the jacket, he shows Orthanc – a black tower – and Minas Morgul – a white tower with the sign of the White Hand beside it.

The production continued through 1953, 1954 and the first half of 1955. Material for the appendices was culled from *The Silmarillion*. Along with a glossary-index, Tolkien wrote more explanatory material that had to be cut for reasons of space. These included *The Quest of Erebor* and *The Hunt for the Rings* which appeared in *Unfinished Tales* (1980).

Christopher Tolkien was brought in to help and, when Tolkien found he could not provide the hundred-word description demanded, unable to get it down to even three hundred words, he called in a friend from Malvern College, George Sayer, who provided ninety-five.

Just 3,000 copies of Volume One: *The Fellowship of the Rings* were published by Allen & Unwin on 29 July 1954. The other 1,500 were published by Houghton Mifflin in the US in 21 October.

Publication was greeted by glowing reviews by C.S. Lewis, of course, though his praise in private was even more unreserved. Even the normally scathing critic Bernard Levin enthused. In the US, the reception was cooler, but the British poet W.H. Auden heaped on glowing praise in the *New York Times*. However, the publishers were not overwhelmed with confidence. When Volume Two: *The Two Towers* was published in the UK on 11 November 1954, Allen & Unwin had a print run of just 3,250, while for the US publication on 21 April 1955, Houghton Mifflin produced just 1,000.

The publication of Volume Three: *The Return of the King* was delayed until 20 October 1955 in the UK and 5 January 1956 in the US, while Tolkien undertook a complete revision of Books Five and Six, along with the appendices, where more material had to be excised due to lack of space.

However, Allen & Unwin had upped the print run to 7,000 copies, while Houghton Mifflin produced 5,000.

The critics who had liked *The Lord of the Rings* to begin with liked it to the end. However, some critics were dismissive. The American author Edmund Wilson dismissed it as 'a children's book which has somehow got out of hand' and saying it would only appeal to British literary taste, while British novelist Edwin Muir pointed out that the characters are boys 'masquerading as adult heroes . . . hardly one of them knows anything about women, except by hearsay'. It seems, from the off, you either loved *The Lord of the Rings* or you hated it.

There was, of course, some substance to Muir's criticism. Tolkien was a man from a bygone age and was uncomfortable writing about women or emotions concerning them. He was also out of step with the modernism that was then in literary vogue. But as Tolkien himself succinctly put it:

> *The Lord of the Rings*
> is one of those things:
> if you like it you do:
> if you don't, then you boo!

Although some of the critics did boo, the book-buying public did not. As early as 3 March 1955, Tolkien wrote to a fan named Dora Marshall: 'It remains an unfailing delight to me to find my own belief justified: that the "fairy-story" is really an adult genre, and one of which a starving audience exists.'

To feed that starving audience, the first volumes of *The Lord of the Rings* were quickly reprinted and early in 1956

Tolkien received a cheque for his share of the profit of nearly £4,000 – the equivalent of over £70,000 ($110,000) and more than his annual salary. For the next ten years, the cheques got bigger and bigger.

In 1957, Marquette University in Milwaukee were quick off the mark and bought the original manuscripts of *The Hobbit* and *The Lord of the Rings*, plus *Farmer Giles of Ham* and the then unpublished *Mr Bliss*, for £1,250 ($2,000).

Despite his sudden success, Tolkien was still the crusty, pipe-sucking, old curmudgeon he always had been. When the BBC dramatized *The Lord of the Rings* on the radio, he complained bitterly, though most people who had heard it praised the production. He held up the publication of a Dutch edition of the book when he found that some of the names had been translated incorrectly. A Swedish publisher got in trouble when, in the foreword, they had the temerity to suggest that *The Lord of the Rings* was allegorical – something Tolkien had always stoutly denied, though it is easy to make a case for. Increasingly feisty, he complained about illustrators, photographers, publishers, journalists . . . claiming he could do all their jobs better himself. In 1968, two hapless journalists sent the copy from an interview they had conducted with him for the *Daily Telegraph* magazine, only to be treated to a 2,000-word essay disputing every fact.

Tolkien was, by then, reaching a larger audience in the US. In 1965, New York science-fiction publisher Ace Books discovered that Houghton Mifflin had broken copyright law by importing more than the legally allowed number of printed sheets from the UK. *The Lord of the Rings* was already a fad among college students in California. Ace quickly produced a paperback edition at just seventy-five cents. Before it was shipped, Houghton Mifflin found out about it and alerted Allen & Unwin. To re-establish copyright, Houghton Mifflin needed to rush out a revised edition. Rayner Unwin was left with the task of explaining the situation to Tolkien. The Ace paperback was in the bookshops and doing great business before Tolkien grasped the severity of the situation. After all, Ace were not paying him a penny in royalties.

Six months after the Ace edition, Ballantine Books brought out a second edition, including Tolkien's revisions. But as they were paying him royalties, they could not undercut Ace and priced their paperback at ninety-five cents. Ace were still doing roaring trade and the situation seemed hopeless. However, Tolkien had always been scrupulous with his fan mail. He responded to every intelligent query, providing that it was politely addressed. Every time he wrote back to an American reader, he complained about the Ace edition as they were not paying him a royalty. Word soon got round. Even those who had bought the seventy-five-cent edition sprung another ninety-five cents for the update. The press also ran the story. While Ace sold 100,000 of their edition, within six months Ballantine had topped a million sales. A decade after it had first been published, *The Lord of the Rings* made the bestsellers list. The updated version was used for subsequent editions by Allen & Unwin and Houghton Mifflin and within three years the new edition had sold three million copies worldwide. Ace were forced to settle out of court, paying Tolkien a lump sum plus a royalty on future sales. Along the way, they had turned *The Lord of the Rings* into a global publishing phenomenon.

Much to his bemusement, Tolkien found himself a cult figure. He found the public interest in him intrusive, even preventing W.H. Auden from writing his biography. Tolkien could not even take praise. In his blurb for *The Lord of the Rings*, C.S. Lewis had compared him to the sixteenth-century Italian poet Ludovico Ariosto. Tolkien huffed: 'I don't know Ariosto and I'd loathe him if I did . . . Cervantes was a weed-killer to romance . . . Dante doesn't interest me. He's full of spite and malice. I don't care for petty relations with petty people in petty cities.'

While he was critical of all those around him, he reserved his harshest criticism for himself. He was acutely aware of all the faults in *The Hobbit* and *The Lord of the Rings* and hoped to write more to explain the anomalies. Once, when asked to make revisions to *The Hobbit*, he nearly began all over again with a narrative poem until he stayed his hand. Any narrative, he believed, should first be rendered as a poem. That was the formula he had used with *The Silmarillion*.

But Tolkien's medieval attitudes made no difference. Suddenly in the 1960s everything British was fashionable – even if it was a tweedy old Oxford professor. Soon there were Tolkien societies from Iceland to North Borneo. There were also reports that tribesmen carrying shields decorated with the Eye of Sauron had been seen in Vietnam. Various versions of this appear in different biographies of Tolkien, so they may be apocryphal. Nevertheless, that such tales circulate still demonstrates how famous *The Lord of the Rings* was. There was no doubt that Tolkien and Middle-earth spoke directly to the hippie movement that was then in full swing.

There were older fans too. When the Tolkiens celebrated

their golden wedding anniversary, after taking a Mediterranean cruise, they held a party in the grounds of Merton College where singer-songwriter Donald Swann performed a selection of songs from Middle-earth.

3

THE INKLINGS

Tolkien himself could not have been more distant from the hippies who read his books. He was much happier in the company of other academics. On 11 May 1926, Tolkien had met the Fellow and Tutor in English Language and Literature at Magdalen College, C.S. Lewis, who would become his closest colleague and confidant.

Christened Clive Staples Lewis, everyone knew him as Jack. Nearly seven years Tolkien's junior, Lewis had also fought in the Great War and had been wounded in 1918. In lifestyle, they were poles apart. At the age of nineteen, Lewis had met a forty-five-year-old divorcee named Jane Moore, an ill-educated Irish woman. They lived together, but anyone visiting their house rarely caught a glimpse of her and Lewis always referred to her distantly as 'Mrs Moore'. However, Lewis shared Tolkien's interest in Old English literature and Norse legends. He was also keen to make his name as a writer.

Professors and college tutors at Oxford did not often meet in the course of their duties. Lewis had been at Magdalen for two terms when he was invited to have tea at Merton College to discuss faculty business. It was there that he met the new Professor of Anglo-Saxon.

'Tolkien managed to get the discussion round to the proposed English Prelim,' Lewis recorded in his diary. 'I had a talk with him afterwards. He is a smooth, pale, fluent little chap . . . thinks all literature is written for the amusement of men between thirty and forty – we ought to vote ourselves out of existence if we were honest – still the sound changes and gobbets are great fun for the dons. His pet abomination is the idea of "liberal studies". Technical hobbies are more in his line. No harm in him: only needs a smack or so.'

Jack and Tollers, as Tolkien was known at Oxford, were hardly destined to get on. Tolkien was interested in the English language and rarely read anything later than Chaucer. That was Lewis's sphere. However, they shared an interest in William Morris and Lewis was a fan of the Arthurian myths of Sir Thomas Mallory. Both despised modernism. Lewis also agreed with Tolkien that students should know more than gobbets – passages set for examinations – of Anglo-Saxon and learn the rules of medieval sound changes. As a result, Lewis held 'Beer and Beowulf' evenings, where students were exposed to Anglo-Saxon literature outside the syllabus. Nevertheless, Lewis initially opposed Tolkien's idea that students who had opted to study early and medieval literature did not have to read later writers.

Tolkien thought that Old Icelandic, also known as Old

Norse, should have a more prominent position in the curriculum, especially for specialists in early and medieval literature. To promote this idea, he started an Icelandic reading group called Coalbiters. The name came from the Icelandic word *kolbíter*, meaning those who get so close to the fire they bite the coal. They met once a week to drink beer and read sagas. Tolkien invited Lewis to join, even though he knew no more than a few words of Icelandic. It did not matter. During the evening, those present would take turns translating. Tolkien, who knew the texts well, would translate up to a dozen pages. Others would offer a page or two, or just a paragraph if they were beginners. One eminent scholar was caught with a crib and was not invited back again.

After three years, Lewis began to share Tolkien's passion for Norse mythology. On 3 December 1929, he wrote to his life-long friend Arthur Greeves, saying: 'One week up till 2.30 on Monday, talking to Anglo-Saxon professor Tolkien, who came back to College from the society and sat discoursing the gods and giants of Asgard [home of the Norse gods] for three hours, then departing in the wind and rain – who could turn him out, for the fire was bright and the talk was good.'

While Tolkien had taught himself Norse in Birmingham after reading 'The Story of Sigurd', Lewis had come to Norse mythology through the Norse ballads of Henry Wadsworth Longfellow. He had then written pastiches of existing Norse stories, while Tolkien was intent on writing a new mythology all of his own.

Soon after their first late-night tête-à-tête in Lewis's rooms in Magdalen College, Tolkien showed his new confidant 'The Gest of Beren and Lúthien'. As yet unfinished, it then appeared in rhyming couplets. Lewis stayed up late to read it and got as far as where 'Beren and his gnomish allies defeat the patrol of orcs above the source of the Narog and disguise themselves in the reaf'. He went on to say that 'it is ages since I have had an evening of such delight', insisting that this had nothing to do with the fact that the poem had been written by a friend – 'I should have enjoyed it just as well if I'd picked it up in a bookshop, by an unknown author'.

'The two things that come out clearly are the sense of reality in the background and the mythical value,' he said, 'the essence of myth being that it should have no taint of allegory to the maker and yet should suggest incipient allegories to the reader.'

This is something that Tolkien always sought. After such high praise, Lewis promised more detailed criticisms later, 'including grumbles at individual lines'. When they arrived, Lewis had adopted the pretence that the Gest was the transcription of an ancient work. He ascribed weaknesses in the text as if they were the result of the copying error of a scribe, or other corruptions of the manuscripts, and the text was wreathed in annotation as if it had been pored over by a bevy of scholars with names like 'Bentley', 'Schick', 'Peabody' and 'Pumpernickel'. In some places, Lewis replaced entire passages, ascribing his own version to an alternative historical source.

Tolkien rarely incorporated Lewis's emendations, finding his use of language too modern. However, he respected Lewis's opinions and paid renewed attention to passages that had drawn his fire.

With growing confidence, Tolkien began to read more of *The Silmarillion* to Lewis and produced maps so that he could follow the stories.

'The unpayable debt that I owe to him was not his "influence" as it is ordinarily understood,' Tolkien wrote later, 'but sheer encouragement. He was for a long time my only audience. Only from him did I ever get the idea that my "stuff" could be more than a private hobby.'

He could certainly expect little encouragement at home. Edith had always resented being forced to convert to Catholicism. When they had met, she was an accomplished pianist with ambitions to turn professional. But he had no interest in music, gave her no encouragement and seldom heard her play. And by 1929, she had her hands full with four children.

'Friendship with Lewis compensates for much,' Tolkien lamented in his diary. However, Lewis was more dismissive. Tolkien was 'one of my friends of the second class,' he wrote to Arthur Greeves. Greeves himself was obviously first class, along with the solicitor, philosopher and author Owen Barfield. Undergraduates together, Lewis and Barfield often took walking holidays in the English countryside together.

Barfield was an influence on Lewis and, indirectly, on Tolkien. In 1928, he published *Poetic Diction: A Study in Meaning*, which sought to show that mythology was at the heart of language. He was also a member of Rudolf Steiner's Anthroposophical Society.

Tolkien ought to have made a perfect companion for Lewis and Barford on their walking holidays. However, they liked to cover twenty miles a day even when carrying a heavy pack. Tolkien preferred to dawdle, stopping frequently to examine the insects and flowers. This irritated Lewis. Once Tolkien went on a walking tour of the Malverns with Lewis and Jack's older brother Warren 'Warnie' Lewis, a retired army officer. Warnie recorded: 'His one fault turned out to be that he wouldn't trot at our pace in harness; he will keep going all day on a walk, but to him, with his botanical and entomological interests, a walk, no matter what its length, is what we would call an extended stroll, while he calls us "ruthless walkers".' At pubs along the way, they talked of dragons.

In 1930, Lewis, Janie Moore and Warnie moved into The Kilns, a house at the foot of Shotover Hill, five minutes outside Oxford. There they had a pond where Jack and Tollers would go swimming in the summer.

On 19 September 1931, Lewis invited Tolkien to have dinner with him at Magdalen. Also present was Henry Dyson, a lecturer in English Literature at Reading University. Badly injured in the First World War, he had been introduced to Lewis by teacher and theatre producer Nevill Coghill. After dinner, they took a stroll beside the River Cherwell while they discussed metaphor and myth.

Brought up as an Ulster Protestant, Lewis had become an agnostic, though he had begun to become interested in Eastern religions. He began to accept the idea of God as a universal spirit, but was by no means a Christian. To him, Christianity was a 'cock-and-bull story'. It was a myth and myths are 'lies and therefore worthless, even though breathed through with silver'.

Tolkien's riposte was succinct. Myths were not lies. They always contained the seed of a truth as the language they were couched in was simply another way of looking at the world. For Tolkien, God spoke through, not just the story of Christ's crucifixion and resurrection, but also the pagan myths he had been studying. Indeed, God spoke through the myths of Middle-earth he was creating. He believed that God expressed himself through the minds of poets, though in the million words or so that Tolkien wrote about Middle-earth the word 'God' does not appear even once. However, Tolkien's remarks were the beginning of Lewis's conversion.

'I have just passed on from believing in God to definitely believing in Christ – in Christianity,' Lewis wrote to Greeves twelve days later. 'My long night talk with Dyson and Tolkien had a good deal to do with it.'

Lewis went on to become a well-known Christian writer, though he did not become a Catholic as Tolkien had hoped. Instead, he reverted to Ulster Protestantism, which Tolkien despised. After taking his first communion since childhood on Christmas Day 1931, Lewis began, with what Tolkien considered indecent haste, *The Pilgrim's Regress: An Allegorical Apology for Christianity, Reason and Romanticism*. While Tolkien took endless pain over his work, Lewis wrote prose fast in one draft with minimal revisions. Tolkien kept his drafts and notes, while Lewis tore up everything as he went along. He even tore up other people's work. Tolkien complained: 'He "lost" not only official documents sent to him by me, but sole manuscripts of at least two stories.'

Despite this and Lewis's return to Protestantism, Tolkien admired *The Pilgrim's Regress*. In his diary in October 1933, he wrote that his friendship with Lewis, 'besides giving me constant pleasure and comfort, has done me much good from the contact with a man at once honest, brave, intellectual – a scholar, a poet, and a philosopher – and a lover, at least after a long pilgrimage, of Our Lord'. However, the question of religion remained a sore between them, not least because Jack and Warnie, in unguarded moments, would refer to Irish Catholics and 'bog-trotters'.

Warnie would spend his mornings in one of Jack's two

rooms at Magdalen, typing up the Lewis family papers. He would often be interrupted by Dyson who would take him out for a drink. Tolkien would also be a regular caller. He and Jack would usually spend an hour together on a Monday morning, concluding with a pint in the Eastgate Hotel opposite. According to Jack: 'This is one of the pleasantest spots in the week. Sometimes we talk English School politics; sometimes we criticize one another's poetry; other days we drift into theology or "the state of the nation"; rarely we fly no higher than bawdy or puns.'

Tolkien was the master of the bawdy in several languages, often delighting the Coalbiters with risqué stories in Icelandic. However, the 'English School politics' dropped off after Tolkien won his battle to reform the syllabus in 1931.

Lewis and Tolkien would often go for a walk in the afternoon together. Warnie grew jealous, but Jack tried to make him feel included in whatever they were doing. Once when Lewis and Tolkien decided to spend the evening reciting the libretto of Wagner's *Die Walkire*, Warnie was also invited, though he knew no German and could only participate with an English translation. They began after tea and broke off for dinner in the Eastgate, where, according to Warnie's diary, 'we had fried fish and a savoury omelette, with beer'. Then they returned to Lewis's room to finish the reading, along with 'the best part of a decanter of a very inferior whiskey'.

Of course, no evening would be complete without a learned debate.

'Arising from the perplexities of Wotan we had a long and interesting discussion on religion,' said Warnie, 'which lasted until about half past eleven.'

Warnie recorded another bibulous evening with Jack, Tolkien, Dyson and Nevill Coghill at Exeter College. Afterwards, as they strolled back to Magdalen, they saw a deer. Tolkien swept off his hat and said: 'Hail fallow, well met.'

There were plenty of other informal groupings of academics. The Oyster Club would meet to celebrate the end of exams marking by eating oysters. Then there was a larger group called The Cave.

As they exhausted all the major sagas, the Coalbiters wound down, and Tolkien and Lewis moved on to another literary group called the Inklings, in which aspiring authors read their unpublished manuscripts. It had been started by Edward Tangye Lean, an ambitious undergraduate with literary leanings. The editor of the university magazine *Isis*, he published a couple of novels while still an undergraduate. The Inklings met at University College and a number of dons attended. Tolkien read his poem 'Errantry' there. Afterwards it was published in the *Oxford Magazine*.

Around that time Tolkien gave Lewis the manuscript of *The Hobbit* to read. On 4 February 1933, Lewis wrote to his childhood friend Arthur Greeves, saying: 'Since term began [on 15 January] I have had a delightful time reading a children's story which Tolkien has just written . . . he also grew up on W Morris and George MacDonald. Reading his fairy tale has been uncanny – it is so exactly like what we would both have longed to write (or read) in 1916: so that one feels he is not making it up but merely describing the same world into which the three of us have the entry.'

But Lewis added a caveat: 'Whether it is really good (I think it is until the end) is of course another question: still more, whether it will succeed with modern children.'

When *The Hobbit* was published in September 1937, he betrayed no such qualms, writing in *The Times Literary Supplement*: 'No common recipe for children's stories will give you creatures so rooted in their own soil and history as those of Professor Tolkien – who obviously knows much more about them than he needs for this tale.'

By then Lewis had read much of *The Silmarillion*. He was himself hankering to write fiction. According to Tolkien: 'Lewis said to me one day: "Tollers, there is too little of what we really like in stories. I am afraid we shall have to write some ourselves."'

They discussed the idea of creating myths, thinly disguised as popular thrillers. Then Lewis decided to dabble in science fiction and Tolkien began *The Lost Road*, which tells of a father and son who travel through time and become involved in the downfall of Númenor, an island in the Sundering Sea to the west of Middle-earth. But he gave up after four chapters. It appears in *The Lost Road and Other Writings*, the fifth volume of *The History of Middle-earth* edited by Christopher Tolkien. So he returned to what he thought of as *The New Hobbit* – the one he had started with 'A Long-Expected Party', something that would make a story out of the material he had collected for *The Silmarillion*.

Lewis finished *Out of the Silent Planet* by the autumn of 1937, but the publishers of *The Pilgrim's Regress*, J.M. Dent, turned it down. Tolkien recommended it to Allen & Unwin.

Writing to Stanley Unwin, he said: 'I read it, of course; and I have since heard it pass a rather different test: that of being read aloud to our local club . . . It proved an exciting serial, and was highly approved. But then of course we are all rather like-minded.'

The hero was a philologist and, by coincidence, named

Unwin, though the name was changed to Ransom before publication.

Tolkien wrote a second letter a few weeks later, saying: 'I read the story in the original ms and was so enthralled that I could do nothing until I had finished it.'

When Allen & Unwin decided not to publish it, Stanley Unwin passed it on to The Bodley Head, where he was also chairman. They took it on and published it in autumn 1938.

In June 1938, the Inklings had something else to celebrate. One of their number, the Reverend Adam Fox, had been elected Professor of Poetry at Oxford. Lewis and Tolkien had nominated him. It was, Tolkien said, 'our first literary club of practising poets – before whom *The Hobbit* and other works (such as the *Silent Planet*) had been read. We are slowly getting into print.'

When Tangye Lean graduated and left for a career in journalism and broadcasting, the Inklings wound down. But Tolkien and Lewis resurrected it in Lewis's rooms at Magdalen. The meetings there had little connection to its earlier, undergraduate incarnation, but Tolkien liked the name.

'It was a pleasantly ingenious pun in its way, suggesting people with vague or half-formed intimations and ideas plus those who dabble in ink,' he said.

Warnie had bought a two-berth cabin cruiser that he moored at Salter's boatyard on the Thames at Oxford. But with war looming, he was recalled to duty as a major. Jack and Dyson had been planning a trip up the river, but as neither of them was practical enough to handle a motorboat, they enlisted as pilot Dr R.E. 'Humphrey' Havard – later known as UQ (Useless Quack) Havard – who also became a member of the Inklings. They were on an extended waterborne pub crawl up the Thames when Hitler invaded Poland and had returned to Oxford by the time Britain declared war.

With the onset of hostilities, the London branch of Oxford University Press moved back to Oxford, bringing with it Charles Williams. Fascinated by Rosicrucianism, he became a member of the Order of the Golden Dawn, an occult organization said to have been involved in black magic and necromancy. These interests were reflected in the novels he wrote. In 1936, while Williams was reading Lewis's *Allegory of Love* at OUP, Lewis was, by chance, reading Williams's *The Place of the Lion*, where Platonic archetypes inhabit the countryside. Lewis praised it highly.

No sooner had Williams arrived in Oxford than Lewis invited him along to a meeting of the Inklings in his rooms in Magdalen. They were generally held on Thursday evenings during term time. Williams read his nativity play *The House by the Stable*, followed by a play for Whitsun called *Terror of Light*. He was soon expressing religious views that Tolkien's fellow Anglo-Saxonist Charles Wrenn found so heretical he expressed a wish to burn him. He then read his dense Arthurian poem *Taliessin through Logres*, which everyone but Lewis found incomprehensible.

Tolkien was irritated by Lewis's hero-worship of Williams, who was largely self-educated and followed by a coterie of young women.

'I was and remain wholly unsympathetic to Williams' mind,' Tolkien wrote in 1965. 'I knew Charles Williams only as a friend through CSL . . . owing to the war he spent much of his time in Oxford. We liked one another and enjoyed talking (mostly in jest) but we had nothing to say to one another at deeper (or higher) levels. I doubt if he had read anything of mine then available; I had read or heard a good deal of his work, but found it wholly alien, and sometimes very distasteful, sometimes ridiculous.'

Due to the references to black magic in Williams's books, Tolkien called him the 'witch doctor'. Tolkien believed in the devil and did not think that such ideas should be bandied about in popular novels. What annoyed him more was that Williams frequently turned up for the Monday-morning sessions Tolkien had been having with Lewis in the Eastgate Hotel for nearly ten years. Worse, Lewis and Williams would discuss modern English literature – that is, literature after Chaucer and an anathema to Tolkien. Nevertheless when the Inklings began holding their meetings on Tuesday mornings at a pub called the Eagle and Child, also known as the Bird and Baby, in St Giles, Tolkien and Williams were often seen talking together. The group met in the snug bar at the back of the pub, which was called, appropriately enough, 'The Rabbit Room'. Tolkien and Williams would also walk home together after the Thursday night meetings in Magdalen and it is thought that Tolkien only sought to distance himself from Williams later to quash speculation that the newcomer may have influenced him.

Certainly Tolkien was not being fair when he implied that Williams knew nothing of his work. He was at most of the meetings where Tolkien read *The Lord of the Rings*. Later, Williams borrowed the manuscript, as much of it as was complete at the time, to refresh his memory. In December 1944, Tolkien wrote to his son Christopher, saying: 'C. Williams who is reading it all says the great thing is that its centre is not in strife and war and heroism (though they are all understood and depicted) but freedom, peace, ordinary life and good living. Yet he agrees that these very things

require the existence of a great world outside the Shire – lest
they should grow stale by custom and turn into the
humdrum.'

Tolkien was much more dismissive of Williams's work. He
did not like the Byzantine settings in the *Taliessin* poems.
The random selection of geographical features did not appeal
to him, nor did the fact that they seemed to be related to
parts of the anatomy. He even wrote a long poem ridiculing
Williams's work.

No one recorded what happened at the meetings of the
Inklings and the Thursday-evening sessions in Lewis's rooms
were a closed affair. It is known that the large sitting room
where they were held was rather shabby. Lewis would
eschew ashtrays and flick cigarette ash on the carpet and
armchairs, claiming it was good for them. A table survived.
It had large ring marks from jugs of beer – despite wartime
shortages – and smaller ones from bottles of ink, along with
ink stains and cigarette burns. The books on his shelves were
shabby too. Due to the expense of living with Mrs Moore,
Lewis had long since given up collecting finely bound
editions and stocked his shelves with cheap, second-hand
books. There were not very many of them either. He used
the Bodleian – the university library – for all essential texts.
Lewis did not even keep copies of his own books, giving
them away or throwing them out at the slightest excuse.
However, there were a number of Charles Williams's books,
along with Owen Barfield's children's story *The Silver
Trumpet* and, of course, *The Hobbit*.

In a small adjoining room, there was a typewriter which
Warnie Lewis used to type Jack's letters, after being co-opted
as his secretary. After the first months of the war, he had
returned to Oxford when the army decided they did not

need officers his age. The shelves were also stocked with books on the Bourbon court; Warnie had ambitions to write a book on the court of Louis XIV. There were scraps of paper and scissors, used to crop the ends of short letters when paper was rationed. Jack slept in a second adjoining room during term time. It contained nothing but a bed, a washstand and piles of books.

Members would assemble in the sitting room after nine o'clock when the blackout curtains were closed and a few lumps of coal were put in the grate to revive the fire. Then Warnie would make the tea. There was no formal time for the meetings to begin. Lewis and Tolkien would turn up after Jack had treated Tollers to dinner at the high table in Magdalen. Other members would turn up any time between nine and half-past ten.

There was no fixed membership. Inklings could bring along someone new without prior approval of the others. This did not happen often. Most Thursdays, there was just Tolkien, Williams, Havard and the Lewis brothers. War work would sometimes intervene. As an air-raid warden, Tolkien would have to spend an evening every two weeks or so, manning the telephone in a concrete ARP post in the grounds of St Hugh's College. Six years younger, Lewis was a member of the Home Guard and, sometimes, had to go out on patrol.

Dyson would turn up, if he was in Oxford. Coghill was also a regular, but his attendance dropped off as he was in demand by the university dramatic society, or other groups putting on a production. Adam Fox turned up occasionally, as did Owen Barfield when he could get away from London. Charles Wrenn also looked in. Although Jack Lewis insisted that the raison d'être of the Inklings was to air unpublished work, often no one had anything to read so they simply joined in a general conversation.

Tolkien would sometimes read early drafts of a chapter, before he had many of the details worked out. Even so, he read quite fluently. Sometimes he would stop and correct himself if he spotted something was wrong. A reading would go on for over an hour. A general discussion would then ensue.

In 1942, Lewis published *The Screwtape Letters*, purportedly written by a senior demon named Screwtape to his nephew, Wormwood, a younger and less experienced demon, who is charged with guiding a man toward 'Our Father Below' – that is, the Devil – and away from 'the Enemy' – God. It was dedicated to Tolkien, though he did not like the book. Tolkien believed in the power of evil and thought you should not trifle with such things.

Still the Inklings were pleased with themselves. Parodying the opening lines of *Beowulf*, Tolkien wrote: '*Hwæt! we Inclinga . . .*' or 'Lo! we have heard in old days of the wisdom of cunning-minded Inkings; how those wise ones sat together in their deliberations, skilfully reciting learning and song-craft, earnestly meditating. That was true joy!'

The poem went on to praise Hlothwig, 'dearest of men, board and bright of word'. Hlothwig is the Anglo-Saxon form of the Germanic word that the name Lewis is derived from.

In 1943, Havard was called up into the navy as a medical officer. Due to his ginger beard, he was immediately nicknamed the 'Red Admiral'. However, there was a malaria research unit in Oxford. Tolkien put in a good word and Havard was posted there, allowing Lewis to call Tolkien 'The Lord of the Strings'. As a result, the Thursday evening session could continue as bibulously as ever. Tolkien wrote on 18 November 1944 of the proceedings the previous

Thursday: 'I reached the Mitre at 8 where I was joined by CW and the Red Admiral, resolved to take on fuel before joining the well-oiled diners in Magdalen (CSL and Owen Barfield). CSL was highly flown, but we were also in good fettle; while OB is the only man who can tackle CSL making him define everything, and interrupting his most dogmatic pronouncements with subtle *distingo*s. The result was a most amusing and highly contentious evening, on which had an outsider dropped he would have thought it a meeting of fell enemies hurling deadly insults before drawing their guns.'

One would have thought, after this, there would have been little time for literature that evening. On the contrary, they then enjoyed 'a short play on Jason and Medea by Barfield, two excellent sonnets sent by a young poet to CSL; and some illuminating discussion of "ghosts", and of the special nature of hymns'. Lewis was on a committee revising the Church of England's hymnal *Hymns Ancient and Modern* at the time. Tolkien left at twelve-thirty and was in bed by one.

By the mid-1940s, *The Screwtape Letters* had sold nearly a quarter of a million copies and more science-fiction novels were on their way. Lewis was now a famous writer, while Tolkien and *The Hobbit* were a distant memory. Jealous perhaps, Tolkien began to suspect that Lewis was borrowing his ideas. The Adam and Eve characters in Lewis's *Perelandra (Voyage to Venus)* were called To and Tinidril. Tolkien thought they had a 'certain echo of Tuor and Idril in *The Silmarillion*', and that Tinidril was actually a combination of his of Tinúviel and Idril. In his own copy of *Perelandra*, Tolkien wrote: 'A bottle of sound vintage (?) I hope!' It is interesting, however, to note that Lewis's Wormwood predates Tolkien's Wormtongue from *The Lord of the Rings*.

Lewis was invited to broadcast and lecture on Christianity, but occasionally his growing pomposity was punctured. He had dedicated *Perelandra* 'To some ladies at Wantage' – a congregation of junior nuns he had addressed there. In the Portuguese translation of the book, this appears as 'To some wanton ladies'. The Inklings were irritated by the attention Lewis's broadcasts bought him. Lewis, Tolkien wrote, was 'getting too much publicity for his or any of our tastes'.

Towards the end of the war, the morning meetings of the Inklings were not limited to Tuesdays. Nor were they restricted to the Bird and Baby, which had been drunk dry by American troops in the build up to D-Day. They would congregate in the tap room of the Mitre Hotel, the White Horse next to Blackwell's bookshop in Broad Street or the King's Arms opposite the Bodleian Library.

'The fun was fast and furious,' wrote Lewis, enjoying the thought 'that the company probably thinks we're talking bawdy when in fact we're talking theology.'

By then the Inklings were pared down to Tolkien, Williams, Havard and the Lewis brothers. Fox had left Oxford. Wrenn was working in London and rarely came to the Thursday meetings, while Coghill had dropped out altogether. Tolkien's friend, history tutor at Pembroke College R.B. McCallum, came along, but he was considered too donnish to be convivial while Catholic priest Gervase Mathew stole Tolkien's crown as the fastest and most inaudible speaker. Tolkien had a slight speech impediment and one of his obituaries described him as 'the best and worst talker in Oxford – worst for the rapidity and indistinctness of his speech, and the best for the penetration, learning, humour and "race" of what he said'.

The biographer Lord David Cecil became an honoured

guest, reading his *Two Quiet Lives* at meetings. However, both Mathew and Cecil were more impressed by Williams than Tolkien, who had yet to finish his masterwork. When Williams's book on Dante, *The Figure of Beatrice*, was published, Tolkien wrote:

The sales of Charles Williams
Leapt by the millions,
When a reviewer surmised
He was only Lewis disguised.

Detective writer Dorothy L. Sayers was impressed by *The Figure of Beatrice*. She also wrote Lewis a fan letter. In return, Lewis and Tolkien admired *The Man Born to be King*, a series of plays she had written for the BBC. But she was not invited to meetings of the Inklings. No woman ever was.

'She never met our club,' said Lewis, 'and probably never knew of its existence.'

While Tolkien liked Sayers personally, he could not stand *Gaudy Night*, her detective story set in Oxford, and found her aristocratic sleuth Lord Peter Wimsey had grown tiresome.

'I followed P. Wimsey from his attractive beginnings so far,' he said, 'by which time I conceived a loathing for him not surpassed by any other character in literature known to me, unless by his Harriet.'

They welcomed the author E.R. Edison, another English medievalist, into their number. Tolkien thought him a great writer and read everything he published, but disliked his 'peculiarly bad nomenclature and his personal philosophy'. Lewis and no such qualms and exchanged letters with Edison in medieval English.

In the summer of 1944, when Tolkien was reading aloud from the newly completed Book Four of *The Lord of the Rings*, Edison was reading his romance *The Mezentian Gate*, which Tolkien found to be of 'undiminished power and felicity of expression'. Edison died the following year, leaving the book unfinished.

On 6 October 1944, the American troops had gone and the Bird and Baby became home to the Inklings again. Tolkien and Lewis were in there one Tuesday morning, exchanging bawdy tales, when they were approached by South African writer Roy Campbell, author of *The Flaming Terrapin* and *Flowering Rifle*. He had sought them out. This was embarrassing because Lewis had recently lampooned Campbell in the *Oxford Magazine*.

Campbell had fought in the Spanish Civil War on the side of General Francisco Franco, the fascist leader, and at that Thursday evening's meeting of the Inklings provoked a political falling out between Lewis and Tolkien. While Lewis stuck up for democracy, Tolkien announced: 'I am not a democrat, if only because humility and equality are spiritual principles corrupted by the attempt to mechanize and formalize them, with the result that we get not universal smallness and humility, but universal greatness and pride.'

Both Lewis and Tolkien were conservative in their politics. They feared the rise of communism, as they had feared the rise of the Blackshirts – Oswald Moseley's British fascists. Lewis had attacked them in *The Pilgrim's Regress*. However, Tolkien supported Franco in Spain because he defended the Catholic Church against the predations of the Republicans. While fighting in Spain, Campbell had converted to Catholicism, another thing that gained Tolkien's approval.

Lewis on the other hand 'loathed ... Roy Campbell's

particular blend of Catholicism and fascism'. And he told him so. Tolkien suspected that it was not Campbell's fascism that Lewis loathed but his Catholicism. That evening, Tolkien reported, Lewis had taken a 'fair deal of port and was a little belligerent' and insisted on reading his lampoon of Campbell.

Campbell then responded with tales of the atrocities the Communists had committed against the clergy in Spain. Lewis's 'reactions were odd,' said Tolkien. 'If a Lutheran is put in jail he is up in arms; but if Catholic priests are slaughtered – he disbelieves it, and I daresay really thinks they asked for it. There is a good deal of Ulster still left in CSL, if hidden from himself.'

Williams introduced the American poet T.S. Eliot, but he did not stay long after casually remarking that Lewis looked much older in person than he did in his photograph. Williams was published by Faber & Faber, where Eliot was a director. Eliot also wrote an introduction to *All Hallows' Eve*, which Tolkien heard read aloud at the Inklings. It was Williams's version of Dante's *Purgatorio*.

Lewis was also working on a story about purgatory. Tolkien was not impressed, preferring the first chapter of Warnie's book on the court of Louis XIV. Later they smoked their pipes, stretched their legs out on the Chesterfields while listening to Williams read his latest medievalist work, *The Figure of Arthur*.

With the war drawing to a close and the blackouts removed, Tolkien and Lewis discussed writing a book together on the nature, origins and function of language. The Inklings also agreed on what form their victory celebrations should take. They planned to 'take a whole inn in the countryside for at least a week, and spend it entirely in beer and talk, without any reference to the clock'.

The Oxford University Press reopened its branch in London, so Williams was to return to his old office. Lewis and Tolkien organized a collection of essays as a going-away present. But before he could leave Oxford Williams fell ill and died. That morning, Lewis walked straight from the hospital to the Bird and Baby, where the other Inklings were already enjoying their Tuesday-morning beer. Lewis remarked that the very streets looked different.

'The Inklings can never be the same again,' he said.

Essays Presented to Charles Williams, with a contribution by Tolkien, was published in 1947.

Those Inklings who were available gathered at the Pig and Whistle in Fairford for their victory celebrations as planned.

The Thursday meetings of the Inklings continued. New members included Tolkien's son Christopher who was now twenty-one. By then he was deeply involved in the writing of *The Lord of the Rings*, producing maps and making fair copies of the text. Later, when he was posted abroad by the RAF, Tolkien would send him new parts of the story to solicit his opinion. When Christopher returned to Oxford, Lewis was his tutor for several terms. And by the autumn of 1945, the Inklings proposed that Christopher Tolkien be made a member in his own right, independent of his father's presence or otherwise. Lewis's student John Wain, later a well-known novelist and poet, also joined.

Though the war was over, food rationing continued. Fortunately one of Lewis's American fans sent lavish food parcels, so Thursday evening meetings of the Inklings were accompanied by a ham supper. But Dyson grew irritated with the continuing evolution of *The Lord of the Rings* and would veto further readings if he was present. He would achieve notoriety by giving unscripted talks on Shakespeare on the television and appearing as an elderly writer in John Schlesinger's film *Darling*.

In the spring of 1949, Lewis began reading the beginning of a new children's book he was writing to Tolkien. This would become *The Lion, the Witch and the Wardrobe*. Tolkien disliked it intensely.

'It really won't do, you know,' he said.

He was not convinced by the 'secondary world' Lewis created. He had not worked out every detail of its geography and history as Tolkien was attempting to do with *The Lord of the Rings* and *The Silmarillion*. By Tolkien's standards, it had been hastily constructed and Lewis, in Tolkien's eyes, had not taken it seriously.

When Lewis finished *The Lion, the Witch and the Wardrobe*, publishers were beating a path to his door. Meanwhile, Tolkien's work on *The Lord of the Rings* slowed to a standstill. Lewis still heaped praise on Tolkien's manuscript, saying that, in its grandeur and terror, it was 'almost unequalled in the whole range of the narrative art', while Warnie was amazed by what he called the 'inexhaust-ible fertility' of Tolkien's imagination. They both hoped that Tolkien's twelve years of labour over the book was now over. Six of Lewis's seven Narnia books were published before *The Lord of the Rings* appeared in print.

Mrs Moore had died in 1951. The following year, Lewis met Mrs Joy Gresham, a fan from New York. She was a writer, Jewish and a former communist who, like Lewis, had undergone a religious conversion. After staying with Lewis, she returned to New York, divorced her husband, and came back to England with her two young sons. She installed herself in The Kilns as Lewis's lover. They married. Although Edith and Joy became close friends, Tolkien did not approve and a coolness developed between the two old friends.

In the 1930s, Lewis had supported Tolkien when he had wanted Victorian literature to be removed from the compulsory examinations to make room for Anglo-Saxon and medieval studies in the curriculum. Now the current professors wanted Victorian literature restored. Tolkien went along with this and Lewis was upset that he had deserted the cause. However, at the last minute, before the vote, Lewis managed to talk Tolkien round. Soon after, Lewis left Oxford to take the chair of Medieval and Renaissance English at Cambridge at Tolkien's urging.

The meetings in the Bird and Baby were moved to Mondays, to fit Lewis's schedule. Afterwards, they would eat in the Trout in Godstow before Havard would drive Lewis to the station to get the train back to Cambridge. However, the old spirit of the Inklings was gone. When Lewis died in 1963, Tolkien could not be induced to write an obituary. Nor would he contribute to a memorial collection of essays. The only comment he made about the end of their relationship that had lasted over thirty years was in a letter he wrote to his son Michael shortly after Lewis's death: 'We were separated first by the sudden apparition of Charles Williams, and then by his marriage. Of which he never even told me; I learned of it long after the event. But we owed each a great debt to the other, and that tie with the deep affection it begot, remains. He was a great man of whom the cold-blooded official obituaries have only scraped the surface.'

Tolkien was all too keenly aware of what he owed Lewis.

'But for the encouragement of C.S. Lewis I do not think that I should ever have completed or offered for publication *The Lord of the Rings*,' he wrote.

Tolkien's time in Oxford was now drawing to a close too. Tolkien had retired in 1959 and hoped to spend his remaining years completing *The Silmarillion*. Instead he found himself overwhelmed with fan mail. He received letters from astronauts and Hollywood stars. Fans would phone from California, forgetting the time difference, at 3 a.m. In the summer of 1967, a bunch of American students camped on his lawn at Headington, yelling: 'We want Tolkien.'

The last thing Tolkien ever wanted was fame. Now, he complained, he had become 'a gargoyle to be gaped at'. He had to move to a secret address in Poole in Dorset, far from his beloved Oxford. But Edith was happy. She had never been at home with his highbrow friends in academia. Of the Inklings, only Robert Havard, himself a married man, made any effort to talk with Edith. She disliked the wives of the other dons, who were largely from upper-class or wealthy backgrounds.

Cut off from stimulating conversation, Tolkien continued to work, but during his last ten years he made little real progress with *The Silmarillion*. There were some compensations though. Having been short of money all his life, he could now splash out on silk cravats and hand-made brogues. He was still a staunch enemy of the modern world, furious that a cross-Channel hydrofoil had been given the name *Shadowfax* without his permission, which would certainly not have been forthcoming. On the cheque he sent to the Inland Revenue to pay his income tax in 1971, he wrote: 'Not a penny for Concorde.'

Edith died that year and there was no reason for him to stay in Poole. By that time Christopher was a Fellow at New College, Oxford. He arranged for Tolkien to move into a flat owned by his old college in Merton Street. It was well furnished with plenty of shelf-space for his books and his meals were provided by the college chefs. He now had time for old friends. In 1973, Christopher Wiseman, the only other member of T.C.B.S. who had survived the trenches, visited. Tolkien, in turn, went to visit his brother Hilary who had become a fruit farmer in the Vale of Evesham.

In 1972, he was awarded an honorary DLitt by Oxford University and a CBE. The following year, he was visiting friends in Bournemouth when he drank a glass of champagne. The following morning, he was taken to hospital suffering from a bleeding gastric ulcer. Three days later, he was dead. He is buried alongside his wife in Wolvercote cemetery, just outside Oxford.

4

MAJOR WORKS

J.R.R. Tolkien was a publishing phenomenon. Despite his massive sales, he published comparatively little in his lifetime. Much more of his work has been published since his death.

While at Leeds, he published *A Middle English Vocabulary* and a definitive edition of *Sir Gawain and the Green Knight* with E.V. Gordon. Then in 1936, his lecture 'Beowulf: The Monsters and the Critics' was published in *Proceedings of the British Academy*. Nothing prepared the world for *The Hobbit*.

The Hobbit, or There and Back Again
First published by George Allen & Unwin in the UK on 21 September 1937 to critical acclaim, *The Hobbit* is a fantasy novel for children. The US edition was published by

Houghton Mifflin on 2 March 1938. It was nominated for the Carnegie Medal and awarded a prize from the *New York Herald Tribune* for best juvenile fiction. The book quickly became a classic of children's literature.

The story concerns Bilbo Baggins, a hobbit, who lives near the bustling village of Hobbiton. While some hobbits live in houses, Bilbo follows tradition and lives in a comfortable hole in the ground known as Bag End, which nestles under a hill. It is furnished and has a well-stocked kitchen. Bilbo is smoking his pipe outside when an old man arrives and introduces himself as Gandalf. Bilbo recognizes him as the wizard who provides the firework displays on Midsummer's Eve in Hobbiton. Gandalf asks Bilbo if he would like to go on an adventure that would be very profitable. Bilbo refuses but, not to appear rude, he invites the wizard to come round for tea some time.

The following day at tea time, the front-door bell rings. Bilbo assumes Gandalf has taken him up on his invitation. Instead a dwarf rushes in. He introduces himself as Dwalin. Bilbo does the polite thing and invites him to stay for tea. The front-door bell rings again. Again Bilbo thinks it is Gandalf. But it is another dwarf. Soon Bilbo's home is full of dwarves and he is running out of cakes. There are thirteen of them sat down to tea when Gandalf finally arrives. Together, they begin discussing their plans which seem to involve a dragon. They somehow involve Bilbo too. Gandalf has told the dwarves that he is fierce. They are not impressed. It seems that Gandalf has volunteered Bilbo as a 'burglar'. One dwarf says that he looks more like a grocer. But Gandalf is adamant there has been no mistake.

'There is a lot more in him than you guess,' says Gandalf, 'and a deal more than he has any idea himself.'

Gandalf then brings out a parchment with a map of a mountain on it. It shows the lair of a dragon named Old Smaug. There is a secret entrance. Gandalf hands the key to the hidden door to a dwarf named Thorin Oakenshield and tells him to keep it safe. The map was made by Thorin's grandfather, Thror, who had mined the mountain and found jewels and gold. Fabulously rich, Thror became King under the Mountain and was treated with great reverence by mortal men.

The dragon came to steal the gold and jewels, killing and scattering Thror's followers. Now Thorin and the other dwarves plan to return to the mountain and claim their rightful inheritance. Bilbo fears that the dwarves want him to slay the dragon. He would rather stay at home and smoke his pipe, but he finds that he is excited by the idea of an adventure.

That night he has troubled dreams and wakes in the morning to find, to his relief, that they have left without him. But Gandalf turns up and hands him a note. It is from Thorin and company and is addressed to 'Burglar Bilbo', thanking him for agreeing to help them. In return, Thorin offers him one fourteenth of any profits, plus travel expenses – including funeral expenses, if necessary. He is to meet them at the Green Dragon Inn in Bywater. Gandalf says that he has just ten minutes to get there. Against his better judgement, Bilbo goes. He arrives just in time to join the party as they head off. Later Bilbo notices that Gandalf is not with them.

Soon they are out of respectable hobbit country, into lands where people speak strange languages and there are evil-looking castles looking like they had been built by wicked people. It is gloomy and begins to rain. Then they stop to camp for the night under a clump of trees.

In the distance, they see a light. Bilbo is told, as a burglar, it is his job to go and find out what it is about. He finds three very large trolls sitting around a fire, cooking mutton and drinking beer. They are tired of mutton and long for manflesh. Bilbo remembers that he is supposed to be a burglar and tries to pick one of the troll's pockets, but gets caught.

They discuss cooking and eating him, though Bilbo would hardly make a mouthful once he had been skinned and boned. The trolls fall out and Bilbo escapes during the ensuing altercation. The commotion attracts the dwarves. They approach one by one and are captured. The trolls are about to roast them when Gandalf arrives. Speaking from behind a tree, he stokes up the argument between the three trolls. This goes on until dawn. If trolls are caught by direct rays of sunlight, they turn to stone. The three trolls are so involved with the fight that Gandalf has stirred up that they do not notice the sun peeking over the horizon and they are, literally, petrified. The dwarves are freed. Inside the trolls' cave they find weapons and arm themselves – Gandalf and Thorin with swords and Bilbo with a small dagger which is as big as a sword to him. Then they bury the trolls' gold.

The following morning, they head for the elves' town, Rivendell. The elves invite them to rest and eat with them. They meet the chief elf, Elrond. He examines the weapons they have taken from the trolls. They are old swords, he says, made by the High Elves of the West, his ancestors. He reads the runic symbols on them and says that they were used by the dwarves in the goblin wars. The one that Thorin carries is called Orcrist, the goblin-cleaver.

Examining Thorin's map of the mountain, he notices, beside the runes marking the hidden door, moon-letters.

These can only be read by the light of the moon in the same phase as it was when they were written. They say: 'Stand by the grey stone when the thrush knocks and the setting sun with the last light of Durin's Day will shine upon the key-hole.'

Durin was the father of the eldest race of dwarves and Durin's Day is the first day of the dwarves' New Year. That night they party with the elves and, in the morning, head for the Misty Mountains.

As they make their way up a pass over the mountains, there is a thunderstorm and stone-giants hurl down rocks. They take shelter in a cave where they camp for the night. Bilbo has trouble sleeping. When he does, he dreams that there is a crack in the wall at the back of the cave. When he awakes there is and he sees the last of their ponies disappearing into it. Then out jump goblins who grab them all, except for Gandalf who is forewarned by Bilbo's yell and escapes in a flash that kills several goblins. Bilbo and the dwarves are dragged through the crack which snaps closed behind them.

They are bound and carried down to a great chamber where the Great Goblin sits. He wants to know what they are doing there. Thorin says that they are on their way to visit relatives on the other side of the mountain. One of the goblins who captured them says he is a liar. Their intent is hostile. When the goblins had come to invite them to visit them below, several of their number were killed. Then he holds up Thorin's sword – Orcrist, the goblin-cleaver.

The Great Goblin goes into a rage and threatens them with all manner of horrible deaths. He then rushes at Thorin with his mouth open as if to eat him. At that moment, the torches lighting the chamber go out and the great fire in the middle of the cavern throws out sparks burning the goblins. In the darkness and confusion, a great sword flashes and runs through the Great Goblin. The others run away.

A voice says: 'Follow me.' And Bilbo follows the dwarves out of the goblin-hall, through dark passages. A dwarf named Dori carries Bilbo on his back. They are being led by Gandalf whose sword, Glamdring, the Foe-hammer, glows when goblins are about. The dwarves flee, but the goblins can run faster and know their way. Dori is seized. He falls and Bilbo rolls off his shoulders and hits his head.

When Bilbo comes round, he can see nothing in the darkness. He sets off on all fours. On the floor he finds a ring, which he picks up and puts in his pocket. His sword is an elven dagger, so it, too, glows in the presence of goblins. By its light, he makes his way on down the passage.

He comes across an underground lake. On an island in the middle of its waters lives a small slimy creature named Gollum. He is paddling a little boat across the lake with his feet, looking for fish. He creeps up on Bilbo in the hope of a tasty meal. When Bilbo hears his hissing voice, he draws his sword.

Unable to contend with the sword, Gollum suggests they trade riddles. If Bilbo loses, Gollum will eat him, if he wins Gollum promises to show him the way out. They are evenly matched, but eventually Bilbo runs out of cryptic clues. While he is trying to think of another, he puts his hand in his pocket and feels the ring.

'What have I got in my pocket?' he asks.

Even though he gives Gollum three guesses – and he takes four – Gollum does not come up with the right answer. When Bilbo insists that Gollum honour his promise and shows him the way out, Gollum tells him that Bilbo must wait until he goes out to the island to pick up something that will help them. It is his most precious possession, a 'ring of power' which makes the wearer invisible except in full sunlight. Tired of a diet of fish, he plans to put it on, seize Bilbo and eat him.

When he cannot find it, he suspects Bilbo has stolen it. Returning to the shore in a murderous rage, he demands to know what Bilbo has in his pocket. Bilbo slips his left hand into his pocket, feels for the ring and slips it on – and Gollum runs right past him. It is then that Gollum realizes what Bilbo has in his pocket.

Gollum figures that, as Bilbo is trying to find his way out, he should wait for him by the exit. Bilbo follows him. As they near the exit, they find goblins guarding the passageway. Gollum stops. Bilbo jumps over him. Then, with the help of the ring, he eludes the goblins and slips out of the door.

He has emerged on the other side of the Misty Mountains. On the path he runs into Gandalf and the dwarves who have also escaped. The dwarves were eager to make off without Bilbo, but Gandalf felt responsible for him. Bilbo tells them about his escape from the mountains, but does not tell them about the ring.

As evening is approaching they must make off quickly, before the goblins catch them. They are some way away when night falls and they hear the baying of wolves. Quickly they climb up trees to escape. This is difficult for Bilbo and, again, Dori has to carry him on his back.

Around the trunks yelp Wargs – evil wolves from the Edge of the Wild. They are allies of the goblins. Gandalf tries to fend them off by lighting pine cones and throwing them at the Wargs. Their coats catch fire and they run, spreading the fire through the woods. When the goblins arrive, they put the fires out, except for those around the trees where Gandalf, Bilbo and the dwarves have taken refuge. The goblins then start singing a song, taunting them with their fiery death.

Gandalf climbs to the top of the tree with his wand, planning to dive down onto the goblins, killing as many as he can. But the Lord of the Eagles, who has been watching from the top of the mountain, swoops down and grabs Gandalf in his talons. As they make off, more eagles come to pluck the dwarves from the trees and carry them off. Bilbo almost gets left behind again, but grabs hold of Dori's legs as the eagle carries him away, the last of the dwarves to be rescued.

The eagles carry them back to their eyrie. Bilbo is afraid that the eagles intend to eat them. But it transpires that the eagles, enemies of the goblins, are friends of Gandalf who had once healed their lord after he had been shot with an arrow. Gandalf talks to the Great Eagle who agrees to carry them on their way, but will not take them anywhere near where men live as they shoot at them with bows and arrows. Meanwhile the eagles bring them fresh food and wood, so they can build a fire and cook. In the morning, the eagles carry them further down their route.

They spend the night in a hall, courtesy of a man named Beorn who is a skin-changer – sometimes he is a black-haired man, other times a black bear. He provides them with new ponies and a horse for Gandalf.

They travel on towards the dark and dangerous forest of Mirkwood. Beorn warns them not to eat or drink anything in the forest, and to avoid bathing in the dark water of the stream that runs through it. As they move on, they see a great bear following them. When they reach Mirkwood, Gandalf leaves them again. He is to take the horse and ponies back to Beorn while they cross Mirkwood on foot. They cannot go around it. To the north are the slopes of the Grey Mountains that are stiff with goblins. To the south is the land of the Necromancer, a black sorcerer in a dark tower.

Bilbo and the dwarves plunge on into the forest. It is dark and full of strange sounds. At night, horrible bulbous eyes watch them as they huddle together. After a day or two, they come across the stream Beorn warned them about. There is a boat moored there which they use to cross, but a dwarf named Bombur falls in. They fish him out but he falls into a deep sleep. They have to carry him. There is nothing to eat or drink in the forest after they waste their last arrows firing at elusive deer, but they sometimes hear disquieting laughter or singing at a distance.

Bilbo is delegated to climb a tree to see how far they still have to go, but he can see no end to the forest. Soon they are starving. One night they see lights in the forest. Creeping forward they find a clearing where elvish-looking folk are sitting around fires, eating and drinking. Smelling roast meat, the dwarves rush forward to beg for food. But as soon as they appear, someone kicks the fire out and they are plunged back into darkness. As they settle down to sleep, they see more lights and the same thing happens again. On the third occasion, Bilbo gets lost in the darkness and confusion. He finds himself alone and sits down against a tree. Waking from a dream about food, he finds sticky string around his left hand. The same thing is around his legs and when he tries to walk he falls over. While he had been asleep a giant spider had been wrapping him in its thread.

He manages to draw his sword. Recognizing it as a 'sting',

the spider jumps back. Bilbo cuts his legs free, then stabs the
spider between the eyes. It dies horribly. After this, Bilbo
calls his sword 'Sting'.

Hearing cries for help, Bilbo slips on the ring. Creeping
quietly through the woods, Bilbo finds the spider's lair. It is
ringed with webs and, even though he is invisible, he fears
discovery. He overhears the spiders talking about eating the
dwarves they have bound in thread and are dangling from a
high branch. Inside one of the bundles, Bilbo recognizes
Bombur, who has roused from his slumber and kicks a spider,
making it fall from the branch. Enraged the spider climbs
back onto the branch with the intention of killing him.

Bilbo grabs a stone and throws it. The stone hits the spider
on the head and it drops senseless from the tree. He throws
another at a spider in the middle of a web, causing confusion.
He throws more stones, then starts singing an insulting song
to draw the spiders off. Then he doubles back, kills the spider
that has been left to guard the prisoners, then cuts them free.
The spiders return. Bilbo now has to reveal the secret of the
ring to the dwarves while they fight the spiders off. Just
when the situation looks completely hopeless, the spiders
suddenly pull back, and the dwarves realize that they have
retreated into one of the clearings used by elves. In the
confusion, not only have they lost the path, but they realize
that Thorin is missing.

It transpires that Thorin has been caught by the wood-
elves. They are different from the High Elves of the West,
dangerous but not wicked, just wary of strangers. He is taken
to the king's palace-cave at the edge of the forest. Thorin is
suspected of coming into the forest to steal the elven treasure
and is interrogated. The elf-king orders him to be imprisoned, though he is grateful for being fed.

The other dwarves are also captured by the wood-elves, but Bilbo eludes them by slipping on the ring. He follows as the dwarves are brought to the elvenking's hall. They are imprisoned, too, and fed.

Bilbo discovers that the wood-elves trade with the men in a nearby town. Wine and other things are brought to the elf-king's palace in barrels. Once empty, the barrels are dropped into a river that carries them back to town. Bilbo finds the chief guard tasting a new batch of wine. Having drunk too much, he falls asleep. Bilbo steals his keys and frees the dwarves. He puts each of them in a barrel and drops them in the river, before making his own escape through the water-gate the same way.

Eventually the barrels run aground against a stony pier. While the barrels are being collected by the people on the bank, Bilbo wades ashore unseen. The barrels are then made up into a raft that is floated down to Lake-town, also known as Esgaroth. Bilbo jumps on. On the way to Lake-town Bilbo sees Lonely Mountain, where the dragon Smaug lives and the goal of their quest.

The river empties out into Long Lake. Under the shadow of the mountain lies Lake-town, which stands out in the middle of the water and is connected to the shore by a wooden bridge. The raft is tied up nearby while the boatmen go to feast in Lake-town. Bilbo then cuts the barrels loose, pushes them ashore and opens them. The dwarves inside are bruised and buffeted, but alive.

Thorin then strides into Lake-town and declares that he, grandson of the King under the Mountain, has returned to claim his inheritance. The people of the town have heard the stories of how gold flowed down the river when the King under the Mountain reigned before the dragon Smaug came.

They rejoice at his return and the master of the town gives up his wooden throne to him. Bilbo and the dwarves are fed and grow fat. However, they still have to face the dragon.

As autumn draws on, Bilbo and the dwarves take boats and set off up the lake towards Lonely Mountain. When they disembark, horses and ponies are waiting for them, but none of the men from the town will stay so close to the dragon's lair. As the party heads on towards the mountain, the land grows bleak and barren. The land there had once been green and fair, Thorin says. Now all that is left is the blackened stumps of trees.

They make camp beside the mountain's southern spur. Bilbo and three dwarves set out to reconnoitre the main entrance. This is the gateway Smaug uses and is far too dangerous to approach. But they see dark smoke, indicating that the dragon is alive and at home. They consult the map. Then the dwarves start the dangerous search for the secret entrance. Along a narrow ledge, they find a passageway. It ends in a flat wall. Although they beat on it, push at it and incant spells, it will not budge. They see no sign of a key-hole, but there is no doubt that this is the hidden door.

Hearing a thrush knocking a snail against a stone, Bilbo then remembers the legend on the map. It is the end of autumn, the dwarves' New Year, also known as Durin's Day. As the moon is dipping towards the horizon a ray of sun strikes the smooth rock face. A flake of rock falls away revealing a small hole. Bilbo quickly calls Thorin to bring the key. He puts it in the hole, turns it and the rock face opens.

Again Bilbo is delegated to take the lead. As the official burglar, he is to go inside and look around. As he does so, he slips the ring on his finger, making himself invisible. Proceeding gingerly down the long dark passageway, he finds the dragon's lair where Smaug is asleep on top of piles of treasure. Although he is afraid, Bilbo plucks up the courage to grab a single gold cup and runs back to show the dwarves.

When Smaug awakes and checks his treasure, he notices that the cup is missing and is furious. Determined to get it back, he leaves his mountain lair and flies around looking for the culprits. While Bilbo and the dwarves cower in the secret passage, Smaug spots their ponies and swoops down on them. Then he goes back to his lair to sleep. Bilbo puts his ring back on and goes back to steal some more treasure. But Smaug is only pretending to sleep. He cannot see Bilbo, or hear him, but he can smell him.

Bilbo addresses the dragon in riddles, which amuses him. Smaug boasts of his armour and shows Bilbo his waistcoat that is made of diamonds. But there is a bare patch. As Bilbo escapes back down the passageway, he is pursued by a blast of fire. When he returns to the other dwarves, they are discussing the greatest jewel in the dragon's collection, the Arkenstone of Thrain. While they talk the thrush is listening. Taking shelter from an avalanche, they shut the door and find themselves trapped inside the mountain. Unable to leave the way they came in, they go back down the passageway towards the dragon's lair. Smaug has gone. Bilbo spots the Arkenstone and puts it in his pocket.

Thorin finds a coat of gold-plated chain mail and gets Bilbo to put it on. They find a spring, the source of River Running, and follow it out of the mountain. Meanwhile Smaug has been out on the rampage. He heads for Lake-town and sets it on fire. The inhabitants fire arrows at him, but they bounce off his armoured hide. Then the thrush alights on the shoulder of a man called Bard and tells him of the bare patch on Smaug's waistcoat. Bard shoots his last arrow at the bare patch. The dragon crashes from the sky onto Lake-town, destroying it.

The elvenking hears of Smaug's death and sends an army, assuming that the dwarves are dead and that the dragon's treasure is unattended. Forewarned, the dwarves return to the mountain to guard the treasure. The people of Lake-town join the elves and march on the mountain, feeling that they deserve some of the treasure in compensation for the destruction of their town. But Thorin considers the treasure his inheritance, regardless of how the townspeople have suffered. Bard begs him to give up some of the treasure, but Thorin is adamant. So the elves and men besiege the mountain.

Bilbo is distressed by the dwarves' greed and steals away to the enemy's camp. He gives the Arkenstone to Bard to use as a bargaining chip against Thorin. On the way back to the mountain, Bilbo bumps into Gandalf who congratulates him on his brave deed.

The following day, Bard again asks for gold. When Thorin again refuses, Bard reveals that he has the Arkenstone. Thorin is dumbstruck. Bilbo then admits that he gave the Arkenstone to Bard. Thorin is furious and upbraids Bilbo, but Gandalf appears in Bilbo's defence. Bilbo insists he had done nothing wrong. True, he took the Arkenstone, but it is only the one fourteenth of the treasure that he has been promised.

A dwarf army under the command of Thorin's cousin Dain is now marching on the mountain and he hopes to regain the Arkenstone by force. However, Gandalf warns that an army of goblins and Wargs are also on their way. The Battle of Five Armies ensues. The elves attack the goblins, who fall back. But the Wargs counterattack, driving the elves and men back. Then Thorin joins the fight. Bilbo watches the fight from the elven camp. It seems clear to him that they are on the losing side, but at this moment the eagles are sighted. However, then a stone hits Bilbo on the head and he passes out.

When Bilbo comes round, it is clear that the goblins have been defeated – thanks to the eagles and Beorn who appeared in the shape of a bear – and the dwarves still hold the mountain. A man comes looking for him. Bilbo then remembers to take his ring off. Back in camp, Gandalf is delighted to see Bilbo alive. Thorin is mortally wounded. Bidding farewell to Bilbo, he retracts the harsh words he used earlier.

Thorin is buried in the heart of the mountain with the Arkenstone on his breast and the elvenking lays Orcrist, his elven sword, upon his tomb. Dain becomes the new King under the Mountain. Two of the other dwarves perished in the battle. A fourteenth of the treasure is given to Bard, who passes some of it on to the master of Lake-town and the elvenking.

Bilbo is given two small chests filled with gold and silver, as much as one strong pony could carry. Then he and Gandalf head home. They avoid Mirkwood, even though the elvenking offered to put them up in his hall. Instead they go via the Grey Mountains now the goblins have been defeated. Then they spend the winter at Beorn's house. In the spring, they head for Rivendell where they are welcomed by the elves. Bilbo is tired, but is cured of his weariness by sleeping at Elrond's house. After a week, Bilbo and Gandalf move on. Along the way they pick up the trolls' gold. When they reach Bag End, Bilbo discovers that everyone thought he was dead and the contents of his hole are being sold off at the behest of his relatives, the Sackville-Bagginses.

Few people believe Bilbo's account of his adventures. Undaunted, he sits down to write his memoirs, which he thinks of calling *There and Back Again, a Hobbit's Holiday*.

The Lord of the Rings

Although *The Lord of the Rings* was published in three volumes, Tolkien was adamant that it was not a trilogy. He had written the work as six separate books he intended to be published as a single volume. It was purely a publishing decision to produce it as three separate volumes. Stanley Unwin was not convinced that it would be a success and was limiting his upfront costs. Ultimately it made both Tolkien and his publishers a fortune.

The Fellowship of the Ring

The first volume of *The Lord of the Rings* was published in the UK by Allen & Unwin on 29 July 1954, and in the US by Houghton Mifflin on 21 October.

BOOK ONE

The book begins with Bilbo preparing for his eleventy-first birthday. In the intervening years, he has adopted his young cousin Frodo as his heir. Frodo shares Bilbo's birthday and is about to become thirty-three. Everyone in Hobbiton comes to their birthday party at Bag End. Gandalf provides the fireworks. After the feast, Bilbo makes a speech. At the end, he announces that he is leaving – and disappears. The guests are flabbergasted. Bilbo has, of course, slipped the ring on his finger.

He is packing when Gandalf arrives to remind Bilbo to

leave the ring behind. Bilbo is reluctant to do so, but is eventually persuaded to leave it for Frodo. After Bilbo has left, Frodo arrives. Gandalf tells him that Bilbo has left the ring for him, but warns him not to use it and to keep it safe.

Time passes. Frodo is nearly fifty when rumours spread of an enemy arising in the land of Mordor. Elves are leaving Middle-earth and dwarves are seeking refuge in the west. Then Gandalf returns. He has bad news. The ring that Bilbo had left Frodo is more powerful than he had thought. It was one of the rings of power, made by the elven-smiths long ago. If a mortal uses the ring too often, he will become invisible permanently and will be devoured by the dark power that rules the rings.

Gandalf suspected this when he saw the strange effects the ring had on Bilbo. That is why Bilbo had to go, leaving the ring behind. Gandalf then takes the ring and flings it in the fire, but when he retrieves it from the flames, it is cool to the touch. Inside the band, fiery letters appear. They are in an ancient elvish language used in Mordor. Gandalf translates: 'One Ring to rule them all, One Ring to find them,/One Ring to bring them all and in the darkness bind them.'

This is a quotation from a verse in elven-lore which says that three rings were made for the elves, seven for the dwarves, and nine for men. But the ring that Frodo has is the master ring, the one ring that rules the others. It belonged to Sauron the Great, the dark lord. He has arisen again, left Mirkwood and returned to the dark tower in Mordor. However, he does not have his ring. If he gets it, nothing can stop him from enslaving all of Middle-earth. The elves have hidden the three they possessed, but Sauron has recovered three from the dwarves. The others had been consumed by dragons. The nine he had given to men had ensnared them and they had become his servants as 'Ringwraiths' under his dark shadow. Sauron had believed that the master ring had been destroyed by the elves. But now he knows that it still exists.

Gandalf goes on to explain that the ring was taken from Sauron long ago, in a great battle between Sauron's forces and the allied armies of the elves and the men of Westernesse. Gil-galad, the Elven-king, and Elendil, King of Westernesse, were both killed in the battle, but Elendil's son, Isildur, cut the ring from Sauron's hand. An army of orcs – demons – attacked Isildur. As he was trying to escape, the ring slipped from his finger and was lost in the River Anduin.

Many years later, the ring was found by a young boy named Déagol. His friend Sméagol was with him at the time, and asked Déagol to give him the ring as a birthday present. But Déagol refused, so Sméagol killed him and took it. Sméagol then discovered that the ring made him invisible. He used this power to spy on others and steal from them. Shunned, he went about talking to himself and making a gurgling in his throat. As a result, his family called him 'Gollum' and threw him out. He lived by catching fish and eating them raw, sheltering from the sun in dark caves under the Misty Mountains, where he slowly became a hunched and miserable creature. Eventually, though, the ring slipped from his grasp and he lost it to Bilbo. The ring, Gandalf explains, is trying to make its way back to Sauron, now that he has arisen once more.

After Bilbo's birthday party, Gandalf had tracked down Gollum and forced the truth out of him. But then Gollum made his way back to Mordor, drawn by the power of Sauron. He was captured and questioned. That is how the dark lord learnt that the ring had been found. He was now searching for it in the Shire and the name Baggins had come to his attention.

Frodo is frightened. He wants to get rid of the ring, but it cannot be crushed or melted. The only way to destroy it is to throw it in the Cracks of Doom, in Orodruin, the Fire-mountain in Mordor. Frodo must take it there and put it beyond the grasp of Sauron for ever. Gandalf recommends that Frodo take some reliable companions with him. One immediately presents himself. It is Sam Gamgee, the gardener, who has been listening outside the window.

Frodo sells Bag End to Lobelia Sackville-Baggins and heads for Rivendell with Sam Gamgee and Peregin 'Pippin' Took. Meriadoc 'Merry' Brandybuck and Fredegar 'Fatty' Bolger go on ahead with their baggage. Just as he is leaving Frodo hears someone is looking for him. The stranger asked Sam's father Ham Gamgee, also known as the Gaffer, only to be told that Frodo has sold up and moved to Bucklebury, though in fact he is on his way, first, to Buckland.

After two days on the road, the hobbits hear the sound of hooves behind them. Frodo wonders whether it is Gandalf coming after them. Nevertheless, their instinct is to hide. Watching from the trees they see a large man on a black horse. He is shrouded in a black cloak and his face is hidden. He stops and seems to sniff the air. Frodo feels a desire to put the ring on his finger, but the rider rides off again. Sam says the rider is the man who had asked his father where Frodo had gone.

When night falls, they hear a horse approaching again and hide among the trees. The black rider stops, sniffs the air and starts to approach their hiding place. Then they hear the voices of elves singing. The rider mounts his horse and rides off.

The leader of the elves introduces himself as Gildor
Inglorion. The elves take the hobbits to their camp in the
woods where they eat and drink. There Gildor tells Frodo
that the black riders are servants of the enemy and must be
avoided at all costs.

When the hobbits wake the next morning, the elves are
gone. Frodo decides to take a shortcut across country to
Buckland, via the Brandywine River ferry. As they look back
at the road, they see a black rider on it. Moving on across the
rough terrain, they hear terrible cries, which they assume to
be the black riders signalling each other. Eventually they
stumble onto the land of Farmer Maggot where Frodo was
caught stealing mushrooms when he was young. Farmer
Maggot invites them into the farmhouse and, over a mug of
beer, tells them of a strange, black rider who came earlier
asking for a Mr Baggins. After supper Maggot offers to take
them to the Brandywine River ferry in his wagon. At the
ferry, they hear hooves approaching in the mist and hide. But
the rider turns out to be Merry, who had come across the
river to look for them.

They take the ferry across the Brandywine River, leaving
a black figure on the far bank. At Frodo's new house at
Crickhollow, they meet Merry and Fatty. But they stay there
only one night. It seems that Frodo's friends know about the
ring. Despite the danger, Sam, Merry and Pippin insist on
coming with him, while Fatty stays behind to tell Gandalf
Frodo's plans. That night Frodo dreams of a tall white tower
overlooking the sea and yearns to climb it.

Frodo, Sam, Merry and Pippin set off early under cover of
a thick fog. They head through the Old Forest that borders
Buckland. Soon they lose the path. The trees appear to close
in on them, preventing them from moving northwards as

they planned. They reach the River Withywindle and follow it. The sun is hot and they sit down in the shade of an old willow tree to take a rest. Merry and Pippin rest their backs on the trunk and shut their eyes. After bathing his feet in the river, Frodo goes to sleep against the tree trunk too. Only Sam stays awake. While tending the ponies, he hears a splash, then the sound of a lock closing. Rushing back, he finds Frodo in the river with a tree root holding him down. Sam grabs him and drags him out of the water. When Frodo comes round, he claims that the tree threw him in.

They then find that Pippin has vanished altogether and a crack in the trunk of the tree where he had been leaning has closed up. The crack where Merry had been leaning has closed too, trapping him so that only his legs are visible. They try threatening the tree with fire, but Merry yells that the tree will crush him if they do not put it out.

Frodo then cries out for help and hears someone approaching singing a song. The singer introduces himself as Tom Bombadil. He says he is familiar with the tricks of 'Old Man Willow' and goes up to the tree. First, he sings quietly into the crack where Merry is caught, then orders the tree to give up its captives, and Pippin and Merry are released. Bombadil then invites them home for supper where his wife Goldberry makes them welcome.

That night Frodo dreams of a pinnacle of stone like a natural tower. A man is standing on the top of it when an eagle swoops down and carries him off. He hears wolves cry and the sound of the hooves of the black riders. Pippin and Merry have disturbing dreams too, but are comforted by the voice of Tom Bombadil.

The following day it is raining so Tom Bombadil invites them to stay. He passes the day telling them of kingdoms that had risen and fallen there, the victories and the defeats, the crumbling hill-top fortresses and the burial mounds, or barrows, which are haunted by spirits known as barrow-wrights. Frodo asks Tom who he is. He replies that he is 'eldest', saying that he was there before the river and trees – he remembers 'the first raindrop and the first acorn'. He even remembers a time before the dark lord came.

After supper, Tom asks to see the ring. He puts it on – but does not disappear. He then spins it in the air, making it disappear in a flash. Then he hands it back to Frodo. Suspicious that Tom may not have returned the same ring, Frodo tries it on and vanishes. However, Tom Bombadil can still see him.

The next day is fine and Tom Bombadil advises them to head due north to avoid the barrows. After lunching along the way, they take a nap and wake to find the sun obscured by a mist. As they head on they get separated. Frodo hears a voice calling to him, then cries of 'Help!' He sees a dark figure and a great barrow, then passes out.

Frodo awakes to find that he is inside a barrow. A barrow-wight has captured him. He finds Sam, Pippin and Merry unconscious. They are deathly pale and clad in white, adorned by jewellery. Lying across their three necks is a long sword. Then he sees a hand moving towards the hilt of the sword.

Frodo thinks of putting on the ring and making his escape, but he cannot leave his friends. He seizes the sword and severs the hand. But the sword shatters in his hand. The light goes out and he hears a snarling noise. Then he remembers a song that Tom Bombadil had taught him and begins to sing it. He hears a voice singing in reply, then Tom Bombadil bursts into the barrow. They carry Sam, Pippin and Merry out of the barrow where they revive.

Tom lays out the treasures from the barrow so that passers-by can take their pick, taking only a brooch to give to Goldberry. He then takes them to the road that will lead them to the village of Bree, recommending that they stay at an inn named The Prancing Pony there. On their way, Frodo tells the others not to address him as Mr Baggins in Bree. They should call him Mr Underhill instead.

Both hobbits and big people – humans – live in Bree, and plenty of other travellers pass through. The innkeeper, Barliman Butterbur, provides rooms. After supper, Frodo mixes in the 'common-room' of the inn. The Bree-hobbits are friendly and inquisitive. Frodo notices a man listening intently to their conversation. The landlord says that he is one of the wandering folk they call rangers. He introduces himself as Strider and warns Frodo not to talk too much.

However, Pippin is in full flow, talking of Bilbo's farewell party. Frodo is afraid that this will bring the name Baggins to mind – or that Pippin might even mention the ring.

'You had better do something quick!' Strider whispers in his ear.

Frodo jumps up on a table and makes a speech. Grasping the ring he resists the temptation to slip it on. Then he sings a silly song. After another drink, he sings it again. This time he falls off the table. As he falls, the ring slips on his finger and he disappears. He crawls into a dark corner and takes it off.

Strider says that Frodo has put his foot in it – or rather, his finger – and addresses Frodo as 'Mr Baggins', saying that he wants a word with him. Back in Frodo's room, Strider makes it clear that he knows of their quest and warns them that the black horsemen have passed through Bree. They were looking for someone named 'Baggins'. Frodo's slip has put him in danger. Strider says that the horsemen will return and there are others in Bree who are not to be trusted, particularly one Bill Ferny.

Landlord Butterbur comes to Frodo's room. He has a letter Gandalf left for Frodo. It tells Frodo that Strider is a friend. His real name is Aragorn and Gandalf quotes some ancient poetry which Strider will know so Frodo can confirm his identity. They should head for Rivendell. Frodo must not use the ring again for any reason and they should not travel by night.

Merry has been out taking a stroll and has seen the black riders. Strider says that they will know about Frodo by then. He thinks it best that they do not stay in their rooms. They put bolsters in the beds to make it look like they are occupied and sleep in the parlour where Strider stands guard.

In the morning, the hobbits find that the windows to their bedrooms have been forced and the bolsters slashed to pieces. In the stable, their ponies are gone. They are forced to buy a half-starved creature from Bill Ferny at three times what it is worth.

Crowds turn out to watch them leave Bree. Some way out of town they leave the road and go across country. Their route takes them via Midgewater Marshes, where they are plagued by midges. They make for Weathertop. Once there was a great watch-tower there called Amon Sûl. From the ruins, they get an unimpeded view across the surrounding countryside.

On the top of the cairn, they find a stone with runes scratched on it. Strider says this may have been left by Gandalf. On the road below they see black figures. The black riders are gathering there. For their own protection, they light a fire and wait on the top of the hill. Around the fire,

Strider tells them the tale of Lúthien Tinúviel, a beautiful elven princess who gave up immortality so she could die and join Beren, the man she loved.

In the night they see dark shapes approaching them. The hobbits are terrified. Frodo is seized with the desire to put on the ring and succumbs. But it is clear that he is not invisible to their attackers. In the ensuing altercation, Frodo feels a pain in his left shoulder as if it has been pierced by a dart of poisoned ice. As he loses consciousness, he sees Strider leaping out of darkness with a flaming brand of wood in each hand. Frodo then slips the ring from his finger.

Strider tells the hobbits to keep Frodo warm and bathe his wound. He reassures Sam that Frodo will resist the evil power that will spread from his wound. Strider goes down the hill to collect athelas leaves to tend the wound. Frodo recovers, but is not strong enough to walk. With Frodo on the pony, they move on. In the distance, they hear the cries of the black riders. When they cross the Last Bridge over the River Hoarwell, they find an elf-stone – a pale-green beryl which seems to have been left for them to indicate that it is safe to cross the bridge. Leaving the road, they cut through Trolls' Wood, then climb a slope so steep that Frodo has to get off his mount. Their morale is boosted when they come across three trolls that had been turned to stone in *The Hobbit*.

Returning to the road, they hear the sound of hooves coming up from behind. But it is not a black rider. It is Strider's friend the Elf-lord Glorfindel, sent out from Rivendell to look for them. He says he has seen the servants of Sauron waiting on the bridge. Glorfindel puts Frodo on his own horse to carry him to Rivendell.

Along the way they are ambushed. Frodo makes off on

Glorfindel's white horse, eluding the black riders, who then give chase. Glorfindel's horse carries Frodo across a ford to the outskirts of Rivendell. When they reach the far bank, Frodo turns and brandishes his sword, telling the black riders to go back to Mordor. But the black riders simply cry out: 'The ring! The ring!'

Frodo then evokes elven names. Then, as the black riders try to cross the river, a huge roar of white water comes rushing down the river, washing them away. Frodo, weakened by the effort, passes out again.

BOOK TWO

A few days later, Frodo awakes in the house of Elrond in Rivendell. Gandalf is there. He explains that the black riders are the nine Ringwraiths that he had told him about. When Frodo was stabbed, if the blade had pierced his heart, he would have become a wraith too. Elrond saved Frodo by commanding the flood, with a little help from Gandalf. The black riders are now crippled without their horses, but they cannot be so easily destroyed.

Now Frodo is well again, he and the others dine at Elrond's table with his beautiful daughter Arwen. He sits next to a dwarf named Glóin, one of the three dwarves who had accompanied Bilbo to Lonely Mountain in *The Hobbit*.

After dinner, they move into the great Hall of Fire for songs and merrymaking. Bilbo is there. He has written more of his book. The ring comes up in their conversation. Bilbo asks to see it, but Frodo is reluctant to show it to him. While he was ill, it has been strung on a chain around his neck. Slowly he brings it out. Bilbo puts his hand out, but Frodo pulls back the ring. A shadow falls between them and Bilbo apologizes.

It transpires that Bilbo also knows Strider, under the name Dúnadan, which means 'man of the west'. Strider is also a friend of Lady Arwen.

The following day there is a council meeting. Gandalf summons Frodo and Bilbo. Representatives from all over Middle-earth have come for Elrond's advice. Glóin says that there is disquiet among the dwarves. The dwarf-leader Balin had gone to the Mines of Moria under the Misty Mountains to re-establish the ancient dwarf-kingdom that once flourished there, but no word has been heard from him for many years. A messenger had come to the dwarves from Sauron offering his friendship, along with the return of their rings of power, in exchange for news about a hobbit who has stolen a ring. They had given no reply.

Elrond again tells of the origins of the rings and how the master ring had been lost. Since then the realms of the men of Westernesse had gone into decline. The northern realms were mostly abandoned, while the southern realm of Gondor has been weakened to the point where it had to allow Sauron's forces back into Mordor and cede the territory to the dark lord.

Boromir, a warrior from Minas Tirith, the great city of Gondor, then relates of the rising power of the enemy in Mordor. Gondor had suffered a crippling defeat, but fought on. He tells of a disturbing dream that involves a broken sword, 'Isildur's bane' and a halfling – that is, a hobbit. Strider reveals the meaning of Boromir's dream. He is Aragorn, the heir and direct descendant of Isildur, keeper of the broken sword of Elendil used to cut the ring from Sauron's finger. The halfling is Frodo and Isildur's bane is the ring.

Bilbo and Frodo tell of their parts in the story of the ring.

Then Gandalf relates how he managed to ascertain the identity of the ring. He discovered that Sauron was gaining power again, but Saruman the White, the head of Gandalf's order of wizards, advised against challenging Sauron directly. When the wizards finally decided to challenge Sauron, it was too late. The dark lord had built up his forces in Mordor and fled there.

Gandalf then searched for Gollum and went to the city of Minas Tirith, where Isildur left a description of the ring. After Aragorn found Gollum, Gandalf also learnt that Gollum had been to Mordor, so Sauron heard about Bilbo and the ring. Gollum had ended up in prison in Mirkwood. But Legolas, an elf from Mirkwood, reveals that Gollum escaped from the elves' dungeon when they had been attacked by an army of orcs.

There is more disturbing news. Gandalf then went to Orthanc, the tower of Saruman, who told him that he intended to join forces with Mordor, or wield the ring himself. When Gandalf refused to join him, Saruman locked him in the tower of Orthanc, but was rescued by Gwaihir, the Great Eagle. They took him to the horsemen of Rohan who had preserved their independence by supplying horses to Mordor. It was there that Gandalf obtained his legendary horse Shadowfax.

After a prolonged discussion, the council decide that the ring must be destroyed in the fire that forged it, back in Mordor. Though he admits he does not know the way, Frodo volunteers to take it. Sam, who is not even supposed to be at the council meeting, protests that they cannot send off Frodo on such a task alone. Elrond agrees and says Sam can go with him.

While Elrond sends out elves to find out what the enemy

is up to, Bilbo asks Frodo to help him finish his book and start the next one. Elrond then chooses the company that will set out with Frodo, the ring-bearer. All told, there will be nine in the fellowship: Frodo, Sam, Gandalf, Legolas, Glóin's son Gimli, Aragorn, Boromir, Merry and Pippin.

Elendil's broken sword is re-forged by elven-smiths and Aragorn renames it Andúril, Flame of the West. Bilbo gives Frodo his sword Sting and the coat of mail he used in his own adventures. They also take along the old pony the hobbits bought from Bill Ferny. Now well taken care of, and healthy and strong, he has been named Bill by Sam.

The party set out across the foothills of the Misty Mountains, heading for Mount Doom. They see a flock of large crows flying overhead; Aragorn fears they have been sent to spy on them. To cross the Misty Mountains, they head for the pass of Caradhras. However, Gandalf says that there is a darker and more secret path.

As they climb higher, the road narrows to a treacherous path along the cliff face. Snow fills the air. Then there are cries and the sound of laughter, and stones begin to tumble down the mountainside. When they turn back, deep snow impedes their retreat.

Gandalf suggests that, rather than going over the mountains or around them, they go under them, through the Mines of Moria. However, Moria is thought to be an evil place. Boromir fears that they will be walking into a trap. But Gimli is keen to find what happened to Balin.

That night they have to fight off Wargs. In the morning, they head to the western door of Moria, near a dark lake at the side of the mountain. Gandalf says that they cannot take Bill the pony into the mines and Sam reluctantly has to let him go.

The door to the mine is sealed. There is no keyhole. On the arch are the words in ancient elvish: 'Speak, friend, and enter.'

After several attempts to open the door using spells, Gandalf eventually says '*Mellon*' – elvish for 'friend' – and the door opens. Just as they are about to go in, a tentacle emerges from the lake that tries to drag Frodo into the water. Sam slashes at it with a knife until it lets go. More tentacles appear as they dash for the mine. The door slams behind them.

Fortunately, Gandalf has been in the mines before and leads the way, lighting the passages ahead with his glowing staff. As they walk down miles of twisting passages, Frodo thinks he hears someone following them. Gandalf leads them into an enormous underground hall. The dwarves once mined *mithril* there, a metal of almost magical beauty and strength. Gandalf mentions that Thorin once gave Bilbo a coat of mail made of *mithril*, which was worth more than the entire Shire. It is the coat of mail that Frodo is now wearing.

That night, Frodo thinks he sees two luminous eyes off in the distance. The next day, they come across a large, square chamber, lit by shafts in the mountain above. In the middle of the room is a block of stone, inscribed with runes. It is Balin's tomb.

In the chamber, there are discarded weapons and the remains of a book, detailing Balin's last battle with the orcs there. The dwarves were trapped there and slaughtered. Then the party hear the booming of a drum deep below them and the sound of running feet. They bar the west door of the chamber just as a troop of orcs arrives. A cave-troll tried to force its way through the door, but Frodo stabs it in the foot with his sword. In the ensuing fight, Frodo is speared in the side before Gandalf leads the retreat out of the east door.

Aragon carries Frodo to safety, though he does not believe that he has survived the blow. Gandalf closes the door with a spell as the others flee, but then comes a powerful counter-spell from the other side. In the ensuing battle of wills, Gandalf nearly exhausts his powers.

To reach the gate that leads out of Moria, they must cross the Bridge of Khazad-dûm, a slender arch of rock over a bottomless chasm. They are pursued by a phalanx of orcs and the giant monster known as a Balrog armed with a sword and a whip. Gandalf sends the others on ahead while he holds the bridge. As Balrog steps onto the bridge, Gandalf smites the walkway with his staff. The bridge collapses. Balrog tumbles into the abyss. But as he does so, his whip catches Gandalf around the ankles, dragging him down too.

Eventually Aragorn hurriedly leads the rest of the party out of the Great Gates of Moria. Once they have escaped from the mountain, they are overwhelmed with grief.

Bidding farewell to Gandalf, Aragorn leads the company from the Misty Mountains and towards the elvish forest of Lothlórien, also known as Lórien. They stop briefly to tend to Frodo's injury, only to find that he is uninjured. Bilbo's coat of *mithril* has saved Frodo's life. All he has suffered is bruising.

They enter the woods as night falls and are stopped by a group of elves who have been watching from the trees. Legolas speaks to them in their language. They have also heard something of Frodo's quest and invite the visitors up to the platforms in the trees where they live. There they meet Haldir who knows the common language, the lingua franca of Middle-earth. That night they hear a company of orcs passing below them on the forest floor in pursuit. The elves say that none of the orcs will ever leave Lórien, implying they will be killed. They are followed by another strange creature with pale eyes that makes a hissing sound as it breathes. It slips away and vanishes into the night.

In the morning, the fellowship are taken further into Lórien. The orcs have been destroyed, but the other strange creature has vanished southwards down the river Silverlode.

That night, the company reach Caras Galadhon, the main city of Lórien, where they are brought before Lord Celeborn and Lady Galadriel, the rulers of the country. Their great hall is built on a platform in the largest tree in the forest. Aragorn tells their hosts of the loss of Gandalf in Moria. Galadriel knew Gandalf well. Celeborn blames the dwarves for waking the Balrog, and he regrets having allowed Gimli into Lórien. But Galadriel tells Celeborn that waking the Balrog was not Gimli's fault. She knows the purpose of their quest and the burden that Frodo bears.

As the fellowship stand before her, she seems to read their minds and offers them each the thing they want most, but could get only if they turned aside from the quest. Boromir is reluctant to say what Galadriel offered. He presses Frodo with questions, but he, too, refuses to answer.

One evening, the Lady takes Sam and Frodo to see the Mirror of Galadriel. This is a basin of water where you can glimpse scenes distant in time or space. At first, Frodo is not willing to employ such elf-magic, but Sam has a look and sees Hobbiton where a factory is now belching black smoke from its chimney. Then Frodo has a look too. He sees a wizard, but cannot make out whether it is Gandalf on a journey long ago or Saruman. Then he sees a storm at sea and a tall ship with a torn sail, then a river flowing through a thronging city, then a white fortress with seven towers. After that he sees another ship, and a terrible battle. The surface of the water is then filled with a huge eye which is searching for him and the ring on the chain around his neck grows heavy.

Lady Galadriel is the keeper of one of the rings given to the elves. Frodo offers her the master ring, but she refuses it, knowing that it would corrupt her too and she would become as bad as Sauron himself.

The time comes to move on, but they are not quite sure what their next step should be as they no longer have Gandalf to guide them. Boromir wants to go to Minas Tirith, which is just across the river from Mordor. But then Frodo begins to suspect that Boromir does not want to destroy the ring of power.

Celeborn provides them with boats and they set off down the River Anduin that leads out of Lórien. The elves also supply them with *lembas* – thin cakes that stay fresh and provide enough sustenance for one day's journey – along with elven ropes and cloaks that change colour to match the background and conceal the wearer.

Galadriel then gives Aragorn an ornate sheath for his sword and a green gem in a silver brooch. She gives Boromir a gold belt, and Merry and Pippin a silver one, while Legolas receives a bow strung with elf-hair. Sam, the gardener, gets a box of earth from Galadriel's orchard; sprinkled anywhere, it will cause barren earth to bloom. Galadriel asks Gimli what gift he wants. He asks for a single strand of her hair. She gives him three. Lastly, Galadriel gives Frodo a phial of water which has caught the light of Eärendil, the evening star. It will shine brightly when all other lights have gone out, she says.

As they head down the river, the eastern bank becomes increasingly barren. Sam tells Frodo that he has seen a strange creature in the water which he thinks is Gollum. Frodo says he has been afraid that Gollum has been following them for some time. Aragorn has seen him too, but has not been able to catch him.

As they approach the rapids of Sarn Gebir, they make for the shore. Approaching the eastern bank, they are met by a hail of arrows. One hits Frodo but bounces off his coat of mail. They head back out in the middle of the stream again and try to make their way back up river. Then a dark winged creature appears in the sky. Legolas fires his new bow, bringing the creature down.

Boromir wants to head for Minas Tirith over land, but Aragorn wants to press on down the river. There is a portage path around the rapids, so they could carry their boats and re-launch them after the rapids. Frodo sides with Aragorn, so Boromir has no choice but to go along with them.

Further down the river they pass the Gates of Argonath which is flanked by two giant statues of Aragorn's ancestors Isildur and Anárion. This marks the northern boundary of Gondor. Passing through Argonath, they draw up the boats at the foot of the mountain of Amon Hen on the west bank. This is as far as they can go on the river. Ahead lies the Falls of Rauros.

That night Aragorn is uneasy. He asks Frodo to draw his sword. Sting glows dimly, indicating that there are orcs about. In the morning, Aragorn says that, as the ring bearer, Frodo must decide what to do next. Frodo wanders off on his own to try to make his mind up. Boromir follows him and tries to convince him to go to Minas Tirith and asks to see the ring again. Frodo is suspicious and refuses. Boromir says that they should use the ring against the enemy. It becomes clear that Boromir wants the ring for himself. He tries to take it by force, but Frodo slips the ring on his finger and eludes him.

Boromir then stumbles and weeps, saying that the madness has now left him. But Frodo is already out of earshot. He goes up to the top of Amon Hen. From there, he can see all around him signs of war. He looks over at Mordor and sees Mount Doom. Alongside it is Barad-dûr, Sauron's fortress, and he can feel the eye in the dark tower seeking him out. Then a voice comes into his head telling him to take the ring off. He is torn between the voice and the eye, then somehow finds the strength to take the ring off. The power ring had already corrupted one of the company, Boromir. Frodo realizes that must go on alone. So Frodo puts the ring back on and makes off.

At the riverside, the others are wondering why Frodo is taking so long to make up his mind what to do. When Boromir returns, he says that he tried to convince Frodo to go to Minas Tirith, but he had grown angry and disappeared. They set off to find him. Boromir goes off with Pippin and Merry, while Aragorn accompanies Sam. Aragorn heads off up Amon Hen and Sam cannot keep up. He has faith that Frodo is taking the ring to destroy it in the Crack of Doom. Figuring, in that case, Frodo must cross the river, he rushes back to the boats.

He sees what appears to be an empty boat departing and tries to jump on board, but falls in the water. The boat turns back and Frodo offers his hand, but Sam cannot see it. Frodo grabs Sam and carries him back to shore where he takes off the ring. Then together they head towards Mordor.

The Two Towers
The second volume of *The Lord of the Rings* was published
in the UK by Allen & Unwin on 11 November 1954 and in
the US by Houghton Mifflin on 21 April 1955.

BOOK THREE
From the top of Amon Hen, Aragorn hears cries from the
woodland below, then the sound of Boromir's horn. He
draws his sword and races down the hill, but he is too late.
Boromir is shot with arrows. Still alive, he admits trying to
take the ring from Frodo and tells Aragorn that the orcs have
taken the halflings. Boromir then dies. There is no time to
bury him, so they put him on one of the boats and send it
down the river. Then Aragorn sets off after the orcs with
Legolas and Gimli.

Along the way they find the bodies of five orcs. Aragorn
believes they have been slain by other orcs, fighting among
themselves. In the distance, Legolas spots an eagle. Below it,
he sees a company of orcs moving across the plain on foot.
They are travelling at speed. Among their tracks are hobbits'
footprints and a brooch discarded from the elven-cloak.

After several days' pursuit, they see horsemen in the
distance. They are riders of Rohan, led by Éomer, third
marshal of Riddermark, and are returning from a battle with
the orcs. The orcs have been killed, he reports, but there were
no hobbits among them. Aragorn tells the Riders that
Gandalf is dead. They knew that Shadowfax had returned
and give Aragorn two horses so that they can continue their
search.

That night they camp in the forest of Fangorn where, they
have been warned, it is dangerous to touch the trees. They
must cut no live wood and make a fire only with the dead

wood the Riders of Rohan have left them. Aragorn does not know why this is, but Legolas has heard that creatures called ents lived there long ago. That night, Gimli hears a tree rustle and sees a man with a wide-brimmed hat who then vanishes. He thinks it is Saruman. When Legolas awakes, he finds their horses have bolted.

When Aragorn, Legolas and Gimli first set out to find them, Pippin and Merry were lying captive in the orc camp, bound hand and foot. Pippin hears the orcs talking among themselves. One asks why the hobbits cannot simply be killed. Another replies they have orders to capture them alive.

The orcs come from different clans. One proclaims himself a servant of Saruman the Wise. Another insults Saruman and a fight breaks out. A dead orc falls on top of Pippin, who rubs the bonds tying his hands against the blade of the dead orc's knife, freeing them. The feuding orcs carry the hobbits off. Along the way, Pippin drops the brooch from his cloak.

Eventually, the Riders of Rohan catch up with them and kill the orcs, but the hobbits, not knowing that the Riders are friends, lie hidden under their elven-cloaks. Using discarded weapons they cut themselves free, then flee into the woods.

In the forest of Fangorn, they are surprised to find themselves addressed by a fourteen-foot walking tree who introduces himself as Treebeard. He is an ent and offers to take them home for a nourishing drink – which turns out to be ent-draughts that make them grow taller. As he carries them through the forest, some trees quiver and raise their branches as he approaches. Others appear asleep.

At a meeting, the ents discuss an alliance with Rohan. The orcs have been cruel to the ents, cutting them down for no reason, so they march on Saruman's stronghold at Isengard.

Aragorn, Gimli and Legolas are still on the trail of Pippin
and Merry. Again they come across a man in a wide-
brimmed hat. Gimli says it is Saruman and urges Legolas to
fire an arrow at him, but something prevents him. The man
then reveals himself as Gandalf. Gandalf the Grey has been
reborn as Gandalf the White. He is, he says, what Saruman
should have been.

He explains that Saruman, who had sided with Sauron, has
now betrayed him. Both are intent on having the ring.
Meanwhile Pippin and Merry are with Treebeard and the
ents. Then Shadowfax arrives, along with the two horses the
Riders of Rohan had lent them. Gimli is to ride on
Shadowfax with Gandalf.

They ride to Edoras, the capital of King Théoden of
Rohan. But they are turned away on the orders of someone
called Wormtongue. They get a message to King Théoden
who lets them enter unarmed. But Gandalf insists on taking
his staff as he is an old man and it is, he insists, merely a
walking stick.

King Théoden appears aged. He is accompanied by his
niece Éowyn and his counsellor Gríma Wormtongue, who
immediately attacks them for seeking favours but never
offering aid. Gandalf uses his staff to strike Wormtongue
with a bolt of lightning, sending him sprawling to the floor.
Wormtongue, Gandalf tells Théoden, has been giving him
advice that had allowed Isengard to grow stronger. Théoden
must recover his rightful strength as king and join forces
against Saruman.

Théoden has also been holding Éomer prisoner on the
advice of Wormtongue. He is to be released and Wormtongue is given an ultimatum – either fight against Saruman
or leave. Wormtongue flees. Théoden offers arms to

Aragorn, Legolas and Gimli. Gandalf asks for Shadowfax as he had only borrowed him before.

They arrive at Deeping Wall, a great fortification near Helm's Deep. The battle begins as the area is flooded with orcs. Legolas and Gimli fight valiantly, but the forces of Rohan grow tired. Aragorn is worried that the orcs are using flaming orc-liquor to try and blast through the wall. However, he is reassured that the citadel of the Hornburg has never been taken. The orcs jeer at the Riders in the citadel, but then King Théoden appears in martial splendour and rallies his men. The orcs cannot withstand their charge. Their morale is further boosted by the appearance of Gandalf on Shadowfax.

After their victory Gandalf urges Théoden to take twenty men and head for Isengard. Gandalf, Aragorn, Legolas and Gimli follow. Along the way, they pass through a forest of strange trees. These, Gandalf explains, are ents. Eventually, they reach Saruman's stronghold of Isengard with its tower, Orthanc. Once it was beautiful and fruitful. Now, since Saruman had chosen evil, it is a barren place. Waiting at the gates they find Pippin and Merry. Théoden has not seen a hobbit before.

Merry tells Gandalf that Treebeard is waiting at the north side of Isengard, and Gandalf and Théoden ride off to see him. They relate how the ents destroyed the walls of Saruman's fortress, then diverted the River Isen to flush the orcs from Isengard. However, Saruman has remained in his tower.

Gandalf sets off to speak to him. He calls out Saruman's name. A window opens and Gandalf is answered by Gríma Wormtongue, who now appears as Saruman's henchman. But Gandalf insists on seeing Saruman.

Saruman appears on the tower above them. His hypnotic voice holds Théoden and his men spellbound. But it does not work on Gimli, who speaks up. Saruman then invites Gandalf to come up and speak with him. In response, Gandalf asks Saruman to come down. When he will not, Gandalf upbraids him. Saruman turns to go, but Gandalf commands him to stay. Gandalf explains that he is no longer Gandalf the Grey, whom Saruman betrayed, but Gandalf the White, returned from the dead. He tells Saruman that his staff is broken, and the staff breaks in Saruman's hand. He falls down and crawls away.

Wormtongue then throws a crystal ball down, which narrowly misses Gandalf. Pippin picks it up, but Gandalf takes it from him. Théoden is delighted that the spell of Saruman is now broken. As they leave, Gandalf asks Treebeard to get the ents to flood the area around the tower and guard it so that Saruman can never leave.

That night, when they make camp, Pippin creeps over to where Gandalf is sleeping and takes the crystal ball and looks into it. It is black, then seems to catch fire. Pippin cries out and falls back. The cry wakes Gandalf who asks Pippin what he has done. Pippin says he was looking into the crystal ball and saw nine winged creatures. One of them flew right at him. Then he was asked who he was. He replied a hobbit. His inquisitor laughed.

Gandalf explains that the crystal ball is a palantír, one of the ancient seeing-stones that Sauron has turned to evil uses. Pippin's glimpse into the palantír not only enabled the hobbit to see visions, but allowed Sauron to see Pippin and read his thoughts. Sauron had used it to communicate with Saruman.

Then a huge winged creature flies across the face of the

moon. It is a Nazgûl, one of the nine Ringwraiths that pursued Frodo early on, only they are now mounted on flying horses. Gandalf picks up Pippin and rides away with him on Shadowfax. They will not rest until they reach the court of Théoden at Edoras.

BOOK FOUR

All the while, Frodo and Sam are making their way to Mordor and fear that Gollum is still following them. They are descending when a dark shape passes overhead. There is a crack of thunder, a rush of wind and Sam loses his grip, only to land on a narrow ledge. Frodo then loses his footing and lands on the ledge below. Then Sam remembers that he has the rope the elves gave him. It is just long enough for the two hobbits to lower themselves down the cliff face. When they reach the bottom, the rope miraculously detaches itself. Frodo says that the rope must have frayed or the knot gave way; Sam thinks it untied itself by magic.

That night, Gollum climbs down the cliff. When he falls the last few feet, Sam jumps on him. Frodo draws his sword and threatens to cut Gollum's throat. Gollum begs for mercy. Out of pity, Frodo says he will spare him if he will help them. He agrees, but at the first opportunity, he tries to run off. However, Sam and Frodo are expecting this and tie a rope around his ankle. Gollum complains it hurts. Instead, he says he will do what they want if he is allowed to swear on the ring. But Frodo will not show him it. He swears anyway and leads them on to Mordor.

Gollum guides them through the marshland that surrounds Mordor, though he does not like to travel during the day when the sun is out. He gets hungry, but spits out the *lembas* they give him. After sleeping during the daytime,

Sam and Frodo awake to find that Gollum has gone. But Frodo is sure Gollum will return as he will not want to be parted from the ring. Gollum comes back covered in mud. It is obvious that he has found food.

They travel on through the evil-smelling Dead Marshes where they see lights flickering all around them. These are the candles of corpses, Gollum says, and they should take no notice of them. This was the site of a battle between men, elves and orcs long ago.

Further on, Gollum freezes with fear. They see dark, winged creatures flying back to Mordor. These, Gollum says, are wraiths on wing, and precious – the ring – is their master. Further on, another one passes overhead and Frodo has to threaten Gollum with his sword to make him go on.

When they reach the gate to Mordor, they find it heavily guarded. But Frodo insists that he has to enter Mordor and Gollum eventually admits that there is another way in. He will show them it. To the south there is the Tower of the Moon, known as Minas Ithil. Though it is manned by creatures Gollum calls Silent Watchers, Sauron is not expecting an attack that way. When Gollum had escaped from Mordor years before, there had been stairs to a dark tunnel above the main pass, which is called Cirith Ungol. He says these were not guarded. Meanwhile four Nazgûl appear in the sky. Sauron is watching for them. Then they see more men, evil men, heading towards Mordor, rallying to the dark lord.

Frodo's little party travels on across the bleak landscape. After a few days, they reach a place once known as Ithilien where there is water and greenery. There they stop to drink and bathe. They send Gollum off to hunt for food. He returns with two small rabbits, which he wants to eat raw. But Sam makes a rabbit stew.

They hear voices and Gollum makes himself scarce. Tall men arrive. Their captain introduces himself as Faramir, captain of Gondor. He says that no travellers are allowed there. Frodo explains that they are halflings, friends of Aragorn and Boromir, and quotes the words about a broken sword that Boromir used at Rivendell. Aragorn, he says, is the owner of that sword, the direct descendant of Isildur who is on his way to Minas Tirith.

Faramir warns them that they are in danger and he leaves two men guarding them, while he returns to battle. The Rangers of Ithilien are at war with the Southrons who have joined the hosts at the dark tower. The battle is joined by a huge oliphaunt, a creature the hobbits had only heard about in lore.

When Faramir returns, he interrogates Frodo about Isildur's bane. Frodo refuses to answer, saying only that Elrond of Imladris himself had entrusted him with an errand which he cannot speak of, except to say that those who oppose the enemy should not hinder him.

Frodo says that his friend Boromir would answer all Faramir's questions. But Faramir says that Boromir is dead. He was by the river when he saw a boat carrying his body drift by. Later he found Boromir's horn cut in two as if it had been cleft by a sword or an axe. Frodo says he knows nothing of this and is afraid for his other companions. He tells Faramir to go back to his city and defend it, and leave him to his fate.

But Faramir is not satisfied with Frodo's answers and is determined to take him to Minas Tirith. Whatever Isildur's bane is, Faramir says, Boromir wanted it taken there. As they head off, Sam notes Gollum is following.

When the woodlands begin to grow thinner, Faramir

orders his men to blindfold Frodo and Sam so that they do not know the whereabouts of their hideout. When the blindfolds are removed, the hobbits find themselves in a cave behind a waterfall.

That night, while they eat and drink, Sam lets slip that Boromir wanted the ring. Faramir realizes that he must have tried to take it by force and vows not to do the same. He does not even wish to see it. Frodo explains that he must go to Mordor and throw the ring in the Mountain of Fire.

In the morning Faramir wakes Frodo. Looking down at the river, Frodo sees a small dark creature fishing in what Faramir says is the Forbidden Pool. Faramir asks whether they should shoot it. Frodo begs them not to. If the creature is not to be killed, Faramir says, he must be captured. Frodo goes down to speak to Gollum. Frodo lures him into a trap where he is captured. Gollum promises never to return to that place, or lead anyone else there, and Faramir releases him into the custody of his master, Frodo, as he is to be his guide into Mordor via Cirith Ungol.

Faramir warns Frodo that Gollum is wicked. Worse, the valley of Minas Morgul they have to pass through is full of evil, as is Minas Ithil, once the sister of their own city Minas Tirith. But without Gandalf, Frodo has no choice but to follow that path. And if he does not follow Gollum, then Gollum will follow him.

Heading for Mordor again, Frodo, Sam and Gollum avoid the road and make their way through the undergrowth. In the distance, they hear drumbeats. At a crossroads they find a giant statue. It has been decapitated and defaced. However, the severed stone head has a crown of flowers. Frodo draws comfort from the idea that the force of evil cannot hold sway for ever.

They pass through the valley of Minas Morgul, which reeks of death and decay. Gollum hurries them on. Against the sight of distant volcanic eruptions, there are great flashes of forked lightning. They see a huge army of horsemen led by the Lord of the Nine Riders. Frodo's old wound from Weathertop throbs with pain. Frodo is afraid that the ring might betray him and his hand inches towards it. Then he pulls his hand back and grips the phial of water that Galadriel had given him. The wraith-king then turns and spurs his horse onwards.

Seeing the great army that followed the Ringwraith, Frodo worries that he may be too late. They begin to climb the stairs of Cirith Ungol. High above the tormented land they take a rest. In years to come, they agree their deeds will be retold in a book. Even Gollum will be a hero. But Gollum has sneaked off. When he returns, Frodo says that Gollum has fulfilled his task and can go, but Gollum says that he will go on with them.

They go into a cave which Gollum says is the entrance to the tunnel that leads into Mordor. The stench is foul. Sam fears that there are orcs inside, but Gollum says that it is the only way. In that case, Frodo says, they must take it. Inside Gollum disappears. In the darkness, they hear a hiss. Sam urges Frodo to produce his phial as it will shine brightly when other lights have gone out. In its light they see eyes. As they flee, they run into a wall of cobwebs. Sam hews at them with his sword but the threads will not break. However, Frodo's sword Sting hacks through them.

Once in view of the exit, they run. Frodo pulls ahead. The great spider Shelob attacks him. Sam cries out a warning, but his cry is stifled by the clammy hand of Gollum who has brought them there to feed Shelob and pluck the ring from their remains. Sam fights him off, but Gollum escapes.

Sam then sees Shelob has Frodo bound in thread and is dragging him away. Having dropped his own sword, he grabs Frodo's and attacks the giant spider. He slashes at her legs and stabs her in the eye. Still the spider tries to crush him with her body, but impales herself on his sword. Then Sam, who now has the phial, raises it. Shelob, long unused to light, shrinks back and makes off.

Believing Frodo to be dead, Sam feels that it is now his duty to complete the quest and he takes the ring. When he puts the chain around his own neck, he feels the great weight of it. As he continues towards the exit, he hears orcs and puts on the ring. Cloaked in invisibility, Sam overhears the orcs' conversation and realizes that Frodo is still alive. But the orcs are carrying his master's body through a doorway and bolt it behind them.

The Return of the King
The third and final volume of *The Lord of the Rings* was published in the UK by Allen & Unwin on 20 October 1955 and in the US by Houghton Mifflin on 5 January 1956.

BOOK FIVE
Gandalf and Pippin ride on towards Minas Tirith, the capital of Gondor. Along the way they see dragons and the Ringwraiths fly overhead.

At Minas Tirith, Gandalf is known as Mithrandir. The guards recognize him and, as he knows the passwords to the seven gates, he is allowed to go forward. He says he will vouch for Pippin before the seat of Denethor who is the steward of Gondor in the absence of the king.

The white-stone city is built on seven tiered levels along one side of a hill, each surrounded by a gated wall. At the top of the hill is the Citadel. Within it is the High Court at the foot of a White Tower. Pippin notes that the city is falling into decay and is under-populated. And the emblem of the city, the white tree, is now dead.

Approaching the court, Gandalf warns Pippin to avoid mentioning Aragorn, who maintains a claim to the kingship of Gondor. For the moment the throne remains empty. At its foot sits Denethor, who is holding the broken horn of his dead son Boromir. Pippin describes the circumstances of Boromir's demise. As Boromir died in the defence of the hobbits, Pippin offers his service as recompense to Denethor. He accepts and Pippin swears fealty to him. Then he notices an unspoken tension between Denethor and Gandalf. Denethor will listen to no advice Gandalf has to give. It is his job to rule Gondor alone until the king returns. On the other hand, Gandalf insists that his only concern is for the good of Middle-earth.

Pippin is taken to meet Beregond, a soldier who has been instructed to give the hobbit the passwords of the city. Looking over the city walls, Pippin sees another city. It is the ruins of Osgiliath, Beregond says, destroyed long ago. Gondor retook it, but then the black riders came. Beregond fears that they cannot hold Minas Tirith in the next onslaught. Already a great fleet of the corsairs of Umbar are nearing the mouth of the Anduin.

Beregond sends Pippin to seek out his son, Bergil. They watch as the captains of the outlands arrive with reinforcements. The last and the proudest is Imrahil, Prince of Dol Amroth. That night it is very dark. There are no stars. Gandalf warns there will be no dawn. The darkness has begun.

After Gandalf and Pippin have gone, Aragorn, Merry, Legolas and Gimli ride on with Théoden and the Riders of Rohan. They are joined by Halbarad Dúnadan and thirty Rangers of the North who have come to aid Aragorn. With them are Elrond's two sons, Elladan and Elrohir, who bring the mysterious message: 'If thou art in haste, remember the Paths of the Dead.'

Théoden asks Merry to ride with him for the rest of the journey. Flattered, Merry offers his sword in service of Rohan, and Théoden gladly accepts.

Aragorn fears that it is going to take time to muster troops from Rohan, so he decides to ride on Minas Tirith with his men by the swiftest and most dangerous route – the Paths of the Dead. Aragorn then tells Legolas and Gimli that he has consulted the palantír from Orthanc. As lawful master of the stone, he has the right to use it. He confronted Sauron through the palantír and showed him the sword of Elendil re-forged.

In the stone, he saw a surprise attack on Minas Tirith. If it is not countered, the city will be lost. So they must make haste via the Paths of the Dead. Aragorn then explains the paths' history, citing an ancient song. In the early days of Gondor, Isildur set a great black stone upon the hill of Erech. The king of the mountains swore allegiance to Isildur on that stone. When Sauron returned and waged war on Gondor, Isildur called upon his allies for aid. The men of the mountains broke their oath and worshipped Sauron. So Isildur condemned them never to rest until their oath was fulfilled. They fled. Not daring to go to war on Sauron's behalf, they hid themselves in the barren hills. According to the verse, the sleepless dead, or oathbreakers, must fulfil their oath to Isildur's heir when he returns.

Legolas, Gimli and the rangers follow Aragorn as he rides towards the stone of Erech. Along the way, they meet Théoden's niece, Lady Éowyn, at Dunharrow. She begs Aragorn not to take the Paths of the Dead. But Aragorn is adamant. Then she insists on being allowed to come too as she is a shieldmaiden, but Aragorn will not allow it. When he leaves, she weeps.

Beyond Dunharrow lies the entrance to the Paths of the Dead, which run beneath the mountain there. The horses will not enter the dark path until their riders dismount and lead them. Aragorn halts in a clearing and speaks to the dead, summoning them to follow him to the stone of Erech. Once the company is mounted again, they find the dead marching behind them. Seeing them, the inhabitants of the surrounding countryside flee in terror, calling Aragorn the 'king of the dead'.

Arriving at the large, black stone of Erech, Aragorn addresses the oathbreakers who now agree to fulfil their oath so that they can rest in peace. Aragorn then unfurls a black flag and pronounces himself the heir of Isildur's kingdom.

Théoden musters his men and heads for Dunharrow, where Lady Éowyn awaits. At dinner, Merry sits by Théoden. A messenger from Gondor arrives. He delivers a red arrow which is a summons from Lord Denethor. Théoden says he will set out with 6,000 in the morning, but that they will not reach Minas Tirith for a week.

The sun does not rise the following morning. A great darkness has descended, emanating from Mordor. The war has begun. As Théoden prepares to set out, he asks Merry to stay behind with Lady Éowyn. Fulfilling a promise she made to Aragorn, she outfits him in the armour of the king's guard and bids him farewell. Then a young and slender rider calling himself Dernhelm rides up and takes Merry with him.

In Minas Tirith, Pippin is outfitted as a member of the Tower Guard. Looking out from the battlements, he sees five black riders on their flying mounts wheeling above a small party of men on horseback led by Faramir, Denethor's son. As a Nazgûl swoops on him, Pippin sees what appears to be a brilliant white star in the north. It is Gandalf on Shadowfax. Gandalf raises his hand and sends a shaft of light shooting upwards into one of the Nazgûls. The Nazgûl lets out a cry and circles away. The others follow, as Gandalf and Faramir enter the city.

In Denethor's chambers, Faramir reveals that he has seen two halflings, Frodo and Sam, who were on their way to Cirith Ungol. He left them two days before. They could not have reached Cirith Ungol yet, so the darkness was not due to anything they had done.

Denethor then upbraids Faramir, remarking bitterly that Boromir would have brought him a 'mighty gift', meaning the ring. Gandalf points out that Boromir would not have brought it to Denethor, but kept the 'gift' for himself. Denethor derides Gandalf for sending the ring into the land of the enemy in the hands of a witless hobbit. Then when Gandalf learns that Frodo and Sam are travelling via Cirith Ungol with Gollum, he suspects treachery.

The following morning, Denethor sends Faramir to protect the outlying ruins of Osgiliath, where Mordor's armies are likely to strike first. The army that attacks there is led by the Lord of the Nazgûl, the Black Captain. Gandalf rides off towards Osgiliath to challenge him and returns the next day with many wounded. Faramir has stayed behind to cover their retreat.

Soon the armies of Mordor approach Minas Tirith, driving the last of Gondor's rearguard before them across the Pelennor Fields. As their retreat turns into a rout, Denethor sends out a sortie to protect them. Gandalf rides out with them, using the white fire from his staff to deter the Nazgûl. The retreating men reach the city, but Faramir is struck by one of the Nazgûl's poisoned arrows. He is carried to Deneroth's chamber.

The city is now besieged and siege engines fire missiles over the wall. Meanwhile, Denethor locks himself in the Tower with Faramir, who is now delirious with fever from his arrow wound. Gandalf takes charge of the defence of Minas Tirith. Outside siege towers are built and soon the outer tier of the city is on fire. Men flee. Denethor gives orders that everyone should stay at their posts and burn in the fires. Then he orders funeral pyres to be built for him and his son. But Pippin tells Denethor's servants to bring no wood until he has spoken to Gandalf. Leaving Beregond on guard, he goes to find the wizard.

A great battering ram is brought up. It strikes the Gate of Gondor three times. On the third strike, the gate shatters. The black captain enters and everyone flees except Gandalf who stands alone before him. Gandalf orders the Lord of the Nazgûl to leave, but he just laughs and throws back his hood to reveal a crown on a headless body. Then his sword bursts into flame. At that moment, a cock crows. The sound of horns comes from the north. The Riders of Rohan have arrived, thanks to the Woses, or Wild Men of the Woods, who offered their services to Théoden. All roads to Minas Tirith are blocked, but the Woses showed him a forgotten route through the forest. When they emerge, Théoden's men find the dead body of the messenger from Gondor, still clutching the red arrow, so Deneroth does not know the Riders of Rohan are on their way.

As they approach Minas Tirith, Dernhelm, still carrying Merry behind him, draws closer to Théoden as he looks on the destruction of the city. It appears they are too late. Suddenly, a great flash of lightning springs from within the walls, followed by a great boom. Heartened, Théoden leads his men into battle. They rout the armies of Mordor and a fresh wind from the sea dissipates the darkness.

Seeing the darkness fading, the Lord of the Nazgûl leaves the city. The Battle of the Pelennor Fields continues outside though. Back on his winged mount, the black captain swoops on Théoden's horse. He then approaches Théoden with a black mace to finish him off. Dernhelm comes to his rescue. The Lord of Nazgûl warns Dernhelm not to come between him and his prey, saying that no living man will hinder him. Dernhelm laughs and tells him that he looks on a woman. She is Éowyn, Lady of Rohan.

The black captain's winged steed strikes at Éowyn, but she slices off its head. He dismounts and shatters Éowyn's shield with a single blow, breaking her arm. He raises his mace again. But before he can strike, Merry, who has sneaked up behind him, stabs him in the leg. Bowed over, the creature lets out a terrible shriek. With her last ounce of strength, Éowyn slashes at where his face should be with her sword. The blade shatters and he falls shapeless at Éowyn's feet. His crown rolls away and she falls forward on top of him.

The dying Théoden appoints Éowyn's brother Éomer as his heir. Seeing his sister's fallen body, Éomer leads a furious attack. The men of Minas Tirith, led by Imrahil, Prince of Dol Amroth, emerge from the city and drive the enemy from the gate. Théoden's body is taken to the city, along with

Éowyn, where Imrahil examines her and finds she is not dead.

Mordor and its allies soon reinforce and prepare to take the city. Then ships with black sails are seen in the Anduin and the cry goes up that the corsairs of Umbar are coming. But when the banner on the first ship is unfurled, it has on it the white tree of Gondor and the seven stars and crown of Elendil, the symbols of the ancient kingdom of Gondor. Aragorn has arrived, along with Legolas, Gimli, the Rangers of the North, and reinforcements from the southern kingdoms.

Wielding the legendary sword Andúril, Aragorn wades into the battle. The armies of Mordor are defeated, and Aragorn, Éomer, and Imrahil return to the city.

Meanwhile, Pippin has run to Gandalf to tell him that Denethor has gone mad and Faramir is in danger of being burnt alive. They race to the Citadel. When they reach the door to the House of Stewards, they find Denethor's servants carrying swords and torches. Holding them back is the lone figure of Beregond.

Denethor throws open the door with his sword drawn, but Gandalf lifts his hand and the sword flies from Denethor's grip. Gandalf asks why they are fighting among themselves when the enemy is at the gate. Denethor answers that he is not answerable to Gandalf. Faramir is already burning; the West is lost.

Gandalf pushes past him and finds Faramir lying on the funeral pyre, but it has not been lit yet. He lifts him off. The wizard says Denethor does not have the authority to order Faramir's death. Only a heathen king under the domination of the dark power would do that.

Denethor laughs and produces from his cloak a palantír. The West is doomed, he says; the black ships are coming. He lights the funeral pyre and throws himself onto it, clutching the palantír.

Gandalf and Beregond carry Faramir to the Houses of Healing. As they leave, the House of Stewards collapses in flames. Soon after, they hear a great cry of victory from the battlefield.

Théoden and Éowyn are carried into the city. Pippin runs into Merry who complains that his arm has become paralysed after he stabbed the Nazgûl. So Pippin takes him to the Houses of Healing where Faramir and Éowyn are already being tended.

After the battle, Aragorn furls his banner and camps outside the city. He refuses to claim the throne of Gondor until the war with Mordor is over. However, at Gandalf's request, Aragorn enters the city dressed as a Ranger after an elderly nurse remembers a legend of Gondor that says, 'The hands of the king are the hands of a healer, and so shall the rightful king be known.'

Aragorn is the rightful king. He shows them the green gem that Galadriel gave him and sends for athelas leaves, also known as kingsfoil. He crushes them and puts them in a bowl of hot water. The sweet scent of the herb revives Faramir who immediately recognizes Aragorn as his king. The same treatment revives Éowyn and Merry.

Gimli and Legolas find Merry and Pippin in the Houses of Healing. The hobbits ask about the Paths of the Dead. Gimli refuses to answer, but Legolas says that Aragorn led the army of the dead to the River Anduin, where the fleet of Umbar lay. At Aragorn's command, the dead swept on board as terrified sailors threw themselves overboard. Their oath now fulfilled Aragorn released them, picked up reinforcements and set sail for Minas Tirith.

Meanwhile Aragorn is holding a council of war. Gandalf warns that, although they have won the first battle, they cannot beat the enemy by force of arms. The key is the ring of power. They must attack. That way, Sauron will think that Aragorn has the ring – without it he could not hope to defeat the dark lord. This diversionary tactic will give Frodo a chance to destroy the ring. Otherwise everything is lost.

Two days later, the armies of the West set out for Mordor. The injured Merry cannot go with them, but Pippin marches with the soldiers of Gondor to represent the Shire. As the army nears Mordor, Gandalf instructs the heralds to sound the trumpets to announce the coming of the king of Gondor. They are attacked by orcs, but fight them off. Aragorn concludes that this is just a feint to make them think that the enemy's force is spent. As they move on, they are watched by Nazgûl flying overhead. Some younger men are stricken with fear and Aragorn permits them to turn back. Eventually, the army reaches the Black Gate of Mordor.

Gandalf and Aragorn ride up to the gate. They are accompanied by Gimli, Legolas, Pippin, Éomer, Imrahil and Elrond's sons as representatives of all the races of Middle-earth that are opposed to Sauron. They call for Sauron to come forward and submit to the justice of Gondor. After a long silence, the lieutenant of the dark tower rides out with an escort of black-clad soldiers. Although a living man, his face is like a skull, and flames burn in his eye sockets and nostrils.

He mocks Aragorn and his army, then produces Sam's sword, Frodo's coat of mail and his elven cloak. Sauron, he says, will spare the life of the captured hobbit if the army of Gondor withdraws, Gondor becomes a tributary to Mordor and they rebuild Isengard where a governor from Mordor will rule. Gandalf takes the hobbits' belongings, but rejects the terms.

The lieutenant heads back to Mordor. As he does so, the Black Gate opens and the army of Mordor pours out. Joined by the orcs, they soon outnumber Gondor's forces by ten to one. Pippin joins in the fighting. As a hill-troll attacks Beregond, Pippin stabs the troll who falls on top of him. As Pippin loses consciousness, he hears the shout: 'The Eagles are coming!'

BOOK SIX

Sam wakes to find himself in the dark, outside the door to the orcs' stronghold. He makes his way down the tunnel and puts on the ring. Immediately, he feels its great weight. But his hearing improves and he can hear the orcs in the tower above him. They are fighting. This gives him hope that he may be able to rescue Frodo. As the ring makes his vision hazy, Sam takes it off. In the distance, he sees Orodruin, or the Mountain of Fire. Feeling the pull of the ring, he begins to fantasize about becoming Samwise the Strong, a great hero. His love for Frodo makes him shake off such thoughts. Besides, he does not feel big enough to bear such a burden. He is just a gardener. These delusions of grandeur are just a trick.

Orcs are fleeing and Sam heads towards the gateway to the tower. He draws Sting and charges at the gateway, only to be halted by an invisible barrier. The gate is guarded by two Watchers. Each has three bodies joined together so their heads point in three different directions, but they are as immovable as if they were carved out of stone. Not knowing what else to do Sam pulls out the phial Galadriel had given Frodo. It does the trick. He sprints past the Watchers, who cry out. From above, as if in answer, comes the clang of a bell.

Inside, the place is littered with the bodies of dead orcs, their liveries marked with different badges. He hears the sound of running feet coming towards him. It is an orc. When it sees Sam, it turns and flees. Sam now fancies himself as a great elf-warrior.

He climbs the tower looking for Frodo. Upstairs, Sam hears orcs quarrelling. He confronts one. The power of the ring sends him fleeing. But although he seems to have reached the top of the tower, still he cannot find Frodo, so he sings a song. He hears a voice, but it is an orc's. The orc thinks the singing comes from Frodo and brings a ladder. Sam realizes that he is not at the top of the tower. Frodo is held in a room above that is accessible only through a trap door in the ceiling.

Hearing the orc whipping Frodo, Sam bounds up the ladder. He slashes at the orc, cutting off the hand that is holding the whip. The orc then falls through the trap door.

Frodo is lying naked on a heap of rags in the middle of the room. He is surprised to see Sam, but he thinks the orcs have taken the ring and is delighted to find that Sam has it. Suddenly, Frodo demands that Sam hand over the ring, calling him a thief. He grabs the ring, then realizes that the horrible power of the ring has overcome him and apologizes. Frodo and Sam disguise themselves in filthy orc clothing, climb down the tower and, with the phial of Galadriel, slip out through the gate. The Watchers cry out and the bell sounds again. This time it is answered by the terrifying cry of a Nazgûl in the sky above them.

Sam and Frodo run from the tower. Alarms sound as they dash along a bridge. A Nazgûl is perched on the wall.

Hearing orcs approaching, they have no choice but to jump over the side. They land in thorn bushes.

As the two hobbits struggle on northward, the ring gets heavier still, weighing Frodo down. Around forty miles away, they see Mount Doom. Behind it is Barad-dûr, the Dark Tower where Sauron is watching. The armies of Mordor are forming. Then Sam spots Gollum. Frodo and Sam are overtaken by orcs driving a gang of smaller breeds who seem unwilling to fight the dark lord's wars. The orc guards assume Sam and Frodo are deserters and make them join the column. They travel on at an excruciating pace. Carrying the ring's increasing weight, Frodo struggles to keep up. After some miles, their column meets another. In the confusion, Frodo and Sam hide behind a boulder.

The next morning, Sam and Frodo press on towards Mount Doom. As the troop movements are now at an end, they take to the road again. Frodo is exhausted by the burden he is carrying, but Sam urges him on. He offers to help carry the ring, but Frodo will not give it up. To lighten their load, they fling away everything else they are carrying. They have no need for weapons now.

They travel quite openly as the attention of the Nazgûl and Sauron is focussed elsewhere. But Frodo is so exhausted that he has to crawl. They reach Mount Doom. Above them is the dark tower of Barad-dûr. A piercing eye looks out, but it is not looking at them. It is gazing northwards to where the captains of the West have gathered. But Frodo panics. As his hand reaches out towards the ring strung around his neck, he calls out to Sam for help. Sam then puts his master's hands together, palm to palm, between his own and kisses them.

Frodo is now so weary that Sam has to carry him up the slope. Finally, they near the top. Suddenly, Sam is knocked to the ground. When he gets up and draws his sword, he sees Frodo locked in a struggle with Gollum who is trying to grab the ring. Somehow Frodo finds the strength to throw him off.

Sam holds Gollum at sword-point while Frodo makes his way on to the top. Out of pity, Sam does not kill Gollum, but lets him slink away.

Reaching the Crack of Doom, Frodo announces in a clear, ringing voice that he will not complete the quest. The ring, he says, is his. He puts it on his finger and vanishes. Then Sam is knocked down once again and sees a dark shape leap over him.

Now Frodo has put on the ring, the dark lord notices him. Suddenly, Sauron is aware that he has been tricked. The armies of Mordor halt and the Nazgûl hurtle towards Mount Doom.

Sam watches as Gollum struggles with an invisible enemy on the edge of the Crack of Doom. His white fangs bite at the air. Frodo suddenly reappears. Gollum dances around holding aloft Frodo's severed finger with the ring upon it. Unaware that he is so close to the edge, Gollum slips over and falls in the Crack of Doom. The mountain shakes with a fresh eruption. As Sam pulls Frodo to safety, the mountain's tremor destroys all the dark towers, the battlements, the courts and the prisons of Mordor. The Nazgûl, straying too near Mount Doom, are consumed by the ejecta spewing out of it. The quest is now complete, thanks to Gollum.

While Frodo and Sam were making the last leg of their trek up Mount Doom, Gandalf and the armies of the West were fighting the forces of Mordor outside the Black Gate when the cry went up: 'The Eagles are coming!' They are led by Gwaihir the Windlord.

As they swoop down, the Nazgûl make off back to Mordor. A cry comes from the dark tower and the armies of Mordor quake in terror. The earth shakes and the Black Gate and its ramparts fall down. Sauron is defeated. The ringbearer has completed his quest. Then a huge shadow rises in the sky like a giant hand, only to be blown away by the wind.

The orcs, trolls and fell beasts of Mordor kill themselves, but their human allies fight on, only to be vanquished by Aragorn and his captains. Meanwhile, on the back of Gwaihir, Gandalf soars over Mordor.

In the ruins of Mordor with Mount Doom erupting around them, Frodo and Sam have given up all hope of survival. But Gwaihir spots them as they collapse due to the fumes and heat. Two other eagles swoop down and rescue them.

When Sam wakes, he finds himself on a soft bed in Ithilien. Frodo is beside him and Gandalf, who they thought was dead, is watching over them. He tells them that a great shadow has departed. They are to feast with the king of Gondor, but they should wear the orc-rags they wore in Mordor.

A great cheering crowd awaits the two hobbits. At their emergence, the crowd bursts into thunderous applause, singing songs in praise of the hobbits. Frodo and Sam approach a great throne – to find it occupied, to their surprise, by Strider. Aragorn then bows to the two hobbits, picks them up and puts them on the throne.

Then they are taken to a tent where they change out of their old clothes. Frodo's possessions are returned to him, but he insists on giving Sting to Sam. That evening they are reunited with Pippin, Merry, Legolas and Gimli. The following morning, Aragorn prepares to enter the great city of Gondor as its rightful ruler.

Left behind in Minas Tirith, Faramir had met Lady Éowyn in the Houses of Healing. Éowyn longs to fight against Mordor. Then they hear of Aragorn's victory. She loves Aragorn, but when she hears that Faramir is in love with her, her heart softens and she agrees to marry him.

When Aragorn returns, Faramir, now the steward of Gondor, rides out of Minas Tirith with the crown. Aragorn tells Frodo to bring the crown to him and has Gandalf set it on his head.

Ambassadors from many lands arrive in Gondor. Gandalf explains that the Third Age of Middle-earth has passed and the age of Men has begun.

Gandalf sends Aragorn up a mountain where he finds a sapling that is a scion of the white tree of Minas Tirith. Aragorn takes it back to the Citadel. He has the old, dead tree removed and plants the new one in its place.

The day before Midsummer, the elves arrive in the city. Elrohir and Elladan are followed by Celeborn and Galadriel. Then comes Elrond with his daughter, Arwen. On Midsummer's day, Aragorn, who rules as King Elessar, marries Arwen. As queen, to show her gratitude for all Frodo has done, she says that he can go in her stead to the Havens in the west where all his wounds and weariness will be healed.

When the festivities are over, Frodo wants to return home, stopping at Rivendell on the way to visit Bilbo. First, they must go to Rohan for the funeral of King Théoden. Then they move on to Isengard, only to discover that Saruman has persuaded Treebeard to let him go.

As they move on, they overtake a ragged Saruman on the road. At his heels is Wormtongue. Saruman scorns their pity. The travellers arrive at Rivendell in time to celebrate Bilbo's 129th birthday. After a fortnight, Frodo decides to head on to the Shire. But Bilbo remains in Rivendell, saying he is too old to travel. Bilbo gives Frodo three books of collected lore entitled *Translations from the Elvish*, asking Frodo to finish editing them. Before Frodo leaves, Elrond assures him that he will bring Bilbo with him when he visits the Shire.

Next, their party arrives at Bree, stopping at The Prancing Pony. Gandalf assures Butterbur that now that Sauron has been vanquished, better times are coming. Butterbur asks about the dangerous region known as Deadmen's Dike, but Gandalf asserts that the king will visit the area and it will become safe and prosperous again. He adds that the king is none other than Strider the Ranger. Butterbur is shocked, but is reassured by their conversation. Next day, business is brisk, as many visitors have come to gawk at Gandalf's party. People ask Frodo whether he has written his memoirs. He promises to get to work on them when he gets home, but Butterbur warns that all is not well in the Shire.

On the road, Gandalf leaves them, after telling them that Saruman had taken an interest in the Shire before Mordor did. It is then they are introduced to what Tolkien calls 'The Scouring of the Shire'.

At the Brandywine, the travellers find the bridge closed with a large spiked gate. The gatekeeper says he is under orders from the chief at Bag End to let no one enter between sundown and sunrise. The chief turns out to be Lotho, Lobelia Sackville-Baggins's son. Pippin and Merry climb over the gate. Bill Ferny appears and accuses them of 'gate-breaking'. They force him to open it.

As the four hobbits set out for Hobbiton, they meet a large group of hobbit Shirriffs, who tell them they are under arrest. The four hobbits laugh. As they move on, they meet ruffians who claim to be working for a mysterious boss named Sharkey, who turns out to be Saruman. Frodo tells them that their boss is finished. The other hobbits draw their swords and the ruffians flee.

Sam rides on to find Tom Cotton, the oldest hobbit in the area. He is delighted to hear that Frodo is back. Sam promises that they are going to clear out the ruffians. They raise the entire village to fight. When the ruffians return and try to impose their boss's will on the village, they find they are surrounded by armed villagers. The leader of the ruffians takes on Merry, but is shot down by arrows.

Farmer Cotton explains that, after Frodo and Sam had left, Lotho began buying farms and other property in the area. The produce was sent away, causing shortages in the area. Then the ruffians, men from the south, came and took over, while Lotho started calling himself Chief Shirriff and dealt with anyone who resisted.

The next morning, a large band of ruffians approaches Hobbiton. Pippin arrives with his relatives. In the ensuing fight, nearly seventy of the men die, along with nineteen hobbits. This engagement goes down in hobbit history as the Battle of Bywater.

Frodo leads the other hobbits to Bag End to find Lotho. The place has been ruined and Saruman is standing at the gate. Saruman – aka Sharkey – says that he has come to ruin their home, as they ruined his, and curses any who try to harm him. Frodo assures the other hobbits that Saruman has lost his power, but he forbids them to kill the wizard. But as Saruman and Wormtongue pass by Frodo, Saruman pulls a knife and stabs Frodo. Again Frodo's mail-coat shields him.

Despite the attack, Frodo continues to insist that Saruman is not to be killed. But Frodo's clemency enrages Saruman. As Saruman makes to go, Frodo says that Wormtongue can stay as he has done them no wrong. Then Saruman tells Frodo that Wormtongue has killed Lotho in his sleep, so he had better come with him. Wormtongue cries out that Saruman ordered him to do so. Saruman now orders Wormtongue to follow him and kicks him in the face. But Wormtongue has a knife and cuts the old wizard's throat. As he flees, Wormtongue is cut down by hobbit arrows. A grey mist rises from Saruman's corpse and blows away in the wind.

The hobbits rebuild their villages. With her son dead, Lobelia gives up Bag End. Sam plants saplings to replace the trees the men have cut down, dusting their roots with soil from the box Galadriel gave him. In it, he also finds a small silver seed, which he plants in the Party Field. An elvish mallorn tree springs up, the only one west of the Misty Mountains. Many children are born or begotten that year and there is an abundant crop of fruit.

Sam marries Tom Cotton's daughter Rosie and they live at Bag End with Frodo. But Frodo's injured shoulder never really heals. The following year, Frodo decides to travel to Rivendell to see Bilbo. Before he goes he gives the manuscript of *There and Back Again* and *The Lord of the Rings* to Sam for safekeeping. The tale is almost finished, but Frodo has left the last page for Sam to complete.

Then Frodo and Sam set out together again. On the way, they meet Elrond and Galadriel, who each wear one of the three elven rings. Riding slowly behind them is Bilbo, who is bound for the Havens. Frodo decides to join them. Sam accompanies them to the sea where a ship is waiting. They find Gandalf on the quay wearing the third elven ring.

Then Merry and Pippin turn up to see them all off. They watch as the ship sails away, then ride home in silence.

5

POSTHUMOUS PUBLICATIONS

When Professor Tolkien died in 1973, he had not completed his life's work *The Silmarillion*. However, his son Christopher set to work to pull it together and edit a final manuscript. But what he found in his father's papers would keep him busy for another thirty-five years.

The Silmarillion

Tolkien's life's work *The Silmarillion* was published on 15 September 1977 in the UK by Allen & Unwin and in October that year in the US by Houghton Mifflin. It is supposed to be the three volumes of *Translations from the Elvish* that Bilbo gave to Frodo to edit in Rivendell in *Book Six* of *The Lord of the Rings*. It is actually made up of five parts – *Ainulindalë*, a creation myth; *Valaquenta*, an account of the spirits chosen to go into the world; *Quenta Silmaril-*

lion, the story of three jewels known as the Silmarils; *Akallabêth*, the rise and fall of the island kingdom of Númenor; and *The Rings of Power and the Third Age*, a history of Middle-earth in the Second and Third Ages.

Ainulindalë

In Tolkien's fictional language Quenya, *Ainulindalë* means 'the music of the Ainur'. These beings, the Ainur or Holy Ones, are brought into being by Eru, or the One, later known as Ilúvatar or God, to help in the creation. They are created by Eru's thought alone to produce music. Each Ainu is to play its own part in a great symphony that will fill the primordial void.

However, one of the Ainur named Melkor, which means 'Arises in Might', begins making a tune of his own that does not fit with Ilúvatar's great plan, producing discord. Ilúvatar calls a halt and gives the Ainur a vision of the world that their music is creating. This is where the Ilúvatar's children – elves and men – will live. The mighty among the Ainur like the place that the elves will call Arda. Melkor is the mightiest as he provides heat and cold. He pretends he wants to go to Arda to improve things for Ilúvatar's children. In fact, he wants to rule over them.

Ulmo is the Ainu who deals with water. Melkor with his heat and cold can make water into clouds, snow and rain, though he has not diminished the majesty of the sea. There the vision ends, so that Ainur does not see the later ages, or the end of the world.

Ilúvatar then says the word *Eä* or 'Let these things be', creating the universe which also takes the name *Eä*. Some of the Ainur go to live in the world. They are called the Valar, or 'the Powers of the World'. One of them is Melkor, who kindles great fires and seeks to take over the world as his own kingdom. Manwë, the brother of Melkor, calls the others together and tells Melkor that he cannot take the world for himself as others have also had a hand in making it. Melkor withdraws.

The Valar are invisible to the children of Ilúvatar, so they clothe themselves in physical form. They then spend their time ordering the world, quelling turmoil and turning the Earth into a garden. When Melkor sees this, he returns and the first battle for control of Arda begins. Despite Melkor's interference, the other Valar manage to fashion a world fit for the children of Ilúvatar to live in.

Valaquenta
This is an 'account of the Valar and Maiar' – the lesser Ainur – 'according to the lore of the Eldar', who are 'Star People', the ancient elvenkind who follow the call of the Valar.

There are seven Lords of Valar – Manwë, Ulmo, Anulë, Mandos, Lórien, Tulkas and Oromë. Melkor is not counted among the Valar and his name is no longer spoken in Arda. There are also seven queens of Valar, or Valier – Varda, Yavanna, Nienna, Estë, Vairë, Vána and Nessa. These are their elvish names. Men call them many different things.

Manwë is Ilúvatar's favourite and is the first king. He takes the surname Súlimo and, because he likes the wind and the clouds, is known as the Lord of the Breath of Arda. He lives with Varda, Lady of the Stars. Melkor fears her most of all, while the elves love her and call her Elbereth.

The next most powerful is Ulmo, but he does not like to clothe himself in a physical form and moves from place to place. However, he can be found in the sea, rivers, lakes, wherever there is water.

Next comes Aulë, who is an artisan who fashions the land and teaches the Noldor who are the elvish craftsmen and loremakers. As well as making the mountains and the sea bed, he also produces the gold and gems that are hidden in the earth. Melkor is jealous of him and is always trying to spoil the things he did.

Aulë's wife is Yavanna, the 'Giver of Fruit'. She is responsible for all the things that grow on the Earth, right down to the moss that grows on stones. She wears green and is sometimes seen as a tall tree, whose leaves Manwë speaks through and whose roots are watered by Ulmo. The Eldar calls her Kementári, Queen of the Earth, and she is second only to Varda in the female pantheon.

Mandos is more properly called Námo; Mandos is where he lives in the west of Valinor, the realm of the Valar. One of the Fëanturi, or masters of spirits, he is the keeper of the houses of the dead. His wife is Vairë, the Weaver.

The other master of the spirits is Lórien, more properly known as Irmo, Námo's younger brother. The master of visions and dreams, he lives in Lórien, the garden where Valar comes to rest. His wife is Estë, the healer. She also controls sleep and, herself, rests by day on the island in the lake of Lórellin.

Nienna is the Fëanturi's sister. She controls grief and mourning. Living on the western edge of the world, she rarely visits the Valar, except Námos who lives near her.

The strongest of the Valar is Tulkas, who takes the surname Astaldo, the Valiant. He comes to support the Valar in their battle against Melkor. His wife is Nessa, who can outrun a deer. Her brother is Oromë, the hunter of monsters and other foul creatures. His wife is Vána, the Ever-young, younger sister of Yavanna.

Then there are the Maiar, the lesser spirits, who are the Valars' servants and aides. The elves do not know how many there are as they rarely appear in physical form. Eönwë is Manwë's standard-bearer and herald, and a mighty warrior, while Ilmarë is remembered as the handmaiden of Varda.

The best known to Ilúvatar's children are Ulmo's vassal Ossë, the master of the shallow water around Middle-earth, and his wife Uinen, the Lady of the Seas, whose hair calms the waves. Melkor hates the sea because it will not smash up the land as he wants, so he tries to form an alliance with Ossë, promising him the power of Ulmo. But Uinen restrains him and gets Ulmo to forgive him, but no one really trusts Ossë.

Melian serves both Vána and Estë, and tends the flowering trees in Lórien. Olórin also lives there, but spends a lot of time with Nienna who teaches him patience and pity. Melian appears in the *Quenta Silmarillion*, but Olórin does not because he either remains invisible or disguises himself. However, his presence is felt, particularly in the later days.

Although Melkor is no longer spoken of, the Noldor who have suffered at his hands call him Morgoth, the Dark Enemy. He too has servants – Valaraukar, known in Middle-earth as Balrogs. Once a Maiar of Aulë, the greatest of these is Sauron.

Quenta Silmarillion

The title means 'The Story of the Simarils' and takes place in the First Age. It begins after the Valar have arrived in Arda, but before the world is fully formed. Nothing yet grows or walks on the earth. Melkor still has the upper hand. But Tulkas the strong comes and Melkor flees. The Valar then begin making the land and the sea. Seeds are planted, but as the fire has been hidden under mountains, light is needed. Two huge lamps are raised to the north and south of Middle-earth. The plants flourish and animals inhabit the earth.

Melkor knows what is going on as he has friends among the Maiar. With spirits from the halls of Eä, he returns and builds a fortress called Utumno under the dark mountains. His presence in Arda spoils the spring. Vegetation withers and rots, rivers are choked, and animals become bloodthirsty monsters. Then Melkor knocks down the two great lamps, so the Earth catches fire. Meanwhile the sea batters the land. Then Melkor returns home and hides in Utumno.

The Valar then have to abandon their island home of Alamen and go to live in Aman to the west. There they raise a mountain fortress of their own called Pelóri. Behind its walls they make their home, Valinor. It becomes as nice as Arda had been in its first spring. Two trees grow. One has dark green leaves and drips silver dew. The other has light green leaves and flowers that rain gold.

The Earth is to be populated by the children of Ilúvatar – the elves, who are immortal, and men, who are not. But Aulë cannot wait, so he makes a race of dwarves. Ilúvatar chides Aulë for exceeding his authority, so Aulë takes a hammer to destroy the dwarves. But Ilúvatar likes the dwarves and spares them. However, they are not to come before the firstborn of his own design, the elves. So Aulë takes the Seven Fathers of the Dwarves and puts them out of the way in a distant place, only to be awoken after the elves.

When Yavanna hears what Aulë has done, she is afraid the dwarves will damage her plants. Indeed, this is true of the children of Ilúvatar too. She seeks the protection of Manwë. Manwë has a vision where Eru tells him that spirits will also awake to protect what Yavanna has created. The greatest among these will be the eagles who will overlook Middle-earth from the mountains.

Melkor spends his time in Utumno creating demons, including Balrogs with their whips of flame, and breeding a race of orcs. He also makes a fortress called Angband to defend against any attack from Aman. It is commanded by his lieutenant Sauron. Meanwhile the Valar prepare Arda for the coming of the Ilúvatar's firstborn – the elves. As part of their preparation they decide to attack Melkor. Tulkas wrestles with Melkor and binds him with a chain made by Aulë. Then he is to be imprisoned in Mandos for three ages.

After they have been awoken, the Valar summon the elves to Valinor. Those who are unwilling to leave Middle-earth and stay behind are called the Avari, the unwilling. Those prepared to leave their first homes and make the journey are the Eldar. They comprise the Vanyar, or fair elves; the Noldor, or deep elves; and the Teleri, who tarry on the road. The Vanyar and Noldor eventually reach the sea at the west of Beleriand. Meanwhile, some of the Teleri reach the eastern part of Beleriand, by way of the Misty Mountains.

The beautiful Maia, Melian, then populates Middle-earth with songbirds. Elwë, lord of the Teleri, goes to visit his friend Finwë, who is the first king of the Noldor. On the way he gets lost in the forest of Nan Elmoth and meets Melian, who enchants him. They produce some of the fairest of all the children of Ilúvatar and he becomes known as King Greymantle or Elu Thingol in the elvish language.

The Vanyar move on to Valinor where they enjoy the trees, while the Noldor go to the island of Tol Eressëa, which translates from the Quenya as 'Lonely Island'. When the Teleri eventually reach the coast they are instructed in shipbuilding by Ossë. Then their ships are towed over the windless sea to Aman by swans. Eventually all three clans of Eldars arrive in Valinor.

Finwë has a son called Fëanor, Spirit of Fire. His mother Míriel dies in childbirth, but Finwë lavishes all his love on the boy. Finwë then marries Indis, who gives him two sons, Fingolfin and Finarfin.

Melkor manages to persuade Manwë that he has reformed, so Manwë releases him, though he has to stay in Valmar, the capital of Valinor, where the Valar can keep an eye on him. Ulmo and Tulkas are still suspicious of Melkor, but are bound by Manwë's judgement. Meanwhile Melkor hates the Eldar, blaming them for his downfall.

Fëanor becomes a noted elven craftsman and makes the three Silmarils, jewels which shine with the light of the two trees of Valinor, even after the trees themselves have withered. Melkor covets the Silmarils. To that end, he wants to destroy Fëanor and end the friendship between the Valar and the elves. He spreads the rumour among the elves that Manwë has summoned them to Valinor to keep them captive while men take over Middle-earth. The Noldor begin to believe him. He also says that Fingolfin wants to usurp the leadership of Finwë and exclude him from the succession. At Melkor's instigation, the Noldor begin forging weapons.

Fëanor then raises a rebellion against the Valar. He is then called before Mandos at the Ring of Doom to answer charges of sedition. Melkor's part in the plot is revealed, but Fëanor is not found guiltless. He has drawn a sword on his half-brother Fingolfin and has challenged the authority of Manwë. Fëanor is banished for twelve years and goes into exile with his seven sons. They are banished to the fortress of Formenos in the north where the Silmarils are kept in a strongroom. His father Finwë goes with him, leaving Fingolfin to rule the Noldor.

Knowing that he has been found out, Melkor goes into hiding. Tulkas searches for him, but Valinor grows dark. Melkor then goes to Formenos and tells Fëanor that he has been unjustly banished. But Fëanor curses him and tells him to leave.

Hearing that Melkor has been at Formenos, Tulkas and Oromë go north after him. But Melkor has travelled on to Avathar Fëanor unclad in physical form to join forces with Ungoliant, an evil spirit that takes the form of a giant spider. There he puts on the form again of the dark lord of Utumno and promises Ungoliant anything she wants if she will help him. Ungoliant then spins a cloak of darkness around them.

Manwë summons Fëanor to a festival, but Finwë will not go until his son's banishment is lifted. Fëanor will not dress for the festival and goes, leaving the Silmarils behind. Nevertheless, Fëanor and Fingolfin are reconciled.

When Melkor and Ungoliant arrive in Valmar, they kill the two trees and darkness falls over Valinor. Tulkas and Oromë catch up with them there, but they are powerless against the black vapour that Ungoliant belches and the dark web she spins.

The light of the two trees has been extinguished, but it lives on only in Fëanor's Silmarils. Yavanna praises his foresight, saying that if she had a little of their light she could restore the trees. But under cover of darkness, Melkor has gone to Formenos, killed Finwë and taken the Silmarils. Fëanor then curses Melkor, calling him Morgoth, black foe of the world.

Morgoth and Ungoliant head for Middle-earth. Ungoliant

then demands that Melkor honour their agreement and give her anything she wants. And she wants the Silmarils. But Morgoth will not give them, even though they are burning his hand. Having ingested the life-force from the two trees, Ungoliant has grown powerful. She grabs Morgoth and binds him in a web. He lets out a terrible cry. This is heard by the Balrogs that live in the ruins of Angband. They come to Melkor's aid and Ungoliant goes into hiding in a place called Nan Dungortheb, the Valley of the Dreadful Death.

Morgoth now makes an iron crown with the Silmarils set in it and begins calling himself King of the World. However, handling the Silmarils has burned his hands black.

With Finwë dead, Fëanor assumes the kingship of the Noldor. He tells them that they are to leave Valinor and return to Middle-earth in pursuit of Morgoth and the Silmarils. Then they swear a terrible oath, vowing to pursue with a vengeance anyone or anything that withholds a Silmaril from them. Fingolfin and his son Turgon speak against Fëanor, while Finarfin and his son Orodreth try to calm things down. The woman Galadriel will not swear the oath, but is eager to return to Middle-earth. So, bidding farewell to Manwë, the Noldor set off.

Fëanor tries to persuade the Teleri to join him. They are unmoved and refuse to lend the Noldor their ships. So Fëanor takes them by force. Many are killed. But eventually, the Noldor arrive back in Middle-earth.

In the meantime, in Middle-earth, Thingol and Maia queen Melian have a daughter named Lúthien. Morgoth sends an army of orcs to take their land of Doriath, but Thingol fight them off. Then Melian puts an invisible wall around Doriath known as the Girdle of Melian.

In Valinor, the Valar cannot revive the two trees. However, one bears a silver flower, the other a golden fruit. From these they make the Moon and the Sun. With Middle-earth now bathed in sunlight, the second people, men, awake.

When Fëanor returns to Middle-earth he takes on the orcs in the Dagor-nuin-Giliath, or Battle-under-Stars. He pursues them back to Angband hoping to challenge Morgoth. But the Balrogs are waiting there and mortally wound him. Fingolfin's son Fingon tries to reunite the dissenting houses of Noldor and go to find Fëanor's son Maedhros, who is a friend. But Maedhros has been hung by the wrist from a rock and begs Fingon to kill him. However, Thorondor, king of the eagles, sees him and carries Fingon up to the rock where Maedhros is suspended. Fingon cannot undo Morgoth's bond and has to cut off Maedhros's hand to save him. Then Thorondor carries them to safety.

After the sun has been shining for twenty years, Fingolfin, now king of Noldor, holds the Feast of Reuniting. Another thirty years passes before the Noldor are prepared to attack Morgoth who is still in Angband. They take on an army of orcs and defeat them, eventually reaching Angband's gates. But while the lords of Noldor can keep Morgoth holed up in his fortress they are not strong enough to take it or get the Silmarils back again and the siege of Angband lasts for four hundred years.

About three hundred years after the Noldor arrived in Middle-earth and established themselves around north and central Beleriand, men begin arriving over the Blue Mountains to the east. When the elves see lights one evening and hear singing they fear that orcs are on the move again. Finrod Felagun, eldest son of Finarfin who has built the stronghold at Nargothrond, is out hunting and looks down on the camp of these strange people. He waits until they go to sleep then goes down among them and plays the harp. They awake to his singing and are struck by the beauty of his song.

When Morgoth hears about it, he leaves Sauron in command at Angband and comes to see for himself. It is important for him to turn men and the Eldars into enemies. While some elves hide from the incoming men, Fingolfin, king of the Noldor, sends messengers welcoming them. Although King Thingol is happy for men to live in the north, he cannot allow any into Doriath. However, Melian does not think she has the power to stop them.

Seeing men getting friendly with the elves, Morgoth sends out orcs to attack them. Meanwhile Fingolfin makes an alliance with the men and begins to consider another attack on Angband. But Morgoth has used the long siege to prepare his own army. He sends great rivers of flame running down from the Mountain of Iron. This begins Dagor Bragollach, the Battle of Sudden Flame. Then Morgoth unleashes the dragon Glaurung, followed by Balrogs and an army of orcs. They assail the besiegers and the Noldor are scattered.

Seeing this, Fingolfin goes to the gates of Angband to challenge Morgoth to single combat. Morgoth throws his mighty hammer, Grond, at Fingolfin, but he jumps out of the way. Fingolfin then wounds Morgoth seven times. But soon he grows tired and Morgoth pushes him to his knees with his shield. Then Fingolfin stumbles and Morgoth puts his foot on Fingolfin's neck. With his last stroke, Fingolfin strikes back, wounding Morgoth on the foot. Then he dies.

Morgoth intends to feed Fingolfin's body to the wolves, but Thorondor comes to the rescue. He slashes at Morgoth's face with his talons, then carries Fingolfin's body away to be buried by his son. Morgoth remains lame and injured, but he is now in command of the Northlands. Sauron is then unleashed. He takes Minas Tirith in the south and makes it into a watchtower for Morgoth.

A man named Beren swears an oath of vengeance after his father is killed by Morgoth and his orcs. For four years he hides out killing orcs until Morgoth puts a price on his head. An army is sent against him under the command of Sauron, so Beren seeks the safety of the hidden kingdom of Doriath. On his way there, he has to pass through the realm of Ungoliant. Having avoided her webs, he then has to find his way through the mazes Melian has set.

By the time he finds his way into the Doriath, he is grey and bowed. In the woods there he sees the beautiful elfmaiden Lúthien dancing and is instantly smitten. When King Thingol hears that Beren has been seen with his daughter Lúthien he is angry and threatens him with death. Melian begs him for mercy. Thingol gives in, but says that Beren can only have his daughter's hand in marriage if he brings one of the Silmarils from Morgoth's crown. Beren agrees.

Beren goes to visit his father's ally Finrod Felagund who says that Thingol has effectively condemned him. Even if he succeeds in getting the Silmaril from Morgoth, those who have sworn the oath of Fëanor will then be duty bound to kill him.

Nevertheless, Felagund sets out with Beren and ten escorts. They come across a company of orcs, kill them and disguise themselves in their clothes. But Sauron in his tower sees this and has them thrown into a deep pit where a werewolf is set on them. When the werewolf attacks Beren, Felagund kills it, but is mortally wounded in the process.

Lúthien rides to the rescue. With the help of Huan, the hound of Valinor, she sees off the werewolves Sauron has sent against her. But when Sauron lunges at Lúthien, Huan is afraid and leaps aside. Lúthien faints. However, she has already made a spell that makes Sauron drowsy. Despite shape-shifting, in that state, Sauron cannot beat Huan and eventually surrenders.

Once Lúthien has rescued Beren, they travel together to Angband. There they are confronted by Carcharoth, the giant wolf that guards the fortress. At Lúthien's command, the giant wolf falls asleep. Eventually, they find their way to the throne where Morgoth is sitting. Her beauty blinds him and she casts a spell putting him and his minions to sleep.

Using a knife, Beren prises one of the Silmarils from Morgoth's crown. Then he decides to go further and take all three, but the knife snaps. The broken blade hits Morgoth on the cheek, waking him. Beren and Lúthien flee. Carcharoth has awoken too. Beren holds out Silmaril in an attempt to quell him, but Carcharoth bites his hand off and swallows the Silmaril.

Lúthien tries to suck the venom from Carcharoth's teeth out of Beren's wound, but she cannot staunch the bleeding. Eagles carry them back to Doriath, where Thingol asks the dying Beren about his quest. Beren replies that it has been fulfilled. The jewel is in his hand. With the help of Huan, Thingol has Carcharoth tracked down and killed. When his belly is opened, they find the Silmaril. It is then placed in Beren's other hand. This revives him. He then gives it to Thingol in fulfilment of his quest.

Lúthien then kisses Beren and asks him to wait for her beyond the western sea. He waits for her in the halls of Mandos. Lúthien dies of grief and her spirit follows him there. It kneels before Mandos and sings to him. Enchanted, Manwë takes pity on her and gives her a choice. Either she can come and live with the Valar in Valimar until the end of the world, or she can return to Middle-earth with Beren. However, she would become mortal and, like him, die a second death. This is what she chooses.

Hearing the tale of Beren and Lúthien, Maedhros realizes that Morgoth is not invulnerable. However, as Fëanor's son, he is now a sworn enemy of Thingol who has one of the Silmarils. Melian advises her husband to give it up, but he refuses. First, though, Maedhros and Fingon attack Angband in what becomes the Dagor Nírnaeth Arnoediad, or the Battle of Unnumbered Tears, the fifth battle of the Wars of Beleriand. During the onslaught, a party of elves under Gwindor of Nargothrond bursts through the gates. They reach the door of Morgoth's chamber where they find themselves trapped. Everyone is killed, except for Gwindor, who is captured. Meanwhile Fingon is driven back with great losses.

The elves and men manage to hold off the orcs. But then Morgoth sends wolves, Balrogs and the dragon Glaurung. And there is treachery in the ranks. The Easterlings attack the Eastern Army from within and Maedhros's forces are scattered. Gothmog, the leader of the Balrogs, kills Fingon with a black axe and the King of the Noldor is trampled into the earth.

In the end only the great hero Húrin is left alive. He has killed seventy of Gothmog's troll-guard and so many orcs that he is finally buried beneath them. Morgoth gives the order that he should be taken alive and Gothmog captures him, ties him up and takes him to Angband.

However Turgon, son of Fingolfin, has escaped. Morgoth knows that Húrin is a friend of Turgon, now the king of the hidden city of Gondolin.

When Húrin is brought before Morgoth, he mocks him. Morgoth then curses Húrin's family and has him bound to a stone chair high up in the mountains of Thangorodrim so that he can see the evil and despair Morgoth will bring to the lands below. Then Morgoth has all the dead from the battlefields collected together in a huge pile called the Hill of the Slain, or the Hill of Tears. Grass grows on it and it becomes the only green hill in the desert that Morgoth has left.

Húrin's son Túrin is just eight years old when his father is captured at the Battle of Unnumbered Tears. His mother Morwen begs King Thingol to give Túrin sanctuary in Doriath. But she stays behind in the house in Hithlum where she lives with Húrin and gives birth to a daughter she names Nienor.

Túrin is headstrong and has a falling out with one of the king's counsels, Saeros, resulting in Saeros's death. Túrin then flees. Thingol forgives him and sends Túrin's friend, the elf Beleg, out to find him. By then Túrin has become leader of a band of outlaws. Beleg arrives at their camp while Túrin is away. The outlaws seize him, believing him to be a spy for Thingol. When Túrin returns, he has Beleg released, but he refuses Thingol's pardon.

Túrin is betrayed to the orcs by a dwarf named Mîm and is captured. Though wounded, Beleg trails the orcs. Along the way he comes across Gwindor, who is now a shadow of his former self. He had been put to work in the mines but, via a secret passage, has managed to escape. While hiding in the woods, Gwindor sees a tall man being taken north by a company of orcs. Together they follow the orcs and find that camp which is guarded by wolves. Beleg shoots the wolves one by one. When they find Túrin, he is unconscious. When

Beleg is cutting him free, his sword slips, cutting Túrin. As he awakes, Túrin thinks he is being attacked by orcs, grabs the sword and kills Beleg.

Gwindor takes Túrin to Nargothrond where he lives under a false name. There he comes to be loved and respected. But Finduilas, daughter of King Orodreth, who Gwindor loves, falls for Túrin. Gwindor then tells her that he is Túrin, whose kin has been cursed.

When Morgoth moves against the lands of Narog, Túrin goes out with the army. Orodreth is killed and Gwindor mortally wounded. He begs Túrin to return to Nargothrond to protect Finduilas. When he arrives, the sack of Nargothrond is under way. As Túrin fights his way towards the city, he is confronted by Glaurung. When Túrin tries to attack the dragon, Glaurung casts a spell paralysing him. Then, when Túrin is stuck motionless, Glaurung taunts him. Finduilas has been taken, and Glaurung will not release him until she is out of earshot.

As Túrin cannot save Finduilas, Glaurung now gives him the chance to save his mother and sister whose home at Dor-lómin is under threat by orcs. Túrin heads north, but everywhere he goes he seems to hear the cries of Finduilas. When he reaches Dor-lómin, his mother and sister are not there. They have gone to Doriath looking for him. When he learns this at the house of Brodda the Easterling, he kills Brodda and everyone in his household.

Figuring that his mother and sister will be safe behind the Girdle of Melian, Túrin goes looking for Finduilas. But he finds her dead, pinned to a tree by a spear. After recovering from his grief, Túrin then takes the name Turambar, which is elvish for Master of Doom.

News gets back to Dorieth that Túrin has been killed by

the dragon and his mother Morwen is distraught. She rides out to see if she can find her son. His sister Nienor is told to stay behind, but she disguises herself as one of the party Thingol sends out after Morwen.

After a confrontation with Glaurung, Nienor is struck with amnesia. She cannot even remember her own name. Fleeing from orcs, she goes mad with fear and tears her clothes off. Finding herself near Finduilas's grave, she flings herself down on it. Turambar finds her there. Woodmen wraps her in a cloak and takes her to shelter. When asked her name and what has happened to her, all she can do is weep so they call her Níniel, which means Tear-maiden.

After she learns to speak again, Turambar asks her to marry him. They live together as husband and wife in peace until the orcs come. Once they are defeated, Glaurung follows. Turambar goes out to face him and finds him sleeping on a cliff. He climbs up the cliff face and stabs the dragon from beneath. In his death throes, Glaurung throws himself across the chasm with Turambar's famous black sword still stuck in him. Turambar wants it back, so he crosses the chasm and pulls it out, saying that at last Túrin son of Húrin is avenged. But Glaurung's blood splashes on him. Its venom burns him. Then Glaurung stirs and strikes Turambar.

Unwilling to wait for news, Níniel goes out to look for Turambar. She is followed by Ephel Brandir who loves her. He tells her that Turambar is dead and she should come with him. But Níniel wants to see her husband and finds him lying beside the dragon. She is tending his wounds when Glaurung stirs again. The dragon hails her as Nienor daughter of Húrin and says he is delighted that she has found her brother. After Glaurung dies, Nienor's memory returns and she throws herself off the cliff. Túrin revives. He blames Brandir for leading Níniel to her death and kills him. Realizing later that he has killed Brandir unjustly, Túrin falls on his own sword.

Morgoth then releases Húrin, who heads for the hidden city of Gondolin. The eagle Thorondor brings the news to Turgon. On his way, Húrin stands on a high rock and calls out to Turgon, so that Morgoth knows in which direction Gondolin lies.

In his sleep that night, Húrin thinks he hears Morwen calling. He heads for the place where the corpse of Glaurung is burning and both his son and daughter, Túrin and Nienor, have killed themselves. There he finds Morwen. That night she dies.

Húrin travels on to Nargothrond where he finds Mîm the dwarf and kills him. He then takes Nauglamír, the necklace of the dwarves, to Thingol as payment for looking after his wife and children. Afterwards, he dies.

When Thingol examines the Nauglamír he comes up with a plan to remake it with the Silmaril he carries with him. However, the dwarf craftsmen he takes it to question Thingol's right to their heirloom and kill him. Then two of the killers are slain in retaliation by the elves. The widowed Melian then leave Middle-earth and go back to live with the Valar in Lórien, leaving the Silmaril in the hands of Thingol's captain of the guard Mablung.

The dwarves then invade Doriath, kill Mablung and take the Silmaril. But when the dwarves leave, they are ambushed by elves under the command of Beren, who recapture the necklace of the dwarves with the Silmaril in it for Lúthien to wear. It is then passed to Beren's son Dior who inherits Doriath from Thingol. When news of this spreads, the oath of Fëanor is invoked again and his sons come to take the necklace. Dior and his wife Nimoth are killed and their young sons are abandoned in the forest to starve. Maedhros repents of this and searches for them, to no avail. But while Doriath is being destroyed, Dior's daughter Elwing escapes with the Silmaril.

Tuor, the son of Húrin's brother Huor who is killed in the Batttle of the Unnumbered Tears, is sent to Gondolin by Ulmo to warn King Turgon of the city's coming destruction. But Turgon's nephew Maeglin opposes Tuor and Turgon rejects the warning. More warnings come in the form of the news of the fall of Nargothrond and Doriath, but Turgon ignores them. Tuor stays in Gondolin to marry Turgol's daughter Idril Celebrindal. But Maeglin wants her too as she is Turgon's sole heir. Tuor and Idril then have a son called Eärendil.

It is then that, thanks to the cries of Húrin, Morgoth discovers where the hidden kingdom is. The city is still protected by the eagles, but Idril prepares a secret escape route. Maeglin is then captured by orcs and, under torture, tells Morgoth the best way to take the city. He is then sent back to Gondolin to play his part in the plan. Morgoth then sends orcs, Balrogs and the offspring of Glaurung against Gondolin on the night before the festival known as the Gates of Summer. Despite a valiant defence, the city is soon lost.

Maeglin grabs Idril and Eärendil, but Tuor pushes him over the wall into the flames below. Then he and Idril lead the survivors down the escape route she has prepared. They are attacked by orcs and Balrogs, but are rescued by eagles. Nevertheless, Morgoth considers his triumph complete. However, Eärendil grows up to marry Elwing, the current custodian of the Silmaril Beren has taken from Morgoth.

Ulmo takes pity on the elves and goes to Valinor to beg for their pardon, but Manwë will not pardon them until the sons of Fëanor have renounced their oath and given up the Silmarils.

Tuor builds a ship and, with Idril, sails off to the west, leaving Eärendil in charge of the elves and men who remain in Middle-earth. When Tuor and Idril do not return, Eärendil has a ship built and heads off after them.

Maedhros now learns that Elwing is still alive and has the Silmaril. But the survivors of the destruction of Doriath and Gondolin will not give it up, especially while Eärendil is away. So the remaining sons of Fëanor sweep down and elf kills elf. Maedhros and Maglor win the day. They are the only surviving sons of Fëanor, but do not get their hands on the Silmaril. Elwing is still wearing it when she throws herself into the sea. She is rescued by Ulmo who turns her into a white bird so she can fly to her husband Eärendil. Together they head for Valinor. Eärendil carries the Silmaril on his brow when he goes to beg the Valar to pardon the Noldor and helps the remaining elves and men in their war against Morgoth.

As they are mixed human and elvish, Manwë allows Eärendil, Elwing and their sons, Elros and Elrond, to pick what fate they should suffer. Eärendil and Elwing choose to be judged as the Firstborn Children of Ilúvatar. They are sent across the sea to the limits of the world and up into the night sky where Eärendil the mariner becomes a star. Elwing stays nearer the Earth in a tower and, when Eärendil's star comes near the Earth, she flies up to him.

The army of the Valar, led by Eönwë, heads for Middle earth for the Great Battle, also known as the War of Wrath. Morgoth musters all the forces at his disposal, but they are not powerful enough to resist. The Balrogs are destroyed, apart from a few that hide under the earth in deep caves. Only a few orcs survive the slaughter.

Afraid to join battle himself, Morgoth unleashes flying dragons. But Eärendil musters Thorondor and the great birds of the heavens who destroy most of the dragons. Morgoth tries to hide in the pits under Angband, but is captured. Eönwë takes the remaining Silmarils from his crown. The sons of Fëanor ask for them back, but Eönwë says that they have given up their right to them because of all the evil things they have done in their pursuit.

However, Maedhros and Maglor cannot break their oath. They enter Eönwë's camp, kill the guards and steal the Silmarils, taking one each. But the jewels burn their hands. Finding the pain unbearable, Maedhros throws himself into a chasm of fire, while Maglor throws his jewel into the sea and spends the rest of his days wandering the seashore, singing. The Eldar are allowed to return to the west, settling on the Lonely Isle of Eressëa, while Morgoth is thrust into the timeless void.

Akallabêth

The story is subtitled 'The Downfall of Númenor', which is an island kingdom inhabited by the Dúnedain. In the Great Battle, the Edain are the only clan of men who fight on the side of the Valar. Others fight for Morgoth. The survivors flee to the east where there are men who fight for neither side and corrupt them.

The Valar make a new land called Andor for the Edain to live in. It is an island near to Valinor. To get there, they set sail and follow Eärendil's star. The land is also known as Westernesse, or Númenórë. The Númenóreans are also known as Dúnedain. However, the 'kings of men' who live there remain mortal like other men, but suffer no illness and live long.

Eärendil's son Elros is the first king of Númenor. He has chosen to be judged as a man and has been allotted a lifespan of five hundred years. His brother Elrond has chosen to remain an elf and will be immortal.

The Dúnedain are great seamen, but the Valar forbid them sailing westwards out of sight of the coast of Númenor, so they cannot see the Blessed Realm of the Valar, or the Undying Lands of the Eldar. They are allowed to sail eastwards towards Middle-earth though. When they visit, they bring agriculture and civilization. Later they begin to settle.

Although they have been granted long life, the Dúnedain begin to grow jealous of those who live to the west and are immortal. They begin to chafe against the ban on sailing west, especially as the Eldar had earlier rebelled against the Valar and had still escaped death.

Then Sauron rises again in Middle-earth. He fortifies Mordor and builds the Tower of Barad-dûr. He hates the Dúnedain because they have fought against Morgoth. He also fears that they might invade Middle-earth, but it is said that he has ensnared three Númenórean lords with the rings he has forged.

As he grows more powerful, Sauron calls himself the king of men and seeks to drive the Númenóreans from Middle-earth and, perhaps, even destroy Númenor itself. But the Númenorean king Ar-Pharazôn wants the title for himself and to make Sauron his tributary. So he sends an army to Middle-earth. Unable to match Ar-Pharazôn in arms, Sauron abases himself and swears fealty.

Ar-Pharazôn then takes Sauron back to Númenor, where he can keep an eye on him. But Sauron is clever and makes himself a trusted advisor. He uses his influence to sow dissent, telling Ar-Pharazôn that the Valar have deceived him. They have settled men on Númenor to enslave them. Instead of worshiping Eru, he should worship Melkor. Sauron also urges Ar-Pharazôn to cut down the white tree that symbolizes the allegiance with the Eldar and the Valar. Hearing this, Isildur son of Elendil goes to steal a fruit from the tree.

Soon Ar-Pharazôn cuts down the tree and Sauron burns it. Sacrifices are to be made to Melkor to free the Númenóreans from death. However, death seems to come more often when Sauron leads expeditions to Middle-earth where the lords of Númenor enrich themselves.

Ar-Pharazôn is growing old and fears death, so Sauron encourages him to attack the Valar. Elendil's father Amandil resolves to warn the Valar. He sails out of port eastwards but, when he is out of sight of shore, he turns for the west. Elendil is told to put his family and possessions on ships and head east.

As Ar-Pharazôn prepares to sail west eagles come. Nevertheless Ar-Pharazôn sets sail, breaking the ban. After Ar-Pharazôn and his vanguard have stepped on the land of Aman, Manwë calls on Ilúvatar who opens a great chasm in the sea which swallows up the Númenórean fleet. Then an earthquake comes, burying Ar-Pharazôn and his men underground for all time. Aman and Eressëa are put out of reach of men and Númenor is destroyed.

However, Elendil and his flotilla are saved. In the tumult that follows, Elendil and his sons Isildur and Anárion are washed up on the shores of Middle-earth where they found new kingdoms.

In the holocaust, Sauron, a Maia, is stripped of his physical form. Never again able to look fair in the eyes of men, he returns to his home in Mordor where, in Barad-dûr, his ring is waiting.

Of the Rings of Power and the Third Age
This, the book tells us, is where these tales come to the end. It begins with Sauron abasing himself to Eönwë after the downfall of Morgoth. But instead of returning to Aman to receive the judgement of Manwë he hides out in Middle-earth.

During the ensuing peace, the dwarves and the elfs remain friends and both grow rich. But now that the Valar have withdrawn from Middle-earth Sauron sees his opportunity to seize power. In Eregion, the elves listen to his counsel. While they make many rings, he forges one secretly in the Mountain of Fire that will rule all the others. But when Sauron puts this one ring on his finger, the elves realize that he means to rule them, so they take off their rings. He then demands that they hand over the rings they had made. Afraid, they flee with three of them. From then on, he is constantly at war with the elves.

He gathers up the other rings, however, and gives them to the other inhabitants of Middle-earth in the hope of having power over them too. Seven go to the dwarves; nine to the men who are easier to control. The dwarves only use their rings to make gold. Much of this is taken by dragons. Sauron manages to recover some of the rings; the rest are consumed by fire. Meanwhile, the men who have taken the rings become his servants, the Ringwraiths or Nazgûls.

The elfs flee from him and the story of how he deals with the challenge of the Númenóreans is told in the *Akallabëth*. After being sucked down into the abyss, Sauron returns to Middle-earth.

Having travelled up the River Anduin, Isildur and his brother Anárion found Arnor and Gondor. Elendil's people also build Osgiliath and the bridge there and Minas Ithil with its Tower of the Rising Moon, Isildur's home. Anárion lives in Minas Anor, the Tower of the Setting Sun. Their thrones sit side-by-side in Osgiliath, the chief city of Gondor.

They have brought with them a white tree grown from the fruit Isildur has stolen. It is planted at Minas Ithil. They also have seven palantíri, given to them by the Eldar. Elendil has three; his sons two each.

Sauron gathers his forces, including some dissident Númenóreans. He takes Minas Ithil and destroys the white tree there, but Isildur escapes. Elves and men form an alliance against Sauron, with dwarves on both sides, and Sauron is defeated in what is known as the War of the Alliance. But Sauron retreats into Mordor and they lay siege to him there for seven years, with heavy losses. Anárion is killed, Isildur planting a white tree in his memory at Minas Anor. However, Isildur manages to cut the ruling ring from Sauron's hand with his father's broken sword. His servants routed, Sauron again sheds his mortal flesh. The Dark Tower is levelled and the Third Age begins.

Sauron is not forgotten though. Although the ring is out of circulation, Isildur will not surrender it, or have it destroyed. Then Isildur is attacked by orcs in the Misty Mountains. Isildur escapes using the ring to make himself invisible, but the orcs can smell him. Crossing the river, the ring slips from his finger and he is killed.

Elendil's broken sword Narsil is handed on to Isildur's heir Valandil, though Elrond foretells that it will be re-forged when the ruling ring is found and Sauron returns. In the meantime, the Dúnedain dwindles. Gondor flourishes briefly, before it too goes into decline as the bloodline of Anárion is diluted and their lifespan grows shorter.

When King Eärnil comes to the throne, the nine Ringwraiths come out of Mordor and take over Minas Ithil, which then becomes Minas Morgul, the Tower of Sorcery, and makes war on Minas Anor to the west. This, too, is renamed. It becomes Minas Tirith, the Tower of the Guard, after the kings there build a white tower in the citadel. The white tree still flourishes there, even after Eärnur, the last king of Gondor is captured and never seen again. Minas Tirith is then run by a line of stewards. They were allied to the horsemen of the north, the Rohirrim, who occupy Rohan, the northern grasslands of Gondor.

After the fall of Gil-galad, the heirs of Isildur take refuge in the house of Elrond and, when the Dúnedain become nomads, he takes possession of the shattered pieces of the sword of Elendil. He also has one of the elven rings in Imladris, or Rivendell. Another is with Lady Galadriel in Lórien. The third remains hidden.

The shadow of Sauron returns to Mirkwood, where it grows. At around the same time, Istari, or wizards, arrive in the west of Middle-earth. It is thought that they have been sent by the Valar to fight Sauron when he reappears. Among them are Saruman and Gandalf. While Saruman dwells at Orthanc in the Ring of Isengard, built by the Númenóreans, Gandalf roams freely giving advice to Elrond and the elves.

Saruman is appointed head of the White Council, or the Council of the Wise, and begins studying the lore concerning the rings of power. With the rise of Sauron, Gandalf urges that the Council take action against him, but Saruman says that the ruling ring that has fallen into the Anduin has been carried out to the sea, so nothing is done. In fact, Saruman is hoping to find the ruling ring and take power himself. The ring, he believes, will be drawn to Sauron. Without telling the council, he recruits an army of spies, many of them birds, to keep an eye on Sauron.

Gandalf warns that, even without the ruling ring, Sauron is dangerous and they must attack. But Sauron is forewarned, flees Mirkwood and returns to safety in Mordor. Saruman then withdraws to Isengard and listens to the council no further. But the ruling ring has been found, though they do not know it; it is in the possession of one of the halflings of whom the men and elves take no account. Soon Sauron hears of it and sends the Nazgûl out to get it. It is then that the War of the Ring begins.

In preparation Aragorn, the thirty-ninth heir of Isildur, has Elendil's sword re-forged. There is a battle in Rohan. Saruman is defeated. Another great battle takes place in front of Minas Tirith, where Sauron's captain is destroyed. Then Aragon leads the forces of the West against Mordor. Despite the alliance of Gondor, Rohan, Elrond, Gandalf and the Dúnedain, they come near to defeat. But, at the behest of Gandalf, a halfling named Frodo takes the ruling ring to Mount Doom and throws it back into the fire where it has been made. This saps Sauron's power and he is defeated.

Peace returns. Aragorn takes the crown of Gondor and Arnor, and the white tree flourishes again. Gandalf has been responsible for this because Círdan, lord of the Havens, gives him the third elven ring which he has in his safekeeping. The bearers of the three remaining rings and the last of the Noldor leave Middle-earth and sail to the west.

Unfinished Tales of Númenor and Middle-earth
Christopher Tolkien had already edited *The Silmarillion* for publication after his father's death. But still an enormous amount of material remained unpublished. Tolkien senior

had not been happy with the appendices published in *The Lord of the Rings*, finding them truncated and compressed. His son felt that, by publishing more of the material his father had written, even though it was unfinished, readers of his work would have a clearer insight into the world of fantasy he was creating.

First published by Allen & Unwin in the UK on 2 October 1980 and by Houghton Mifflin in the US on 18 November, *Unfinished Tales* comes in four parts. Part One is titled 'The First Age'. The first story is 'Of Tuor and His Coming to Gondolin'. It gives a more detailed account of the tale told in chapter twenty-three of the *Quenta Silmarillion*, 'Of Tuor and the Fall of Gondolin'. Tolkien originally wrote 'The Fall of Gondolin', the first tale of the First Age he composed, during his sick leave from the First World War in 1917. Sometime in the late 1920s, he produced a shortened version that appears in *The Silmarillion*. The refashioned 'Of Tuor and His Coming to Gondolin' seems to have been written around 1951.

It begins in Dor-lómin, the Land of Echoes in Hithlum, where Rían, wife of Huor, has just given birth to a son, whom she names Tuor. When Rían hears that Huor has been killed in the Battle of Unnumbered Tears, she leaves Tuor with the elves of Mithrim, lays herself on the Hill of the Slain and dies. When he is sixteen years of age he leaves to seek Turgon, the high king of Noldor in Gondolin. He and the elves set off to find someone who knows where to find the hidden kingdom. However, they are attacked by orcs and Easterlings. Tuor is captured. He has been a slave for three years before he sees a chance to escape. For the next four years, he is an outlaw. Then he sets out again to find the Gate of Noldor. Finding a stream, he follows it towards Nevrast on the coast of the Great Sea, Belegaer the Shoreless. Swans then lead him to Vinyamar, Turgon's old home, where he finds arms. Back on the shore of the Great Sea Belegaer, Ulmo appears to Tuor and gives him a cloak which he must wear. Guided by the mariner Voronwë, who is originally from Gondolin, they set out on an arduous journey. Eventually, they come upon Elemmakil, the captain of the guard, who upbraids Voronwë for showing a mortal man the way to Gondolin. Voronwë says only the king can judge him, while Tuor explains that Ulmo appointed Voronwë as his guide. Under close guard, they are led through the seven gates of Gondolin – Gate of Wood, Gate of Stone, Gate of Bronze, Gate of Writhen Iron, Gate of Silver, Gate of Gold and Gate of Steel. At the last one, they are greeted by Ethelion, lord of the fountains and warden of the great gate. Tuor warns the lord of the fountains not to impede the messenger of the lord of the waters. When he passes through, he drops his cloak revealing that he bears arms from Nevrast. Ecthelion then says that no further proof is needed that Tuor has come from Ulmo. There the story ends.

It is followed by '*Narn I Hîn Húrin* – The Tale of the Children of Húrin'. This is a development of the legend 'Of Túrin Turambar', chapter twenty-one of the *Quenta Silmarillion*. Again it existed in earlier versions, including an unfinished poem in alliterative verse called *The Lay of the Children of Húrin*. Tolkien frequently worked up his stories in verse before redrafting them in prose. It begins with the childhood of Túrin, followed by his father's captivity after the Battle of Unnumbered Tears, Túrin's exile in Doriath, his time as an outlaw, his unintentional incest with his sister Nienor, the slaying of Glaurung and his own suicide. The tale also appears in *The War of the Jewels*, part of the *History of Middle-earth* series where the conclusion, 'The Wanderings of Húrin', is added. Then in 2007, Christopher Tolkien published the complete story in *The Children of Húrin*.

Part Two of the *Unfinished Tales* is called 'The Second Age' and begins with 'A Description of the Island of Númenor'. This starts with a short account of the fictional sources Tolkien purports to have derived his description from. He then gives a detailed description of the geography of the island, its cities, treasures and its flora and fauna. It tells of the people there, their craftsmanship and their weapon-making. They are also great seamen and adventurers.

This leads on to 'Aldarion and Erendis: The Mariner's Wife'. Aldarion's father Meneldur is the fifth king of Númenor. He takes little notice of the sea, instead spending his time studying the stars and the heavens. However, Aldarion loves the sea and is taught seamanship by his maternal grandfather Vëantur. Together they sail to Middle-earth and meet Círdan the shipwright and King Gil-galad. Aldarion forms the Guild of Venturers. Because of his passion for the sea he gradually becomes estranged from his father, who wants him to marry Erendis, daughter of Beregar of the house of Bëor. But Aldarion continues taking long voyages, staying away for years at a time, much to Erendis's displeasure.

Eventually, however, they do get married and have a daughter named Ancalimë. But Aldarion sails away again. When he does not return after two years, Erendis locks up their house in Armenelos, the capital of Númenor and moves with Ancalimë to the inland region of Emerië.

When Aldarion eventually returns after five years, his father is cold towards him. Erendis is not welcoming either and, after one night, he leaves her. Meneldur then receives a letter from King Gil-garad, thanking him for his son's support against Sauron. Having misjudged his son, Meneldur then announces his abdication in his favour. But when he commands Erendis to return to Armenelos, she refuses.

Tolkien left notes about how the narrative should proceed from there. Erendis remains estranged from Aldarion, but he alters the line of succession to allow Ancalimë to rule as queen.

The next chapter is the 'The Line of Elros: Kings of Númenor'. It gives the names and a brief biography of the twenty-five monarchs from the founding of Armenelos to the downfall of Númenor.

According to Christopher Tolkien there was no single text for the next chapter 'The History of Galadriel and Celeborn'. Rather it is an essay exploring his father's conceptions of these characters as well as Amroth, the king of Lórien before the arrival of Galadriel and Celeborn. There is also a section on the Elessar, or green elfstone made either by Enerdhil of Gondolin or Celebrimbor who made the three elven rings.

Part Three is 'The Third Age'. It begins with 'The Disaster of the Gladden Fields', where Isildur loses the ruling ring. Christopher Tolkien said that it was written in his father's final period of writing about Middle-earth – after the publication of *The Lord of the Rings* – around the same time as he was writing 'Cirion and Eorl', 'Battles of the Fords of Isen' and 'The Drúedain' which follow it and the philological essays cited in 'The History of Galadriel and Celeborn'.

The story begins with Isildur's return after the fall of Sauron and assuming sovereignty over Arnor and Gondor. After restoring order, he wants to visit his wife and youngest son, Valandil, in Rivendell and meets Elrond there. He leaves Osgiliath with his three elder sons, Elendur, Aratan and Ciryon, and two hundred men, leaving his nephew Meneldil behind in charge. On the thirtieth day of their journey, they are passing Gladden Fields, marshland on the banks of the river Anduin, when they are attacked by orcs. As they are approaching, Isildur gives Elendil's broken sword Narsil to his squire Ohtar and tells him and his companion to take it to safety. Isildur and his men see off the first onslaught, but when the orcs seem to be withdrawing towards the forests they set off again. The orcs then return and surround them, while keeping out of arrow range.

Elendur tells his father to use the ring to get the orcs to obey him, but he dreads the pain of touching it and aims to give it to Elrond and the elves — the 'keepers of the three'. As darkness falls, the orcs attack again. Ciryon is killed and Aratan is mortally wounded. Elendur then urges Isildur to flee and take the ring to the keepers of the three.

The ring is on a chain around Isildur's neck and he cries out in pain as he slips it on his finger. As Isildur vanishes into the night, Elendur and the rest of the men, except a young squire who is hidden under the bodies, are killed.

Isildur flees from the field, but the orcs can follow his scent. On the bank of the Anduin, he strips off his armour and plunges into the river. But the current is strong and drags him back towards the tangles of Gladden Fields where the ring falls from his finger. There is no chance of finding it in the murky water and he is now visible again. As he rises up out of the water, the orcs, who can see at night, spot him. Their arrows pierce him and he disappears into the water. His body is never found.

A second part of 'The Disaster of the Gladden Fields' is

called 'The sources of the legend of Isildur's death'. Again, Tolkien examines the fictional sources for the story. There were, of course, eyewitnesses to the battle – Ohtar and his companion who makes off with Narsil, and the young squire who survives the slaughter. Others arrive in time to prevent the orcs mutilating the bodies and find him. Woodmen run, carrying the news to the Elvenking Thranduil who lives nearby. It is known that Isildur had made for the river. There were orcs armed with bows and arrows on the other bank. If Isildur had the ring, he could have eluded them. As both he and the ring have been lost, it is plain that the ring must have been lost in the river.

When the Council of Elrond is held, Sauron has already been searching the area. Then when King Elessar comes to power in Gondor, Orthanc is searched. The gold chain that Isildur wore around his neck along with the priceless Elendilmir, his insignia of office, are found. They could only have been lost in shallow water. Isildur's body is not found, but that could have been disposed of in Saruman's furnaces. The chapter concludes with an appendix on Númenorean linear measurement.

The next chapter is called 'Cirion and Eorl and the Friendship of Gondor and Rohan'. Christopher Tolkien said he put this together from scraps that he thought were intended for Appendix A of *The Lord of the Rings* – 'Annals of the Kings and Rulers'. It comes in four parts. The first is called 'The Northmen and the Wainriders' which begins with the first meeting of Cirion, steward of Gondor, and Eoril, the lord of the Éothéod, who are the ancestors of the Rohirrim. They have long been friends of Gondor. Some time after Gondor has been weakened by a great plague, it is attacked by the Wainriders, a confederation of Easterlings.

The Northmen of Rhovanion bear the brunt of the first assaults. Those who survive death or enslavement become the Éothéod. With their lands lost, they move far to the north.

The next part is called 'The Ride of Eorl'. After Cirion becomes steward in 2489, Gondor comes under threat again. This time their chief adversary is the Balchoth, a clan of Easterlings under the sway of Dol Guldur, who now lives in Rhovanion. They cross the river and take the Gondorian province of Calenardhon. Messengers are sent to the Éothéod. Only one, named Borondir, gets through. Eorl calls a council and prepares to ride to the rescue. The Gondoreans are near to defeat at the Battle of the Field of the Celebrant when Eorl arrives. The Balchoth are beaten and the Éothéod hunts them down across the plains of Calenardhon.

As described in 'Cirion and Eorl', they hold a great victory feast in Minas Tirith. Cirion then rewards Eorl by giving him the entire province of Calenardhon which, after the Éothéod settle there, becomes Rohan. Later they swear an allegiance over the tomb of Elendil.

The last part is 'The Tradition of Isildur', which concerns Elendil's tomb. It has been set up by Isildur. By tradition, when the heir to the throne of Gondor reaches manhood he is taken there to be instructed in his duties in a secret rite. However, by bringing Eorl there, the rule has been broken. So after the oath has been sworn, Cirion moves the tomb.

The next chapter 'The Quest of Erebor' was written to be part of *The Lord of the Rings*, explaining more fully the relationship between the book and its forerunner *The Hobbit*. An abridged version appeared in Appendix A, Part III 'Durin's Folk'. There are two versions of the text, both written from the perspective of Frodo. However, the narration is largely Gandalf's. He tells the story to Frodo after the coronation of Aragorn as King Elessar.

Gandalf explains why he persuaded Thorin Oakenshield to take Bilbo Baggins with him on the journey to Erebor, or Lonely Mountain. He knew that Sauron was living in the Dol Guldur, the Hill of Sorcery, in Mirkwood and realized that Smaug the Dragon could pose a serious threat if he was commanded by the dark lord. So at the meeting in Bree, Gandalf backed Thorin's plan to attack the dragon. He selected Bilbo to accompany the expedition because dragons could not smell hobbits and dwarves had a low opinion of hobbits which might prevent Thorin from doing anything too rash. Rather than confront Smaug directly, which would end in disaster, they would have to proceed by stealth.

'The Hunt for the Ring' begins with 'Of the Journey of the Black Riders according to the account that Gandalf gave to Frodo'. This was written after the publication of *The Lord of the Rings* and refers to events in Appendix B, 'The Tale of Years', though some dates differ. It tells of the capture of Gollum in 3017, his torture and interrogation. There are several versions of this story, but it seems that Gollum is so consumed by his love for the ring and his hatred for this tormentor that he gives only garbled answers. However, it seems he mentions the Shire and the name Baggins. This puts the Ringwraiths on the trail. The last section 'Concerning Gandalf, Saruman and the Shire' contains several unfinished accounts of Saruman's earlier involvement with the Shire and the use of pipe-weed.

The next chapter, 'The Battle of the Fords of Isen', was also meant to be part of an appendix to *The Lord of the Rings*. This details a crucial period in Rohan during the War of the Ring before the arrival of Gandalf, Aragorn, Legolas and Gimli in Edoras. It covers Saruman's first and second attacks on the critical crossing of the River Isen when King Théoden's son Théodred was killed. An appendix covers the various ranks of Théoden's commanders and the importance of the Fords of the Isen.

Part Four of *Unfinished Tales* fleshes out the people and things found in Middle-earth. The first chapter is 'The Drúedain'. This is the name the Eldar gives to the Folk of Haleth, who use women warriors. Their leader Haleth is a woman and she has a female bodyguard. They make their way to Beleriand in the First Age. They have a blood feud with the orcs, who fear them, but delight in capturing and torturing them. Although they are illiterate, they are great craftsmen and carve figures in wood and stone. They make figures of orcs fleeing from them and images of themselves which they set up as 'watch stones'. One shows a larger-than-life Drúedain sitting on a dead orc. In a second part of the story called 'The Faithful Stone', one of these watch stones kills two orcs that try and burn a Drúedain's house down.

In 1954, Tolkien sat down to write an index to *The Lord of the Rings*. It rapidly got out of hand and was clearly too expensive to include. No index appeared until the second edition in 1966. Christopher Tolkien also used it as his plan for the index for *The Silmarillion*. He also plundered it for 'The Istari', the second chapter of part four which gives a description of the various wizards, focusing largely on Gandalf and Saruman.

Finally, there is a chapter on 'The Palantíri'. This was taken from amendments to the text of Book Three, Chapter Eleven of *The Lord of the Rings* – 'The Palantir' – which did not appear until the second impression of the revised edition that appeared in 1967. It concerns the origins and use of the stones.

The History of Middle-earth

Christopher Tolkien produced a series of twelve volumes of *The History of Middle-earth*, compiling the massive amount of material his father had left behind. This shows the detailed development of the Middle-earth saga.

The first two volumes make up the *The Book of Lost Tales*. Published in 1983 and 1984, they contain the early versions of the myths that would eventually appear in *The Silmarillion*. They purport to tell the tales that a traveller named Eriol the Mariner brought back after visiting the elves on the island of Tol Eressëa, or the Lonely Isle, in the western ocean. The first volume tells the 'Tales of Valinor, from the Music of the Ainur to the Exile of the Noldoli and the Hiding of Valinor'; the second, the 'Tales of Beren and Tinúviel, of the Fall of Gondolin and the Necklace of the Dwarves'.

The next volume, published in 1985, is called *The Lays of Beleriand*. It contains two long lays, or poems: 'The Lay of the Children of Húrin', telling the saga of Túran Turambar in alliterative verse, and 'The Lay of Leithian', which is the basis of the tale of Beren and Lúthien that appears in *The Silmarillion*. The first version of 'The Lay of Leithian' appears among Tolkien's earliest writing. A second was written during the time he was working on *The Lord of the Rings*. Also included are the unfinished alliterative poems 'The Flight of the Noldoli from Valinor', 'The Lay of Eärendel' and 'The Lay of the Fall of Gondolin'.

The Shaping of Middle-earth in 1986 covers the geography

and chronology of Valinor and Middle-earth. It contains more prose fragments following on from *The Book of Lost Tales*; early versions of *The Silmarillion*, or a 'Sketch of the Mythology', with a map; the 'Ambarkanta' or 'Shape of the World', explaining the nature of Tolkien's imagined universe; and the earliest annals of Valinor and Belerian, giving the chronology of the First Age. These purport to be translations made by Ælfwine the Mariner of England.

Published in 1987, *The Lost Road and Other Writings* contains more material written before Tolkien got to work on *The Lord of the Rings*. The story 'The Lost Road' comes from a discussion Tolkien had with C.S. Lewis, where they lamented the state of modern literature. While Lewis was to try writing about space travel, resulting in *Out of the Silent Planet*, Tolkien was to deal with time travel. In the story, he tries to tell the fall of Númenor as a time-travel tale. The volume also includes 'The Later Annals of Valinor' and 'The Later Annals of Beleriand', where Tolkien continues working on the chronology of the First Age. The 'Ainulindalë' is a reworking of 'The Music of Ainur', which appears in *The Book of Lost Tales, Part One*.

The largest part of the book is taken up with 'Quenta Silmarillion', the version that Tolkien submitted to Allen & Unwin in 1937 as a follow-up to *The Hobbit*. The book also contains essays on language and etymology, with appendices on genealogies, names and a second Silmarillion map.

The sixth volume of *The History of Middle-earth* is the first of the four-volume series *The History of The Lord of the Rings* compiled by Christopher Tolkien. These document the development of the book through its many drafts. The titles of the four volumes come from discarded names for the separate books of *The Lord of the Rings*. The first volume, *The Return of the Shadow*, was published in 1988. It covers the development of the story from its beginnings to the end of *The Fellowship of the Ring*, the first published volume, and shows how Bilbo's magic ring turned into the dangerous ring of the dark lord. There are multiple versions of the opening chapter of *The Fellowship of the Ring*. Four get little further than Bilbo's parting speech. Frodo is still called Bingo and Aragorn, or Strider, Trotter. After reaching Rivendell, Tolkien then goes back to Hobbiton and starts again. He even considers doing this a third time, making Bilbo the main protagonist. But then he heads on with the Council of Elrond and the Mines of Moria.

The Treason of Isengard followed in 1989. Instead of proceeding onwards from Balin's tomb in Moria, Tolkien goes backwards to wrestle with some of the plotting problems, notably Gandalf's delayed return to the Shire. He thought that Gandalf might have been held prisoner by 'Giant Treebeard' – the first appearances of the ents. Or he could have been besieged by the black riders in the western tower of Sarn Ford. Only later is he imprisoned by fellow wizard 'Saruman the White' who has sided with Sauron. This means that 'The Council of Elfrond' has to be rewritten – twice – to incorporate this backstory. Meanwhile, Trotter becomes Strider, but instead of a hobbit he is an elf.

Then he moves on to Lothlórien. After mapping out future storylines, he tackles 'The Breaking of the Fellowship', the last chapter of *The Fellowship of the Ring*. However, *The Treason of Isengard* goes on to introduce the Riders of Rohan and turns Treebeard into a friendly character. It ends where Gandalf and party meet Théoden and Wormtongue.

In 1990, *The War of the Ring* appeared. Part One, 'The

Fall of Saruman', deals with the destruction of Isengard and the introduction of the palantír. Tolkien then stopped work on *The Lord of the Rings* for a year. Resuming in 1944, he made a first stab at Frodo and Sam's journey to Mordor. Gollum appears for the first time. The third part deals with what appears as Book Five of *The Lord of the Rings*: the preparations for war in Minas Tirith, the muster of Rohan, the siege of Gondor, the Battle of the Pelannor Fields and the march on the Black Gate.

The final part of *The History of The Lord of the Rings*, published in 1992, is called *Sauron Defeated*. This takes the story from Sam rescuing Frodo from the Tower of Cirith Ungol to Mount Doom, though the idea of dropping the ring into the Crack of Doom had been around from the beginning, when Tolkien first discovered the significance of Bilbo's ring. However, we now get Frodo's final refusal to part with the ring, and Gollum's intervention and demise. This scene was reworked repeatedly. A very different version of 'The Scouring of the Shire', where the returning hobbits discover what has been going on in their absence, appears. Only in later drafts does Saruman, aka Sharkey, make an appearance. This is followed by an unpublished 'Epilogue' where Sam attempts to answer questions asked by his children.

Part Two is called 'The Notion Club Papers'. Dating from 1944–5, it deals with time travel. Supposedly mysterious papers discovered in the early years of the twenty-first century, these report the discussions of an Oxford club in the years 1986–7 that tie the drowning of Númenor to the legend of Atlantis and modern history. This is continued in the third part, 'The Drowning of Anadûnê'.

Volume ten of *The History of Middle-earth* is *Morgoth's*

Ring. Published in 1993, it is the first of two companion volumes subtitled *The Later Silmarillion*. After finishing *The Lord of the Rings*, Tolkien went back to the myths and legends that appear in *The Silmarillion*, reworking stories that he had produced before and adding new material. It includes two new versions of 'Ainulindalë', 'The Annals of Aman', two versions of 'Quenta Silmarillion' and '*Athrabeth Finrod Ah Andreth*' or 'The Debate of Finrod and Andreth'. The final section 'Myths Transformed' deals with notes and rewritings that re-evaluate much of the earlier material.

The second of the companion volumes, *The War of the Jewels*, was published in 1994. It contains 'The Grey Annals', giving a chronology of Middle-earth from the awakening of the elves to the death of Túrin Turambar; later reworkings of 'Quenta Silmarillion'; 'The Wandering of Húrin', covering the period after his release; and an essay on the languages of elves.

Then in 1995 a compilation of Tolkien's artwork was published as *J.R.R. Tolkien: Artist and Illustrator*.

The final volume of *The History of Middle-earth* – *The Peoples of the Middle-earth* – was published in 1996. The first part covers the writing of the prologue and appendices to *The Lord of the Rings* and including early drafts. Part two covers Tolkien's later essays, mostly after 1969, on Middle-earth and its inhabitants. The book ends with two more unfinished tales. The first is an attempt to write a sequel to *The Lord of the Rings*, beginning 105 years after the fall of the dark tower. The second is called 'Tal-Elmar'. Set in the Second Age, it tells of the Númenórean colonization of Middle-earth written from the point of view of the wild men who live there.

The Children of Húrin

Published on 17 April 2007 by HarperCollins in the UK and Canada, and by Houghton Mifflin in the US, *The Children of Húrin* was the first full-length novel set in Middle-earth since the publication of *The Silmarillion* in 1977. Tolkien had begun the tale in 1918, but never completed it to his satisfaction. The tale of Túrin Turambar and his sister Nienor from the First Age first appeared in a truncated form in *The Silmarillion*, covering just thirty pages. An eighty-page version appears in *Unfinished Tales*. An early version, 'Turambar and Foalókë' appears in *The Book of Lost Tales, Part Two* and an unfinished version in verse, 'The Lay of the Children of Húrin', appears in *The Lays of Beleriand*, the third volume of *The History of Middle-earth*.

Christopher Tolkien spent nearly thirty years conjuring the complete story from his father's writings. He claimed that he did not have to invent anything to complete the work, only provide bridging passages to connect the pieces he had culled from various drafts.

The Legend of Sigurd and Gudrún

Throughout his life Tolkien wrote poetry. Much of it has appeared in the various books bearing his name. Then on 5 May 2009, HarperCollins in the UK and Houghton Mifflin Harcourt in the US published *The Legend of Sigurd and Gudrún*, a tale in alliterative verse written in the style of thirteenth-century Icelandic poetry. It tells the tale of the Sigurd and the fall of the Niflungs, or Niblungs, from Norse mythology. William Morris had covered the same ground in 1876 with his epic poem *The Story of Sigurd the Volsung and the Fall of the Niblungs*.

Tolkien's version comprises two related poems: 'The New

Lay of the Volsungs' and 'The New Lay of Gudrun', with related commentaries.

'The New Lay of the Volsungs' tells of the ancestry of the great hero Sigurd, who slews the most celebrated of dragons, Fafnir, and takes his treasure for his own. He then awakes the Valkyrie Brynhild who is sleeping behind a wall of fire. When he tells her that he has killed Fafnir, she says that the gods await his arrival in Valhalla and agrees to marry him if he wins a kingdom for himself. He heads to the court of the great princes, the Niflungs. Their mother, the evil Queen Grimhild, says that, to seal their alliance, Sigurd should marry their sister Princess Gudrún, achieving this with a love potion. Using another spell, Brynhild is tricked into marrying King Gunnar, thinking that it is Sigurd, thereby fulfilling her oath. When she discovers the truth, she curses Sigurd. As a result, Sigurd is killed and Brynhild kills herself. Her corpse is then burnt on Sigurd's funeral pyre and they enter Valhalla together.

'The New Lay of Gudrún' tells of her fate after the death of Sigurd. Against her will, Gudrún is forced to marry the mighty Atli, ruler of the Huns, the Attila of history. He demands Fafnir's treasure. When her brothers will not give it to him, he kills them. She then kills the two sons she has had with Atli and makes goblets from their skulls. These are filled with their blood and honey. Atli collapses in the mead hall and is carried to his bed. Gudrún then stabs him in the chest. Once he is dead, she throws herself in the sea.

Other works
Tolkien published other works intended for children where he began experimenting with some of the ideas that came to fruition in *The Hobbit*, *The Lord of the Rings* and *The*

Silmarillion. In 1949, he published *Farmer Giles of Ham*, which is set, not in Middle-earth, but the Middle Kingdom – a medieval England where there are dragons as well as blunderbusses, giants and swords with names. He also plays verbal games with made-up languages.

In 1962, he published *The Adventures of Tom Bombadil*, a collection of poems. Only two of the sixteen poems feature Tom Bombadil, a character who also appears in *The Fellowship of the Ring*. The poem 'Errantry' is said to be a hobbit poem from Middle-earth, while Tolkien said that 'The Man in the Moon Stayed Up Too Late' is the complete version of the poem that Frodo could only remember part of at The Prancing Pony. The hobbit poem 'The Mewlips' tells of a race of evil creatures who feed on passers-by and collect their bones in a sack. There is a poem called 'Oliphaunt', a creature that appears in *The Lord of the Rings*. 'Fastitoclan' is about a turtle-like creature from Middle-earth, so large that sailors land on its back. But when they build a fire, it dives, drowning them. And 'The Sea Bell' is subtitled 'Frodo's Dreme'. Although Tolkien said that it was not by Frodo, it is thought to reflect the dark dreams that plagued his final years.

Tree and Leaf was published in 1964. It contains an essay called 'On Fairy Stories', first published in the collection *Essays Presented to Charles Williams* in 1947, and 'Leaf by Niggle', first published in the *Dublin Review* in 1945. The mythic poem 'Mythopoeia', written around 1931, was added in the 1988 edition. Later editions also include 'The Homecoming of Beorhtnoth Beorhthelm's Son', a play in alliterative verse, first published in *Essays and Studies by members of the English Association* in 1953. This was also published – along with 'On Fairy Stories', 'Leaf by Niggle',

'Farmer Giles of Ham' and 'The Adventures of Tom Bombadil' – in *The Tolkien Reader* in 1966.

Tolkien published *The Road Goes Ever On* with singer-songwriter Donald Swann in 1967. It contains a cycle of songs taken, largely, from *The Lord of the Rings*. They have also been issued on an LP and, in a limited edition, CD. Tolkien's novella *Smith of Wootton Major* was also published in 1967 by Allen & Unwin, after appearing as a short story in New York's *Redbook* magazine on 23 November that year. Again it is unrelated to Middle-earth, but set in an England beset by faeries.

Tolkien's translations of *Sir Gawain and the Green Knight, Pearl and Sir Orfeo* were published in 1975, after his death. His *Father Christmas Letters*, relating the misadventures of Father Christmas and his helpers, was published the following year.

The Letters of J.R.R. Tolkien was published in 1981. The following year *Finn and Hengest*, featuring two Anglo-Saxon heroes from *Beowulf*, and the children's story *Mr Bliss* were published. The essay collection *The Monsters and the Critics* followed in 1983. Another children's story, *Roverandom*, was published in 1998. It also appeared in *Tales from the Perilous Realm* in 2008, along with 'Farmer Giles of Ham', 'The Adventures of Tom Bombadil', 'Leaf by Niggle' and 'Smith of Wootton Major'.

Throughout his life, Tolkien also published many learned works in his various academic fields. And since the publication of *The Lord of the Rings*, bookshops worldwide have been full of books detailing the world that Tolkien created. There was also a famous parody, *Bored of the Rings*, published in 1969 by two writers from the *Harvard Lampoon*.

6

LIVING IN MIDDLE-EARTH

Tolkien began writing stories and poems about Middle-earth in 1914. Presumably, he began thinking about it sometime before that. So the history and geography of Middle-earth had over sixty years to evolve. Indeed, he was still revising *The Silmarillion* when he died so that he would get every detail of the world that he had created in his head correct. This may have been an impossible task, or maybe just too much to be achieved in one lifetime. After Christopher Tolkien oversaw the publication of *The Silmarillion* in 1977 and *Unfinished Tales of Númenor and Middle-earth* in 1980, he went back over his father's notes and drafts and put together the twelve-volume *History of Middle-earth*. These books traced the development of Middle-earth in his father's imagination. Taken together, for all those who have read his work, Tolkien's overarching creation of an entirely separate reality is breathtaking. However, according to Tolkien, Middle-earth was not an invention. 'It's just an old-fashioned word for this world we live in,' he said, 'at a different stage of imagination.'

If Middle-earth is on our earth, the question must be asked: where exactly is it? It seems clear that the Shire is a distorted view of England, while the countries surrounding it are a contorted version of Europe. Indeed maps of Middle-earth always show it perched on the western edge of a landmass. To the east is 'Rhûn'. Asked about the geography of Middle-earth, Tolkien explained that 'Rhûn' was the elvish word for east. That included Asia, China, Japan, all the places that people in the West consider far away. To the south of Harad is Africa and other hot countries. So Middle-earth, he agreed, was northwest Europe. Mordor, he later remarked, was somewhere in the Balkans and, while holidaying in Venice in 1955, he described the city as Gondor.

The Shire

Once, driving with author Clyde Kilby along the London road to the east of Oxford, Tolkien pointed to the small hills to the north and said that was just right for hobbit territory. And in a letter to Rayner Unwin, Tolkien confirmed that the Shire was 'based on rural England and not any other country in the world'. The fictional Shire measured some forty leagues (120 Númenórean miles, 193 kilometres) from the Far Downs in the west to the Baranduin, or Brandywine, River in the east, and some fifty leagues (150 miles, 241 kilometres) from the moors to the north, to the marshes to the south. So it covered roughly 18,000 square miles (47,000 square kilometres).

The Shire is divided into four quarters, known as the Farthings. A farthing was a quarter of a penny in the old British currency. It had been in use since the thirteenth century, but ceased to be legal tender in 1960. The four Farthings were simply North-farthing, South-farthing, East-farthing and West-farthing. Each was further divided into 'folklands' bearing the name of an old family in the vicinity. Nearly all the Tooks, for example, lived in Tookland.

Beyond the Farthings were the East and West Marches. These were added in the year 1452 by Shire Reckoning – that is the Middle-earth calendar that begins with the founding of the Shire – or year 31 of the Fourth Age. It was the sparsely populated region between West-farthing and the Tower Hills, granted to the Shire-dwellers by King Elessar, Aragorn II.

The East Marches also officially became part of the Shire that year. It was also known as Buckland and had been settled in around SR740 by Gorhendad Oldbuck who changed his name to Brandybuck after excavating their ancestral *smial* or hobbit-hole Brandy Hall. Part of the Old Forest, its chief village was Bucklebury on the slopes behind Brandy Hall. Some of the inhabitants could swim and they liked to take boats on the Baranduin. Being on the east of the Shire, they were vulnerable to attack, so they planted a twenty-mile hedge, which became known as the High Hay and ran all the way from Brandywine Bridge along the river to where the Withywindle flowed out of the forest. The Bucklanders also locked Buckland Gate and their own front doors at night.

Buckland was administered by the head of the Brandybuck family, who was known as the Master of Buckland. Otherwise, hobbits did not go in much for government.

Families were generally occupied in growing food. The land was fertile and the hobbits grew fruit, cereals and pipe-weed. Along with the farms, there were workshops and small businesses. But these practically ran themselves and remained unchanged for generations.

There was something of a class system with a landed gentry who did not have to work for a living, but most hobbits were farmers, tradesmen or labourers. There were some relatively poor hobbits but, in the absence of war or famine, their situation was not dire.

Laws, or The Rules, came down from the kings of Fornost, or Norbury, far to the north of the Shire – that is, the kings of Arnor – though there had been no king there for over a thousand years when we first visit the Shire. The chief Took carried the honorary title 'Thain'. Technically he was master of the Shire-moot and captain of the Shire-muster, but as these only happened during an emergency, the thainship was merely nominal.

The only official who actually did anything was the Mayor of Michel Delving, the chief township of the Shire, located on the White Downs in the West-farthing. He was elected at the midsummer festival, Lithe, for a seven-year term. But his main function was to preside at feasts on the frequent Shire holidays. He was also postmaster and First Shirriff in charge of the watch. His police force comprised three men in each Farthing. Their main duty was as haywards who prevented cattle straying and their only uniform was a feather in their caps. There was also a force of Bounders who guarded the borders.

The Shire lay to the northwest of Middle-earth in the region of Eriador. This was bounded on the west by the Blue Mountains and in the east by the Misty Mountains and, in the Third Age, was home to all the free people of Middle-earth. The Shire had been part of Arnor, but was deserted during the waning years of the kingdom. When Arnor broke up, it was part of the province of Arthedain and was the king's hunting ground until King Argeleb II of Arthedain (1473–1670 in the Third Age) granted hobbits migrating from Dunland the lands up to the Baranduin. The settlers were led by the Bree hobbits Marcho and Blanco in TA1601, year one Shire Reckoning. It was divided into its four Farthings some thirty years later. By then, most of the hobbits of Middle-earth lived in the Shire.

The hobbits lived there comfortably enough during the Third Age, though they suffered in the Great Plague of TA1636 (SR36) and the Battle of Green Fields where the game of golf was invented in TA2747. Then there was the Long Winter of TA2758, followed by the Days of Dearth when famine struck Middle-earth, though losses in the Shires were minimized by the intervention of Gandalf. And in the Fell Winter of TA2911, when the Brandywine froze, the Shire was invaded by white wolves.

The Shire was well protected by the Dúnedain Rangers of the North and so untroubled by war that the hobbits almost forgot that the outside world existed, despite the dwarves who travelled along the Great East Road that ran through the middle of the Shire on their way to their mines in the Blue Mountains and elves on their way to the port of Grey Havens.

The hobbits of the Shire had lived in peace for over 250 years before the Ringwraiths visited looking for Frodo. Then, during the War of the Ring when the Rangers were occupied elsewhere, the Shire was left defenceless, prey to Lotho Sackville-Baggins, his evil ruffians and Saruman himself. But peace was returned by Frodo, Sam, Merry and Pippin after the Battle of Bywater in TA3019. After that, the rapid industrialization introduced by Saruman was quickly undone.

The fertility of the land was restored by the soil from Lórien, given to Sam by Galadriel, and the year TA3020 was known as the 'Great Year of Plenty'. Then in year 17 of the Fourth Age (SR1427) King Elessar signed an edict preventing men from entering the Shire and making the Shire a free land under the protection of the Northern Sceptre.

The most authoritative history of the Shire was contained in the Red Book of Westmarch, written largely by Bilbo, Frodo and Sam. A large book with a red leather cover, it contains the story of Bilbo's adventures with Thorin, as related in *The Hobbit*, and an account of the War of the Ring told from the hobbits' point of view, as related in *The Lord of the Rings*. Also attached is Bilbo's *Translations from the Elvish*, the basis of *The Silmarillion*, and a volume of genealogies and other annals compiled by one of Sam's descendants. Sam gave the original Red Book to his daughter Elanor and it was kept by the Fairbairns in Westmarch, hence its name. While the original was lost, copies had been made. The most important was the Thain's Book, which was kept at the Great Smials, the many-tunnelled mansion of the Took family in Tuckborough in West-farthing. It had been corrected and amended by scholars from Gondor and various marginalia had been added by generations of hobbits. This seems to be the copy studied by Professor Tolkien. It was also known in Gondor as the Red Book of Periannath – their word for a hobbit.

Bree

To the east of the Shire lay the village of Bree. It was settled by both men and hobbits. Around the time of the War of the Rings, there were around a hundred stone houses for 'Big Folk', with a smaller number of *smials* in the hillside where the hobbits dwelt. It was surrounded by a hedge and a dike. At an important crossroads, its gates were shut at night.

Bree was an important trading centre. It lay on the East Road that ran from the Dale in the east to the Blue Mountains and the coast in the west. The North Road that connected Arnor to Gondor also ran through Bree, but that was not used so much after the fall of Arnor which, at that time, had become known as the Greenway due to the encroaching vegetation. Nevertheless, The Prancing Pony at Bree still provided an important meeting place and the Rangers of the North used the village for resupply.

Surrounding Bree Hill was Bree-land, which extended from Buckland in the west to the Weather Hills in the east. Along with Bree, it comprised the villages of Staddle, a settlement of hobbits on the eastern slopes of Bree-hill; Combe, which lay in the deep valley east of Staddle; and Archet, which was further to the east on the edge of Chetwood. It was mostly inhabited by men, but some hobbits lived there too.

Rivendell

Known as Imladris – 'Deep-cloven-valley' in the Sindarin language – Rivendell was located in the foothills of the Misty Mountains, at the edge of a narrow gorge of the Bruinen, or Loudwater, river. Its main tributary, the Mitheithel or Hoarwell, ran to the west.

Elrond sought refuge there in the hidden valley in 1697 of the Second Age after Sauron's destruction of the elvish settlement of Eregion to the south. Elrond's house there became known at the 'Last Homely House East of the Sea'. It stood behind the fast-running stream and was surrounded by pines.

Tolkien gives us a clue where this might be. In a letter to his son Michael in 1968, he wrote: 'I am ... delighted that you have made the acquaintance of Switzerland, and of the very part that I once knew best and which had the deepest effect on me. The hobbit's journey from Rivendell to the other side of the Misty Mountains, including the glissade down the slithering stones into the pine woods, is based on my adventures in 1911.' At the age of nineteen, Tolkien had travelled to the Lauterbrunnen valley with a party of twelve.

Arnor

The surrounding territory of Arnor was the more northerly of the two Númenórean realms founded by Elendil the Tall in the year SA3320. At its greatest extent, it included all the lands from the River Bruinen, which joins the Mitheithel at Tharbad to form the Gwathlo, to the River Lhún, the boundary with the elvish and dwarvish lands to the west. Until Arnor broke into three separate states, its capital was Annúminas. After the death of Elendil, the realm of Arnor passed to Isildur, but he never reach Annúminas to take up the sceptre. The realm then passed to his fourth son Valandil.

Arnor broke up after the death of the tenth king Eärendur in TA861. His three sons then quarrelled over the kingdom and divided it into Arthedain, Cardolan and Rhudaur. Five hundred years later, Argeleb I of Arthedain realized that the line of Isildur was extinct in Cardolan and Rhudaur and laid claim to them. But Rhudaur made a secret pact with Angmar, the witch-realm to the north. Eventually, the great fortress at Fornost, Arthedain's capital, fell in TA1974. The surviving Dúnedain of the North became the Rangers.

Gondor

The southerly realm founded by Elendil the Tall was Gondor. It was ruled by Isildur's brother Anárion. Its chief port, Pelargar on the river Anduin, had been founded by Númenórian sailors in SA2350. While Isildur had raised the tower of Minas Ithil near the border of Mordor, Anárion had built Minas Anor, or the Tower of the Setting Sun, to defend against the Wild Men to the west. Between them, they built Osgiliath, where the two brothers' thrones sat side by side.

During the first part of the Third Age, Minas Ithil and Osgiliath decreased in importance and Minas Anor became the chief city of Gondor and it was rebuilt in TA420. At its zenith in TA1100, Gondor extended north to the river Celebrant, east to the Sea of Rhûn which marked the edge of the known world, west to the river Gwathlo and south to the river Harnen inland and Umbar on the coast. At that time, Gondor was so powerful that several of the realms to the east and south were tributary states.

Since its founding, Gondor was constantly under attack by Sauron or his allies in Rhûn, Harad or Umbar. In SA3429, Sauron took Minas Ithil and burnt the white tree. Isildur escaped down the Anduin, while Anárion defended Osgiliath and Minas Anor. In TA2000, the Nazgûl came out of Mordor and besieged Minas Ithil, which fell two years later. The palantír that was kept there was captured and Minas Ithil was renamed Minas Morgul, the Tower of Sorcery, which the orcs held until their defeat in the War of the Ring. Meanwhile Minas Anor was renamed Minas Tirith, or Tower of the Guard.

During the Third Age Gondor suffered other reversals. Between TA1432 and 1448, there was a civil war known as the Kin-strife. When King Valacar died, his son Eldacar succeeded, but he was deemed unfit to rule because he was not of pure Dúnadan blood. There was a rebellion in the south led by Castamir, the captain of ships. He besieged Eldacar in Osgiliath. In TA1437, Eldacar was forced to seek refuge with his mother's family in Rhovanian and Osgiliath was burnt. The Dome of the Stars, also known as the Tower of Stone, was destroyed and the palantír lost. Castamir also captured and killed Eldacar's son Ornendil, and took the throne.

However, Castamir the Usurper, as he became known, was cruel and sought to move the capital to Pelargir. In TA1447, after ten years of exile, Eldacar returned to Gondor with an army of Northmen. He was joined by men from the two fiefdoms of Anórien and Ithilien, and northern grasslands of Calenardhon. Battle was joined at the crossings of the River Erui in the southern fiefdom of Lebennin. Castamir was killed, but his sons escaped. Besieged in Pelargir, they escaped with the fleet to Umbar, where they became pirates.

Gondor was further weakened by the Great Plague of TA1636. After that, Osgiliath fell into ruin and Mordor was left unguarded. Further troubles ensued when the Wainriders invaded between TA1851 and 1954. Then in TA2050, King Eärnur rode out to face the Witch-king of Angmar and was never seen again. Eärnur was the last of the line of Anárion, so Gondor was ruled by stewards until Aragorn took back the kingdom as King Elessar.

Rohan

To the northeast of Gondor, beyond the White Mountains, was Rohan, the 'Land of the Horse', Gondor's most important ally. It was the home of the Rohirrim, the 'Masters of Horses' who were farmers and herdsmen. Their horses were said to be the best in Middle-earth and roamed free in great herds. Consequently, the Rohirrim were born horsemen and their cavalry was known as the Riders of Rohan. While the Gondoreans called their land Rohan, the Rohirrim called it Riddermark – 'Land of the Knights' – the Mark of the Riders, or just the Mark. The orcs called it horse-country.

Their territory was bounded on the west by the Misty Mountains and the river Isen, where it flows through the Gap of Rohan forming the border with Dunland, the forest of Fangorn and the River Limlight to the north and the Anduin to the east. The River Entwash divided Rohan into Westfold and Eastfold, also known as Westemnet and Eastemnet. There the ground was firmer and the Rohirrim kept many herds and stud, living in tents there even in wintertime. Rohan had once been the province of Calenardhon, the 'Green Region', but Cirion of Gondor had given it to the Éothéod, the ancestors of the Rohirrim, after the Battle of the Field of Celebrant in TA2510. While raising their horses on the green plains there, the Rohirrim restored the ancient fortresses. The most important were Dunharrow, overlooking the pass of Harrowdale in the White Mountains, and Hornburg above the gorge of Helm's Deep in the Ered Nimrais, or White Horn Mountains.

Eorl, the leader of the Éothéod, built the first city Aldburg, but his son, Bego, built a large hall to the west below Dunharrow. This was known as Meduseld, derived of the Old English *Maeduselde* meaning 'mead hall'. It had a straw roof that looked golden from a distance, so it was also known as the Golden Hall. Around it was built the capital Edoras, a hill fort on the slopes of the White Mountains. However, most of the Rohirrim lived on farms or in small villages. During the reign of King Goldwine (TA2680–99) the Dunlendings, who the Rohirrim had driven out, began to return, occupying the south of the forest of Fangorn and the Ring of Isengard at the southern end of the Misty Mountains. King Déor (TA2699–2718) rode against them, but was unable to recapture the Ring of Isengard.

In TA2758, Rohan was overrun by Dunlendings. King Helm Hammerhand (TA2741–59) took refuge in Hornburg. However, his nephew Fréaláf led a daring raid to retake Edoras, before driving the Dunlendings out of Rohan. After Helm Hammerhand died, Fréaláf became king (TA 2759–98). It was Fréaláf who advised Beren, then steward of Gondor, to lend the keys of Orthanc, the tower of Isengard, to Saruman so that he could protect Rohan from any further encroachment by the Dunlendings.

After the Battle of Nanduhirion, also known as the Battle of Azanulbizar, where the dwarves defeated the orcs in TA2799, the surviving orcs tried to find refuge in the White Mountains. Fréaláf's son King Brytta (2798–2842) fought to rid Rohan of orcs. The task was completed by King Folca (TA2851–64).

Around TA2960 Saruman turned against Rohan, trying to undermine King Théoden (TA2980–3019). Some time before TA3014, he sent his henchman Gríma Wormtongue to be Théoden's aide. In TA3019, Saruman launched a full-scale invasion of Rohan. During the First Battle at the Fords of Isen, Théoden's son Théodred was killed. However, Saruman's forces were defeated at the Battle of Hornburg, also known as the Battle of Helm's Deep.

Théoden was killed at the Battle of Pelennor Fields in front of Minas Tirith and was succeeded by his nephew Éomer (TA3019–FA63). After the War of the Ring was won, he continued to honour the Oath of Eorl and Rohan recovered from the war and became rich and fruitful again.

Forest of Fangorn

To the east of the southern end of the Misty Mountains, the Forest of Fangorn was the eastern remnant of the great forest that once covered the whole of Eriador. Fangorn was the home of the ents. The word in Sindarin, the language of the grey elves, meant 'beard-tree', or Treebeard, which was also the name of the oldest of the ents who was the guardian of the forest. The Rohirrim called Fangorn Entwood, while Treebeard himself called it variously Ambarona, Aldalómë, Tauremorna and Tauremornalómë. Indeed, at one point he said: '*Taurelilómëa-tumbalemorna Tumbaletaurëa Lórmëanor*,' which means 'Forestmanyshadowed-deep-valleyblack Deepvalleyforested Gloomyland'. But what Treebeard, aka Fangorn, was trying to convey was that in the deep valleys of the forest there were places where the Great Darkness of the Elder Days, or the First Age when Morgoth ruled in Middle-earth, had not been lifted.

This was true for the ents as, during the Third Age, the orcs of Isengard did great damage to the forest. That ended with their defeat in the War of the Ring.

Rhovanion

Otherwise known as Wilderland, Rhovanion was a large area of northeast Middle-earth between the Misty Mountains and the Celduin or River Running which emptied into the Sea of Rhûn. The upper reaches of the Anduin ran through it. It was also the home of Greenwood the Great, later known as Mirkwood.

Rhovanion had been known of in the First Age when the elves passed through it after their awakening, followed by the fathers of men. In the Second Age there were two elf kingdoms there. To the south, Rhovanion bordered on Mordor and the Battle of Dagorlad – the dusty plain outside the Black Gate of Morannon – took place there. Also in the south were the great falls of Sarn Gerbir which overlooked Rohan and northern Gondor.

Early in the Third Age the dwarfish kingdom of Erebor was there. It was re-established after the death of Smaug. The Éothéod came from Rohanion before moving to Rohan and the Stoors, one of three breeds of hobbits, also came from the valleys of the Anduin in Rhovanion, before moving to the Shire. Silvan elves lived there and Northmen inhabited the city of Dale. They were distantly related to the Dúnedain and often allied themselves with Gondor, which ceded some of their northern lands to these Northmen.

In the year TA490, the Northmen founded the Kingdom of Rhovanion. For Gondor, this acted as a buffer state against the predations of the Easterlings. However, the closeness between the rulers of Gondor and Rhovanion unsettled those in the southern fiefdoms. This was exacerbated when Prince Valacar of Gondor married Princess Vidumavi of Rhovanion. When their son Eldacar took the throne of Gondor the Kin-strife began.

After the Great Plague had weakened Rhovanion further, it fell prey to the Easterlings and Wainriders. Sauron sought refuge in Mirkwood, further depopulating the region. Then in TA2510 the Balchoth arrived, effectively ending Rhovanion as an independent kingdom.

Mirkwood

Once part of the great forest that covered Middle-earth, it was then called Greenwood the Great and extended from the Grey Mountains in the north to the loop in the Anduin where the Limlight joined it, known as the North Undeep, in the south. Its western boundary was the vale of the Auduin; the eastern the River Running.

The Old Forest Road ran across it from west to east. When that became usable, a new path was made further to the north. The Forest River flowed in from its source in the Grey Mountains to the north. Joining the Enchanted River flowing from the Mountains of Mirkwood, it ran on past the elvenking's Hall out to Long Lake.

South of the Old Forest Road, the forest narrowed where the Northmen from Rhovanion felled the trees, leaving the East Bite. The Forest was just one hundred miles across at that point. Then, near the southwest tip of the forest lay Amon Lanc, the Naked Hill. When Sauron came there in TA1050 and built a fortress, the hill and fortress became known as Dol Guldur, the Hill of Sorcery. It was then that Greenwood the Great became known as Mirkwood.

Lothlórien

Also known as Lórien, the elven realm of Lothlórien was a wooded area lying on either side of the Celeborn river west of its confluence with the Anduin. Its name meant 'dreamflower'. The forest there was home to the mellyrn or mallorn trees whose golden leaves meant that it is sometimes called the Golden Wood. They had silver-grey boughs similar to birches. The inhabitants of the wood wove the branches of the mellryn together to form platforms or *telain* where they lived. Hence the elves of Lothlórien were called *Gadadhrim* or 'Tree-people'.

The first settlers were Nandor elves who refused to cross the Hithaeglir or Misty Mountains. There were no mallorn trees there then. They came from Númenor. Tar-Aldarion, the sixth king of Númenor, gave some seeds to King Gil-galad of Lindon, but they would not grow there, so he gave some to his kinswoman Galadriel. With her care, they grew in the fertile soil of Lothlórien. The breaking of the Thangorodrim, the volcanic mountains raised by Melkor, the Sindar or Grey Elves emigrated eastwards and settled alongside the Silvan Elves already living there. Eventually the Sindarin language took over from Silvan.

A Sindar named Amdir became king of Lórien and ruled until he took a small contingent of silvan archers to the Battle of Dagorlad in SA3434 where he was killed. His son Amroth then took the throne. He fell in love with a beautiful silvan girl named Nimrodel who lived beside the falls that later bore her name. She rejected his suit. However, when the dwarves awakened the Balrog in Moria and Sauron occupied Dol Guldur, Amroth and Nimrodel escaped together. When the ship he was fleeing on left her on shore, he jumped overboard and both were lost.

Then another Sindar named Celeborn married Galadriel and came to live in Lórien. They lived in the Cara Galadhon, or City of Trees, where the mellyrn grew tallest. The elves of Lórien then became estranged from the other Silvan Elves, though they maintained contact with the wizards and chief of the Eldar. Lothlórien then became a secret realm. Galadriel was from a noble race and possessed one of the clven rings, the Nenya, or Ring of Adamant. With it, she set Lórien outside the stream of time.

Despite the onslaught of the orcs, Lórien survived throughout the Third Age. After the members of the Fellowship of the Ring moved on, the orc hosts launched three separate assaults on Lórien, but the elves held them off. Then they crossed the Anduin and eventually destroyed Dol Guldur.

At the end of the Third Age, Galariel sailed west with Gandalf and Elrond. Some time after, Celeborn also left Lórien and took ship westwards. Only a few elves remained behind in Lothlórien 'and there was no longer light or song in Caras Galadhon', according to Tolkien.

Mordor

Even before Sauron the Great chose it as his home, Mordor – the 'Black Land' or 'Land of Shadow' – was a bleak and desolate place. The land there was barren and infertile, but from Sauron's point of view it had its advantages. It was a natural fortress, bounded to the north by the Ered Lithui, or Ash Mountains, and to the west and south by the Ephel Dúeth, the Mountains of the Shadow. Only to the east was it open to the world.

Mordor measured 300 miles (480 kilometres) from north to south and 450 miles (720 kilometres) from east to west. In the northwest corner where the Ered Lithui met the Epthel Dúeth was the deep valley of the Udún, or Pit. Within the walls of Mordor, there were other mountain ranges that separated the plain of Gorgoroth in the northwest corner. In the middle of the plain stood Orodruin, Mount Doom. Beyond the mountains stretched the plain of Nurn with at its centre and inland sea.

When Sauron first came to Mordor in the Second Age, he fortified the passes. Then on a south-facing spur of Ered Lithui that stretched out across Gorgoroth towards Mount Doom, he built the mighty fortress of Barad-dûr, the dark tower that dominated the plain around it.

In SA1590, he used Oroduin's fires to forge the ruling ring. This gave him the power to assault the Westlands. However, at the end of the Second Age, an alliance of elves and men forced him to flee Mordor. The Dúnedain then built their own fortresses there to garrison the desolate land there and prevent evil creatures entering or leaving. These fortifications included the Tower of Cirith Ungol, a pass on the western side of Mordor; Durthang that sits on the pass of Isenmouthe which connects the Udûn to Gorgoroth; and Carchost and Narchost that stood either side of Morannon, or the Black Gate of Mordor, and were known as the Towers of the Teeth or the Teeth of Mordor. Mordor's other fortification, Minas Ithril or the Tower of the Rising Moon, had been built by Isildur on a high spur of the western wall of the Ephel Dúarth in SA3320 to keep Mordor at bay. Sauron took it in SA3429. At the beginning of the Third Age, it was reoccupied by Gondor. The Nagûl retook it in TA2002, seizing the palantír that was kept there. They renamed it Minas Morgul, the Tower of Sorcery.

Still, for nearly a thousand years there was peace. Even Mount Doom remained quiescent.

Exiled in Dol Guldur, Sauron longed to return to Mordor. He sent his Ringwraiths to prepare the way. Then he stirred up the Easterlings. When they attacked Gondor, the Dúnedain withdrew their garrisons from the castles of Mordor, leaving the way open for Sauron to return. Back in his natural fortress, his power grew and he felt invulnerable.

Indeed, he would probably have withstood the onslaught of men and elves that assailed his gates, but he was outsmarted by two resourceful hobbits who, with the help of Gollum, brought his empire of evil crashing down.

After his fall, the land around the Sea of Nurnen to the south was settled by emancipated slaves. But Udûn, Gorgorth and the north-east corner, Lithlad, remained uninhabitable. Although it had been built by the legendary Isildur, Minas Ithil was not reoccupied again in the Fourth Age because of the dread that seemed to lurk there.

Moria

One of the most extraordinary constructions in Middle-earth was the Mines of Moria. Although the dwarves extracted the precious silver-coloured metal mithril, which was stronger than steel, it was more than a series of mine workings. They excavated an entire underground city which the dwarves called the Khazâd-dûm, or the Dwarves' Mansion. However, in later years, the elves called it Moria, which means the black pit or black chasm. It was also known as Dwarrowdelf, Hadhodrond, Casarrondo and Phurunargian in the various languages of Middle-earth.

The excavations began in the First Age when Durin the Deathless arrived at Azanulbizar, a wide valley on the eastern side of the Misty Mountains. There he found the lake of Kheled-zâram, or Mirrormere. When he looked into it, even though it was daytime, he saw in his reflection a crown of seven stars around his head. He took this as a sign and went to live in the caves above the lake.

More dwarves came to join him and they began to expand the caves by hollowing out great halls and passageways. A great gateway was built overlooking the lake and the dwellings constructed on countless levels in the mountain below were known as deeps.

The first and second halls were on the same level as the gates. Between them was a chasm so deep that in all the centuries the dwarves occupied Moria, they could not sound the bottom of it. To cross it they constructed a fifty-foot bridge, so narrow that they had to cross the curving span single-file. This was known as Durin's Bridge, or the Bridge of Khazâd-dûm. They also cut a stairway up to a chamber inside the peak of Zirakzigil, Celebdil the White or Silvertine. This was destroyed during the Battle of the Peak in TA3019 when Gandalf faced the Balrog. From the chamber you could see out across the wide planes of Eriador. The so-called Endless Stairs also descended to the deepest level of the deeps.

Moria was damaged in the earthquakes resulting from the destruction of Thangorodrim, the three peaks above Angband, which also destroyed Belegost and Nogrod, two other dwarf cities in the Blue Mountains, the westerly range of Eriador. Survivors from those cities also came to Moria, further expanding Dwarrowdelf until it occupied three peaks of the Misty Mountains.

Throughout their excavations, the dwarves had sought gold and silver, which they considered toys. They also looked for iron, which they used to make tools. But, early in the Second Age, they found a previously unknown ore which produced a silvery metal that was light, strong and malleable. This became known by the Sindarin word for 'grey flame', *mithril*.

News of the discovery quickly spread to the elvish realm of Lindon, prompting the descendants of the master craftsman Fëanor, who created the Silmarils, to settle nearby on the western slopes of the Misty Mountains in Eregion. It was there that Sauron taught the elves to forge the rings of power. Later, when the elves discovered that Sauron had secretly forged the ruling ring and hidden their own three rings, Sauron destroyed Eregion.

To facilitate trade with the elves in Eregion, the dwarves extended their underground city westwards to give them another entryway to the west. It was here that they built the Doors of Durin. The legend there in old elvish was inscribed by Celebrimbor, the fifth son of Fëanor and the forger of the rings, to symbolize the friendship between dwarves and elves.

When Sauron destroyed Eregion, the dwarves closed the Doors of Durin and remained safe in their subterranean fortress while war raged outside. At the end of the Second Age, with the rest of Middle-earth devastated and the dwarves controlling an abundance of *mithril*, Moria was at its height. However, in TA1980, miners broke through in the cavern where the Balrog of Morgoth had been imprisoned in the Elder days. It killed King Durin VI (TA1731–1980), so this nameless terror became known as Durin's Bane. The other dwarves fled.

Some five hundred years later, orcs from the north occupied the mines. More orcs and trolls in the service of Sauron joined them. During TA2793–2799, the War of the Dwarves and Orcs raged. The final battle – the Battle of Nanduhirion, also known as the Battle of Azanulbizar – was fought in the valley beneath the east gate of Moria. The dwarves won, but their losses were so great that they were in no position to take on the Balrog.

In TA2989, Balin, who had accompanied Thorin

Oakenshield and Bilbo Baggins on the Quest for Erebor in
The Hobbit, led an expedition to Moria. His men beat the
remaining orcs occupying the mines. But the dwarf colony
there was overwhelmed in TA2994. During their attempt to
traverse the mines in TA3019, Gandalf's expedition found his
tomb in the Chamber of Mazarbul. It is not recorded where
the dwarves returned to Moria in the Fourth Age.

Númenor

Also known as Elenna-nórë or Westernesse, Númenor was a
large island in the Sundering Seas to the west of Middle-
earth. It lay closer to Valinor, the lands of the Valar, than to
Endor, another name for Middle-earth. According to the
Akallabêth you could see Avallonë on the island of Tol
Eressëa, the easternmost island of the Undying Lands, from
the top of Númenor's sacred mountain, Meneltarma. That
lay in the central part of the island, which was shaped like a
five-pointed star.

The Númenóreans were farmers and horse-breeders.
Surrounded by the great sea of Belegaer, they were also great
fishermen and, later, great mariners. The land was fertile. The
western part was known for its fragrant trees. The white tree
that grew in the king's palace in the capital Armenelos was
brought as a seedling from Tol Eressëa as a symbol of
friendship between the elves and men. When it was cut down
and burnt at the instigation of Sauron around SA3262,
Isildur took a stolen fruit to Middle-earth to cultivate new
trees there. They were also fine craftsmen who made armour
and weapons that frightened even Sauron.

Nevertheless, by deception, Sauron persuaded the
Númenóreans to break the Ban of Valar and sail west to
Valinor. As a result, Númenor sank into the sea. The only

people who were saved were the Faithful who continued to respect the ban. Under Elendil, they sailed eastwards to Middle-earth where they were known as the Drúnedain, or Edain of the west.

The destruction of Númenor is thought to be based on the legendary city of Atlantis. The inhabitants there, too, were supposed to be superior to modern men. *The Lord of the Rings* and *The Silmarillion*, together, tell the history of the world, ending just where our history begins, which is also the time that Atlantis was supposed to have existed. There are also legends that the human inhabitants of Western Europe came from Atlantis. The Atlanteans, like the Númenóreans, were supposed to have had a lifespan longer than that of modern men. Both were reputed to have a superior civilization that led to arrogance, inviting their destruction by God.

Beleriand

In the First Age, Beleriand was the most westerly part of Middle-earth, around the Bay of Balar to the west of the Blue Mountains. It was discovered by the elves who were making their way westwards at the call of the Valar. However, the Grey elves or Sindar liked the land there so much they decided to stay. It was also home to the Sindar of Doriath and the city of Nevrast is thought to be a part of Beleriand.

In FA583, Beleriand was destroyed in the War of the Wrath of the Valar against Morgoth and sunk into the sea, leaving only part of the easterly province of Ossiriand. This became the elven kingdom of Lindon, ruled over by Gil-galad, son of Fingon and the last High-eleven king of Middle-earth.

Fulfilling a prophecy made by the Edain, the graves of Túrin Turambar and his mother Morwen had remained on the island of Tol Morwen, off the coast, along with the Stone of the Hapless, a memorial to Túrin and Nienor.

7

THE INHABITANTS OF
MIDDLE-EARTH

Middle-earth – indeed, the whole realm of Arda – is inhabited by strange creatures. Some are conjured directly from Tolkien's imagination. Others already inhabited fairy tales and legends, but have been given new life in Tolkien's work. He gives them new form with their own history and languages. He also interrelates them to create a complete universe of myth.

Hobbits
Tolkien's most famous creation was the hobbit. The name appears to have come unbidden to his mind one summer around 1929. As the first thing Tolkien knew about these creatures was that they live in holes in the ground, some reviewers suggested that they were in some way related to

rabbits. This can hardly be the case as in *The Two Towers*, Book Four, Chapter Four 'Of Herbs and Stewed Rabbits', they eat two coneys that Gollum has caught and Sam cooks with no mention of the possibility of cannibalism.

Tolkien himself covered this point in a letter concerning illustrations to *The Hobbit* to Houghton Mifflin in 1938: 'I picture a fairly human figure, not a kind of 'fairy' rabbit as some of my British reviewers seem to fancy: fattish in the stomach, shortish in the leg. A round, jovial face; ears only slightly pointed and 'elvish'; hair short and curling (brown). The feet from the ankles down, covered with brown hairy fur. Clothing: green velvet breeches; red or yellow waistcoat; brown or green jacket; gold (or brass) buttons; a dark green hood and cloak (belonging to a dwarf).'

Elsewhere he admitted that hobbits were based on himself, though he was certainly not between two and four feet (0.6–1.2 metres) tall. Indeed, he says in *The Lord of the Rings* that they seldom reached three feet in those days. They were an ancient people and had once been taller. However, their existence is not mentioned until the Third Age. As they do not seem to have been created independently, like dwarves or elves, it is supposed that they are among the Younger Children of Ilúvatar, created at the same time as men. The Red Book records that Bandobras 'Bullroarer' Took was four foot five and could ride a horse. He died at the Battle of Greenfields in TA2747, barely two generations before the War of the Ring in hobbit terms. It would be reasonable to assume that they had been with the men on Númenor as they display extraordinary longevity. Bilbo Baggins was 130 years old when he sailed to the west in TA3021. They were certainly not of elven stock as they are not immortal.

As well as being about half the height of a human, they were a little stout around the stomach and liked to wear bright colours, notably yellow and green. Generally they eschewed shoes and had hairy feet with leathery soles. Their hair was usually brown and curly, and they had good-natured faces and were prone to laugh, particularly after dinner. Tolkien also notes that they had 'clever brown fingers'.

The first mention of the Periannath, as hobbits are also known in Sindarin, in the historical record is in TA1050, when the Harfoots leave the upper vales of Anduin and arrive in Eriador. It was not clear why they climbed the Misty Mountains, but according to their own lore there was an increase in the human population of the region and a shadow fell across Greenwood the Great, which then became Mirkwood. The Harfoots were one of three breeds of hobbit, or halfling. They were even smaller and shorter than the others, with browner skin. They had no beards and wore no shoes. Both their feet and hands were nimble. They were friendly with the dwarves and preferred to live along the foothills of the mountains. But soon they were so numerous that they had spread as far as Weathertop, while others remained in Rhovanian on the other side of the Misty Mountains.

Harfoots were the commonest type of hobbits in the Shire and could count Bilbo and Frodo among their number. They liked to settle in one place and maintained the tradition of living in holes – resulting in the name hobbit, which derives from the word 'holbytla' (plural 'holbyltan') in Old English, which means 'hole dweller'. But their *smials*, or holes, were not dirty, damp, smelly or filled with worms. They were comfortable places with doors and carpets, kitchens and bathrooms.

King Théoden said that his people also came out of the north and had heard tell of halfings who live in holes in sand-dunes, so things must have been more primitive back then. There were no legends about them, because they did not do much. They were shy creatures and vanished when caught sight of. Pippin granted that, in all the lands he had been through in his travels, he had not found anyone who knew anything about hobbits. Frodo and his friends would change all that.

The Stoors were less shy of humans and stayed behind in the vale of Anduin, only later crossing the Misty Mountains via the Redhorn Pass. Then they followed the course of the Bruinen, or Loudwater, southwards, settling south of Tharbad, along the borders of Dunland, before moving on northwards again. Later it is recorded that they lived in the Angle, between the Loudwater and the Hoarwell. However, when the Witch-king of Angmar attacked Rivendell in TA1409, some of the Stoors sought refuge back across the Misty Mountains and settled near Gladden Fields, surviving there until well after TA2460.

The Dunland Stoors remained there until the founding of the Shire in TA1601, then went to join the other hobbits west of the Brandywine. They settled in South-farthing, East-farthing and, later, in Buckland. It seems that they brought some of the language and culture of Dunlendings with them and were regarded as somewhat foreign by the other hobbits.

The Stoors were more heavily built than the Harfoots with larger hands and feet. They were the only breed of hobbit that could grow beards. Some wore boots in muddy weather. They preferred riversides and flatlands to the hills. They even liked boating and swimming. It seems likely that Déagol and

Sméagol were descended from Stoors as they went boating at Gladden Fields, back in the vale of Anduin.

The last to make the move were the Fallohides who were taller and lighter than the other hobbits. They loved trees and woodlands, and enjoyed hunting. Their other accomplishments were singing and handicrafts. There were fewer of them than the other breeds of hobbit. They lived to the north of the Shire and were more friendly with the elves.

They also mingled with the other hobbits a good deal and were natural leaders. Marcho and Blanco, who founded the Shire in TA1601, were both Fallohides. The Tooks, Brandybuck and Bolgers were also Fallohides and both Bilbo and Frodo had Fallohide blood in them. This may well have helped them in their adventures and it must certainly have helped them when it came to recording their deeds in the Red Book. While Fallohides have a capacity for language, most hobbits had little love of learning, though some older families studied their own books and collected stories from distant lands.

When they first arrived in the Shire, the hobbits were required to swear allegiance to the kings of Arnor, acknowledging their lordship. They were then dutybound to maintain their bridges, repair their roads and speed Arnor's messengers. During the final fight against Angmar at the last Battle of Fornost in TA1974, the hobbits said they sent a company of archers, but this was not recorded. After the Dúnedain's defeat, the kingdom of Arnor was destroyed. Although they still nominally swore allegiance to the king of Fornost, the hobbits then elected a thain as titular head of the Shire.

The first thain of the Shire was Bucca of the Marrish, patriach of the Oldbuck family. Later on the Oldbuck family

crossed the Brandywine River to establish Buckland and
changed the family name to Brandybuck. The head of the
family then became Master of Buckland. The thainship then
passed to the Took family – eventually to Pippin Took
himself. The thain was technically in charge of Shire-moot
and Shire-muster – that is, the Hobbitry-in-Arms – but until
the coming of the War of the Ring the hobbits of the Shire
led entirely peaceful, uneventful lives so the title of thain was
little more than a formality.

Hobbits enjoyed socializing, especially at feasts and parties.
They tended to eat communally and would eat six meals a day
when they could get them. Generally, they preferred plain
food – meat, bread, potatoes, cake – though Sam insisted that
Gollum find him some herbs for seasoning when he was
making rabbit stew. They also drank tea at tea-time, though
generally they preferred ale and pipe-weed. Tolkien himself,
of course, was a pipe-smoker and an ale-drinker.

Elves

The first of the speaking races, the elves were known as the
Firstborn, or the Elder Children of Ilúvatar. They were
created by Elu alone as the third theme of the Ainulindalë.
When Varda, Queen of the Valier, had finished creating the
stars, they were awoken from the sleep of Yavanna by the
lake Cuiviénen far to the east of Middle-earth. They called
themselves Quendi, which means 'the Speakers'. Oromë, the
huntsman of the Valar, heard them singing and called them
Eldar, or 'People of the Stars'. But it seems that Melkor
captured some of them and turned them into orcs.

The Eldar were then called westwards. Those that stayed
behind in the east were known as the Avari, or 'the
Unwilling', and little more was heard of them. The Nandor,

or 'Valley People', reached the Vale of Auduin and refused to cross the Misty Mountains. When some of them later moved into Beleriand, they became the Laiquendi, or 'Green-elves'. Others remained behind in the forests of Wilderland, where they were joined by some of the Avari and became the Silvan Elves.

Those who crossed in Beleriand, but would not go on across the Great Sea to Aman were called the Sindar, or 'Grey-elves'. The Vanyar went on to Aman, where they remained in bliss, while the Noldor also reached Aman, but later returned to Middle-earth.

The elves were good-looking people, about six feet (1.8 metres) tall, slender, graceful and strong. There are a few references to elvish ears being slightly more leaf-shaped and pointed than humans'. The Vanyar were said to have golden hair, though they were not seen back in Middle-earth. The Noldor, Sindar and Avari had dark-brown or black hair, while Celeborn, and some others, had silver hair. Elven eyes were usually grey.

Immortal under most circumstances, they were extremely resilient under all extremes of nature. While they could be killed or die of grief, they did not succumb to aging or disease. When elves lost their life, they went to live in the halls of Mandos, but could not leave the world until the end of time. Elves who married mortals inherited the 'gift of men' – death, that is, a chance to escape everlasting life. Despite their immortality, Middle-earth was not over-stocked with elves because they had few children.

Their eyesight and hearing were more acute than men's and they could speak to one another directly, mind to mind, without the need for spoken words. One of their great achievements was to teach the ents to talk.

They did not sleep, but rested their minds by contemplating beautiful things. This gave them an intense love of nature, particularly of moving water – the first sounds they heard upon awakening – and the stars – the first thing they saw. They were insatiably curious and accomplished craftsmen. By nature, they were good, but they could be tricked. Sauron duped them into making the rings of power in the first place. However, because of their incorruptible nature, they were resistant to the power of the ruling ring and hid their own three rings from Sauron.

Dwarves

The dwarves were the one speaking race of the free peoples of Middle-earth not made by Eru Ilúvatar. They were fashioned by the artisan Aulë who could not wait for the Children of Ilúvatar to awake. To resist the power of Melkor, he had made them tough. They could suffer more hardship and injury than the other speaking peoples, and in spirit they were stubborn, proud and hardy – faithful in friendship, implacable in enmity. When Ilúvatar saw them, he would not have them destroyed, but instead gave them life. However, so that they would not come before the Firstborn – the elves – the seven fathers of the dwarf race, usually with their wives, were put in distant places to be awoken later. From these patriarchs the seven clans of dwarves were descended.

The Longbeards had forked beards that were tucked into their belts. These were seen as a sign of wisdom, age and maturity. They were descended from Durin I, known as 'the Deathless' because of his longevity, and seven of his successors were also called Durin and were said to be his reincarnation. He was said to have been the eldest of the seven fathers and had been put to sleep under Mount

Gundabad at the northern end of the Misty Mountains. In the draft of a letter Tolkien wrote in 1958, he said that Durin was the only one of the seven fathers not to be put to sleep with a mate – he had none. Nevertheless, he founded the underground city of Khazad-dûm and the greatest of the seven dwarf clans. The others were the Firebeard clans, Broadbeams, Ironfists, Stiffbeards, Blacklocks and Stonefoots. There were also the Petty-dwarves who were said to have been exiles from several clans who were smaller and more unsociable. They seem to have been hunted to extinction in the First Age. The last known were Mîm and his sons Ibun and Khîm.

Dwarves were usually four and a half to five feet (1.4–1.5 metres) tall, around the same height as hobbits, but stockier. They lived longer than humankind, but not forever. The average lifespan seems to have been 250 years. They were also less corruptible than men and were generally resistant to the power of the seven rings, which only made them more greedy for gold.

Not many dwarves married as only around one third of the population was female – though it must have been hard to tell. Female dwarves looked, sounded and dressed like the males. They also had beards. Even dwarves themselves could not tell the difference. The only female dwarf mentioned by Tolkien was Dis, sister of Thorin and mother of Kili and Fili.

They had a fierce fighting tradition, favouring the battle-axe, but they were also adept with other weapons. Accomplished metalworkers, they had no difficulty arming themselves. Living underground, they had little opportunity for agriculture, so provisioned themselves by trading with elves and men.

Men

Humankind were the Secondborn Children of Ilúvatar and the last of the speaking races. They awoke in the land of Hildórien far to the east of Middle-earth with the first rising of the Sun. They made friends with the Dark Elves – that is, those elves who did not travel on the Aman but remained in Middle-earth. The shadow of Melkor also fell upon them, making them more easily corruptible. During the First Age, they split into many races, though only the Edain, who travelled into Beleriand, and the Easterlings are mentioned.

Only the Edain, who allied themselves with the elves, rose above the shadow. The rest remained living in fear of Melkor, or worshipping him. The Edain gave rise to the Dúnedain, the Rohirrim, and the men of Dale. But, according to Tolkien, the vast hordes of Rhûn and Harad, along with many men of the west-lands, remained mired in ignorance and barbarity.

Men were clearly inferior to elves. However, they had unquenchable ambition and the 'gift of men' – death. In the Fourth Age, they would become the dominant race of Middle-earth.

Ents

These 'tree-herds' were created in response to a prayer of the Vala Yavanna to protect the growing things that she had placed upon the Earth. They grew to resemble the specific type of tree they sought to marshal. Later the elves taught them how to speak. In the First Age they roamed Beleriand and the east lands. Sometimes in the First or Second Age, they became estranged from their womenfolk and entings grew fewer.

The male ents loved great trees and the slopes of high hills, while the entwives preferred smaller trees, so they crossed the Auduin to create gardens. However, the darkness came from the north and the gardens they created became what men called the Brown Lands and the entwives were lost.

By the Third Age, ents were few in number and confined to the forest of Fanghorn where some had turned 'treeish' – that is, they had ceased to move or talk. Generally, they were around fourteen feet (4.2 metres) tall and a cross between a tree and a man. They did not die naturally, but could be burnt and had a natural fear of axes. They were nourished by ent-draughts, a potent type of water which, when Merry and Pippin drank it, added three inches or more to their height.

Although ents moved and thought slowly, when they chose to act they were immensely powerful. Hurling slabs of stone, they managed to tear down the walls of Isengard.

Orcs

Also known as goblins, orcs were the evil race of Middle-earth. Tolkien suggested several origins for orcs, but it is widely accepted that they were originally elves captured by Melkor near Cuiviénen soon after they were awakened and broken and corrupted in his dungeons. However, as they suffered an inordinately high casualty rate, this presupposes that they reproduced. In his correspondence, on one occasion, apparently, Tolkien mentions the possibility that there were 'orc-women'. A more satisfying explanation appears in *The Book of Lost Tales: Part Two*, where it says orcs were 'bred from the heats and slimes of the earth'. However, this contradicts Tolkien's other statements that only Eru-Ilúvatar could create new life.

From the First Battle of Beleriand on, they were on hand to fight for whichever dark force needed them. There are few descriptions of orcs. However, in a letter concerning the first film treatment of *The Lord of the Rings*, Tolkien complains that the film-makers have put beaks and feathers on them – Tolkien insists that they are orcs not auks. He goes on to say that they are supposed to be corruptions of the human form, as seen in elves and men.

'They are (or were) squat, broad, flatnosed, sallow-skinned, with wide mouths and slant eyes: in fact degraded and repulsive versions of the (to Europeans) least lovely Mongol types,' he wrote. This opened him to the accusation of racism.

Elsewhere the text implies that they were short and squat, with bow legs, yellow fangs, dark faces and longer arms than hobbits. The largest were around human size but, in disguise, Frodo and Sam could pass themselves off as one of the smaller breeds. Elsewhere there were 'snufflers', smaller orcs trained – or bred – to follow a scent. Saruman also seemed to have had a battalion of half-orcs, cross-bred with men. They were 'man-high, but with goblin-faces, sallow, leering, squint-eyed'.

Orcs wore foul, coarse clothing and heavy shoes. Most orcs were weakened by sunlight and only went out after dark. They ate raw flesh – ponies, men, other orcs – and were all too eager to try hobbit. They also favoured strong liquor. When they gave Pippin a drink, it burnt his throat. He then felt a 'hot fierce glow' inside and the pain that he felt from having his legs and ankles tied disappeared. They also had some powerful medicine. When 'dark stuff' from a small wooden box was applied on a gash on Merry's forehead, he cried out and struggled wildly. It left a brown scar that he carried until the end of his days.

Orcs were also proficient at tunnelling and making

weapons. But basically they were fighting machines who carried bows, spears, curved scimitars, long knives and stabbing swords. They relished killing and enjoyed destroying anything that was beautiful or good. However, they were easily scattered and broke up into small squabbling tribes when their dark lord was defeated. After the overthrow of Morgoth, they survived in the Misty Mountains and even seem to have created a capital there on Mount Gundabad. They even managed to multiply there before being summoned back to Mordor. They also inhabited Mirkwood when Sauron was there, and they occupied the Mines of Moria when the dwarves left them deserted, retaking them after Balin tried to re-establish a dwarf colony there.

Wandering bands of orcs waylaid travellers in the passes of the Misty Mountains and raided eastern Eriador, even penetrating as far as the Shire in TA2747. They invaded Rohan in 2800 and troubled the Silvan Elves of Lórien and Mirkwood.

There were various tribes of orc. The most dangerous were the Uruk-hai who appeared towards the end of the Third Age. They also made up much of Saruman's army and he promised them man-flesh as a treat. They could travel during the day and were larger, stronger and smarter than other orcs. There is some suggestion that they were a hybrid of orcs and men, though Saruman's half-orcs seemed to be a cross between Uruk-hai and men.

Saruman's Uruk-hai had an S elf-rune in white metal on the front of their helmets and the white hand – Saruman's symbol – on their black shields. Sauron also had Uruk-hai among his elite troops, but they fought under the symbol of the red eye.

Trolls

Created before the First Age by Morgoth, they were said to have been made 'in mockery of ents as orcs were made of elves'. As they were made in the Great Darkness, they were afraid of sunlight and lived in caves and under stones. Direct sunlight turned them to stone. Strong, ugly and stupid, they had strong, scaly hides and black blood. They hoarded treasure, killed for pleasure and ate raw flesh of all kinds.

After Morgoth was defeated, their numbers dwindled and various varieties sprang up. The cave-trolls of Moria had green scales and toe-less feet. The hill-trolls of Gorgoroth and Eriador bellowed like beasts and wielded great hammers. During the Battle of the Pelennor Fields, mountain trolls manned the great battering ram. Troll-men were also present on the battlefield, along with Variags, mercenaries from Khand. Among the Dunlendings, there was talk of snow-trolls. There were stone-trolls who worked for Sauron alongside orcs.

Towards the end of the Third Age, the Olog-hai appeared in southern Mirkwood. These were bred by Sauron and were bigger, stronger and fiercer than other trolls. They were also cunning and inured to sunlight.

Nazgûl

The word Nazgûl from black speech translates as Ringwraith. There were nine of them, slaves of the nine rings. They had once been men. Three of them were Black Númenóreans who had remained faithful to King Ar-Pharazôn when he had sailed for Valinor. Being ambitious, they were easy to corrupt. Initially the rings gave them power, prestige and great wealth. But under the domination of the ruling ring they became the slaves of Sauron. They first appeared under that guise in SA2251.

By then, the men they had once been had completely disappeared. Only their black cloaks and hauberks of silver mail gave them physical form. This made them practically invulnerable to normal weaponry. They could only be wounded with weapons that had a special spell on them; other blades melted on contact. However, they were afraid of fire and the name Elbereth. When chasing Frodo, their black steeds were washed away in the Ford of Bruinen, but the Nazgûl returned on flying beasts.

Blind by normal standards, they had an acute sense of smell. They wielded a variety of weapons and had poisonous 'black breath'. But their major weapon was the terror that they inspired, making loud, piercing cries in the night.

When Sauron was overthrown at the end of the Second Age, the Nazgûl scattered. The Lord of the Nazgûl became the Witch-king of Angmar, while his deputy, the only one to be named, was Khamûl, king of the Easterlings. He and the other seven stayed in the east until they secretly entered Mordor in around TA1640 to prepare the way for Sauron.

Wargs

Wargs were a breed of demonic wolves, perhaps related to werewolves as they did not appear in the daytime. Thought to have been bred by Morgoth in the Elder Days, they were part of Sauron's cohorts in the Third Age.

They first appear in *The Hobbit* where they chase Bilbo and his band up trees. In *The Lord of the Rings* they appear alongside werewolves, orcs and trolls. Packs inhabit the Misty Mountains and have to be seen off with fire and steel when they surround the Fellowship's camp.

Balrogs

Originally Maiar, they became servants of Morgoth in the First Age. About twice the height of a man, they were spirits of fire, armed with whips of flame. A number stalked Beleriand during the War of the Jewels, but most perished in the destruction of the fortress of Angband. Those that survived hid, or were imprisoned, deep underground. It was one of those that the dwarves unearthed in Moria. It was eventually destroyed in a ten-day battle against Gandalf.

Dragons

Created by Morgoth when he returned to Angband with the Silmarils, dragons were going to be his secret weapon after he realized his orcs were not sufficient to protect him from the Noldor. The dragons of the First Age were Urulóki, or fire serpents, like Glaurung. They could breathe fire, but could not fly.

Dragons did not appear again until TA2570, when they inhabited the Grey Mountains and began menacing the dwarves and Éothéod. The cold-drakes there did not seem to have breathed fire, but may have been responsible for swallowing four of the seven dwarf-rings.

Smaug appears to have been the greatest dragon of his day. A fire-drake, he could both breathe fire and fly. However, he may have been the last of his kind. After he had been killed by Bard the Bowman, Gandalf told Frodo: 'It has been said that dragon-fire could melt and consume the rings of power, but there is not now any dragon left on earth in which the old fire is hot enough . . .'

Giant Spiders

They seem to have had more than their fair share of giant spiders in Middle-earth. The first, Ungoliant, helped Melkor destroy to the two trees of Valinor, but she turned against him when he would not give her the Silmarils. Driven off by balrogs, she fled to Nan Dungortheb and lived in a mountain there, which then became known as Ered Gorgoroth, the Mountain of Terror. Infesting the area with her offspring, she made off to the south where it is thought she devoured herself out of hunger.

Giant spiders had moved into Mirkwood and caught Bilbo and Thorin's band of dwarves when they were on their way to Lonely Mountain. Another giant spider, Shelob the Great, lived in a cave on the top of Cirith Ungol. Around TA3000 she caught Gollum escaping from Mordor, but let him go provided that he bring her food. As a result, Gollum lured Frodo and Sam there, hoping that he could repossess the ruling ring once Frodo had been consumed.

Eagles

The eagles of Middle-earth could speak in the languages of both the elves and men. They were created by Manwë as the lords of the animals' world. During the First Age, they were sent, under Thorondor, to Middle-earth to watch over the elves that had been exiled there.

In the Second Ages, eagles kept watch on the Númenóreans. By the end of the Third Age, they were living in eyries on the northern parts of the Misty Mountains. They harassed the goblins who lived under the High Pass there and helped the elves of Rivendell and Radagast the wizard. However, because they stole sheep, they were no friends of the woodmen of Mirkwood.

They played a key role in Thorin's expedition to Lonely Mountain and returned to help out during the Battle of the Five Armies. Later, the Lord of the Eagles Gwair rescued

Gandalf from Isengard and from the peak of Zirakzigil after he had defeated the Balrog. The eagles were also on hand to rescue Frodo and Sam from Mount Doom after they had disposed of the ring.

The eagles were large enough to carry a man, or a hobbit plus a dwarf. The largest, Thorondor, had a wingspan of 180 feet (55 metres) and a lifespan of nearly 600 years.

Wizards

The Istari, or wizards, were spirits of the order of the Maiar. Five of them were sent to Middle-earth in TA1000 to fight Sauron, a fellow Maiar spirit. They were cloaked in the bodies of old men and were forbidden to try to dominate the free peoples of Middle-earth as Sauron had done.

The leader of their order was Saruman the White, then came Gandalf the Grey, Radagast the Brown and two blue wizards, thought to have been named Alatar and Pallando. Despite appearing to be old men, they were surprisingly agile and showed no signs of further aging. Indeed, as Maiar, they were immortal. Nevertheless, they felt all the hunger, pain and emotions of men. Indeed, Saruman fell prey to the lust for power and was corrupted by it. No more was heard of the two blue wizards and it was thought that they too succumbed to the blandishments of Sauron.

The Istari had magical powers, but these were strictly limited and largely focussed through the staffs they carried. Thought to be wise, they were certainly cunning and charismatic.

8

THE CHARACTERS OF
MIDDLE-EARTH

In *The Hobbit* and *The Lord of the Rings*, particularly, Tolkien created some memorable characters. None are more memorable than the small cast of hobbits he assembles. While the other characters are either unmitigatingly wise, good or evil, the hobbits are packed with endearing human frailty – curiously unlike the humans themselves.

Bilbo Baggins

The first hobbit we are introduced to – indeed the first hobbit in the history of literature – is Bilbo Baggins. He was scarcely cut out to be an action hero. Born on 22 September TA2890, he was already fifty-one when his involvement in the history of Middle-earth began. A solid, sensible, respectable and altogether unadventurous hobbit, he allowed himself to be talked into being a 'burglar' for a gang of dwarves.

He was comfortably off, living in a luxurious hole in Hobbiton called Bag End. It had been built by his father Bungo with money from his mother Belladonna Took. Bilbo inherited it seven years earlier after both his parents were dead. It had a round green door with a brass knob in the middle of it. The tunnels were carpeted and tiled. A kitchen, dining-room, sitting-room and bedrooms all opened off the main passageway. Those to the left had windows overlooking the garden and the field sloping down to the river. There were pegs for coats and hats, and plenty of chairs because he enjoyed having visitors.

That was part of his downfall. When Thorin and his band of dwarves arrived at tea time, he could not turn them away. Consequently, despite his better judgement, he found himself swept up in their plans. It was because of the Took blood he inherited from his mother, he decided.

Bilbo was a typical hobbit. The hair on his toes was neatly brushed and he smoked a long pipe, when he was at home at least. He was also adept at blowing smoke rings. But when it came to adventures his initial reaction was 'no thank you'. He was not much good at climbing trees, perhaps because of his small stature. Like other hobbits, he enjoyed parties, inviting almost everyone in the Shire to his 111th birthday bash. When the dwarves turn up uninvited at the beginning of *The Hobbit*, he is happy to provide them with tea and cake. He proved himself equally generous, adopting his orphaned cousin Frodo and, eventually, leaving him his house, his sword Sting and his valuable coat of chain mail made out of *mithril* – along with a ring of inestimable value.

Though, like most hobbits, Bilbo was not an intellectual,

he proved himself a skilled riddler – outsmarting Gollum with the disarmingly simple question: 'What have I got in my pocket?' Though repeatedly mocked by the dwarves, Bilbo proved himself brave and resourceful. Without him, Thorin's expedition would have been a failure. They would never have escaped from the spiders in Mirkwood, or the dungeons of the elvenking. Bilbo figured out how to open the secret door in Lonely Mountain. And it was Bilbo who discovered the weak point in the dragon's protective hide that allowed Bard the Bowman to kill him.

After this adventure, Bilbo returned to Bag End considerably richer than when he left it. However, the local hobbits were sceptical about his accounts of his exploits. Nevertheless, he spent much of his remaining years committing them to paper. He also set about recording Frodo's adventures. This ambitious project ran to eighty chapters and was called variously *My Diary; My Unexpected Journey; There and Back Again, And What Happened After; Adventures of Five Hobbits; The Tale of the Great Ring, compiled by Bilbo Baggins from his own observations and the accounts of his friends;* and *What We Did in the War of the Ring.* Bilbo also produced a book called *Translations from the Elvish,* which was the basis for *The Silmarillion,* demonstrating his facility for languages.

Armed with Sting, Bilbo became a proficient swordsman and he was the first of the ringbearers, if you discount Gollum. Although by the beginning of *The Lord of the Ring,* he had started to be corrupted by the ring, by that point he has had it for sixty years. With a little gentle persuasion from Gandalf he did leave it behind – along with everything else he knew and loved – when he quit Hobbiton to escape its influence. Finding sanctuary in Rivendell he continued his literary work, writing poetry and studying elven-lore. Unlike most hobbits he remained a bachelor. He lived to be 131 years and eight days old, the oldest hobbit in the history of Middle-earth, before he embarked on his final voyage to the west.

Frodo Baggins

Born on 22 September TA2968, Frodo was the only son of Drogo Baggins, great grandson of Bablo Baggins, Bilbo's great grandfather, and Primula Brandybuck, the youngest daughter of Gorbadoc 'Broadbelt' Brandybuck. He spent his childhood at Brandy Hall in Buckland where he got into trouble stealing mushrooms from Farmer Maggot. His parents died in a boating accident on Brandywine River when Frodo was only twelve – an infant in hobbit years. They had been out on the river after dinner and it was thought that Drogo's weight had sunk the boat, though there were dark rumours that Primula had pushed him in. Frodo remained at Brandybuck in the care of Master Gorbadoc who, by all accounts, played host to hundreds of relatives. Eventually though, his redoubtable cousin Bilbo adopted the child when he was twenty-one and took him to live at Bag End, much to the chagrin of the Sackville-Bagginses who hoped to inherit the aging bachelor's property.

According to Gandalf, via a second-hand description given by Mr Butterbur, landlord of The Prancing Pony at Bree, Frodo was 'a stout little fellow with red cheeks'. He was taller than some hobbits and fairer than most. Otherwise he was a perky chap with a bright eye and a cleft chin. Bilbo thought him the best hobbit in the Shire, a judgement that would be put to the test.

Like Bilbo, Frodo was considered eccentric. During his

seventeen-year sojourn at Bag End, he was known to take long solitary walks across the Shire and, some said, consorted with elves. Consequently, it was not entirely unexpected when, at the age of fifty, he announced that he was going to sell up and return to Buckland. Few guessed the real reason for him leaving the Shire. Indeed, as hobbits were not particularly keen on reading books, few even learnt of his historic trip to Mount Doom. However, along with Merry, Pippin and Sam, he was a local hero for ridding the Shire of the ruffians and the mysterious Sharkey.

He took little part in the reconstruction of the Shire afterwards, apart from serving as deputy mayor for a spell. Like Bilbo he spent his later years in literary work, writing his own Tale of the Ring and editing and completing the works bequeathed to him by Bilbo – much in the way that Christopher Tolkien laboured to complete his father's life's work. Like Bilbo, Frodo was a renowned linguist and his magnum opus, built on Bilbo's earlier work, is modestly entitled: *The Downfall of the Lord of the Rings and the Return of the King (as seen by the Little People; being the memoirs of Bilbo and Frodo of the Shire, supplemented by the accounts of their friends and the learning of the Wise)*. The title page also adds: 'Together with extracts from Books of Lore translated by Bilbo in Rivendell.' This forms the core of the *Red Book of Westmarch*. However, there is nothing in the lineage of the Bagginses that explains this sudden flowering of scholarship.

Amazingly Frodo completed his great contribution to the world of letters in just two years. On his fifty-second birthday – 22 September 1421 Shire Reckoning – he left the Shire for the second and last time and took his own trip over the sea.

Gandalf

Gandalf the Grey was one of five wizards, or Istari, sent to Middle-earth in the Third Age to fight Sauron. He was also known as Olórin, meaning 'dream' or vision, in Valinor; Mirthrandr, meaning 'Grey Pilgrim' or 'Grey Wanderer', to the elves; Tharkûn, meaning either 'Grey man' or 'Staff man', to the dwarves; Incánus to the Haradrim; Greyhame, meaning 'Grey cloak' or 'Grey mantle', or Gandalf Greyhame to the Rohirrim; Stormcrow to Théoden; Láthspell to Gríma Wormtongue and Grey Fool to Denethor II, steward of Gondor. Returning after defeating the Balrog in the Mines of Mora, he became Gandalf the White, having been promoted to the head of his order after the disqualification of Saruman. On his faithful steed Shadowfax, he was also known as the white rider.

When Gandalf first appeared in *The Hobbit*, true to his calling, he was wearing a grey cloak and a silver scarf. However, he was also wearing a blue hat and huge black boots. The other thing that made him stand out among hobbits was his long beard that hung down below his waist. Then there were his tricks. The story was told of a pair of magic diamond studs he gave Gerontius Took, Bilbo's maternal grandfather, that fastened themselves and would not come undone until ordered to do so. He told wonderful tales of goblins and giants, dragons and princesses, and the expected luck of widows' sons.

Gandalf was also renowned for his fireworks that he provided for Gerontius Took's midsummer festivals. He also brought fireworks to Bilbo's 111th birthday party. These were made by Gandalf himself and inscribed with a big red G and his mark in elf runes.

We get a more detailed description of Gandalf in 'Many

Meetings', Chapter One of Book Two of *The Fellowship of the Ring*, where he is at Elrond's house in Rivendell and appears alongside Elrond and the elf Glorfindel. 'Gandalf was shorter in stature than the other two,' Tolkien says, 'but his long white hair, his sweeping silver beard, and his broad shoulders, made him look like some wise king of ancient legend. In his aged face under great snowy brows his eyes were set like coals that could suddenly burst into fire.'

Elsewhere Tolkien wrote that Gandalf had 'a figure strongly built and with broad shoulder, though shorter than the average of men and now stooped with age, leaning on a thick rough-cut staff as he trudged along'. Even bent, Gandalf was five foot six (1.7 metres). Compared to a modern Englishman, or an elf, he would have been short, but hobbits and dwarves would look up to him. To add to his stature, he wore a proper wide-brimmed wizard's hat with a pointed conical crown, though Tolkien insists that it is an unwizardly blue. His cloak was an elven silver-grey – though more grey than silver because it was 'tarnished by wear'. It came down just below his knees, perhaps to the top of the boots he wore when walking in the wild. Though it was said of him that his wizard-like appearance made many who did not know him dismiss him as a cheap conjurer, it was also said that, like most wizards, he was quick to anger, though equally quick to laugh.

Arriving in Middle-earth in TA1000, Gandalf spent over 2,000 years fighting Sauron and was largely responsible for the victory of the free people. Of the five Istari, Gandalf was the closest to the elves and the Elven-lord Círdan gave him Narya, the ring of fire, one of the three elven rings, when he first arrived at Grey Havens to help him in his battle against Sauron. However, it was not until TA2063 that Gandalf went to Dol Guldur to confront the evil there. Sauron was plainly afraid of him as he retreated and hid in the east for the next four centuries.

During the Long Winter of TA2758–9, Gandalf came to the aid of the Shire. But in TA2850, he was back on the case, returning to Dol Guldur to find that Sauron was master there. He had already gathered all the other rings and was now searching for the ruling one. Gandalf found the Dwarf-king Thráin II imprisoned there and got the key to Erebor from him, which he later gave to Thráin's son Thorin when he set out to Lonely Mountain. At a meeting of the White Council, Gandalf urged them to attack Dol Guldur, but Saruman overruled him.

Gandalf then set in chain the expedition to Lonely Mountain when Bilbo found the ring. With the help of Aragorn, Gandalf went in search of Gollum. After seventeen years, he became convinced that the ring Bilbo had found was the ruling ring, persuaded Bilbo to give it up and Frodo to return it to Mount Doom, demonstrating Gandalf's high opinion of hobbits. Along the way, his physical manifestation was killed by the Balrog in the Mines of Moria, but he returned as Gandalf the White. He went on to release King Théoden from the spell of Gríma Wormtongue, then provided counsel to both Rohan and Gondor, and, during the Battle of Pelennor Fields, held the gates of Minas Tirith against the Lord of the Nazgûl until the arrival of the Rohirrim. After Sauron's defeat, Gandalf headed back west over the seas.

To accomplish all this he did not depend on his staff alone, but also on his great elven sword Glamdring, which he acquired from the treasure hoard of the trolls. It had a jewelled hilt and an ornate scabbard, and, like other elven swords, glowed blue in the presence of orcs.

Then there was Shadowfax. A silver-grey horse, he was tireless and swift as the wind. Not even the horses of the Ringwraiths could keep up with him. He was also extremely brave. During the siege of Gondor, everyone fled in the face of the Lord of the Nazgûl except Shadowfax who 'alone among the free horses of the earth endured the terror, unmoving, steadfast as a graven image in Rath Dínen'.

At first Théoden had lent Gandalf a horse, giving him his pick of the horses of Rohan. He was angry with the wizard for taking Shadowfax, the most precious of all his horses and one that only the king or his son may ride. When Shadowfax returned, he was found to be wild and no man could handle him, perhaps because Gandalf rode him without a bridle or saddle. Later, Gandalf asked Théoden for Shadowfax as a gift. According to Tolkien, Shadowfax's blood came from the west and he was sure that Gandalf would have taken Shadowfax with him when he returned there.

Aragorn

Born on 1 March TA 2931, Aragorn was an infant when his father Arathorn II, the fifteenth chieftain of the Dúnedain of Arnor, was killed. His mother Gilraen the Fair took him to Rivendell where he was fostered by Elrond who called him Estel – which means 'Hope' – to conceal his ancestry from Sauron whose minions were scouring Middle-earth looking for the heir of Isildur. Elrond told Aragorn of his true identity when he was twenty and gave him the shards of Elendil's sword Narsil, along with the ancient ring of Barahir that Elendil had passed on to Isildur. Aragorn then went out into the wilds to become a Ranger, but before he left he was out in the woods when he met Elrond's daughter Arwen who had just returned from Lórien.

For seventy years Aragorn pitted himself against Sauron in a number of roles. Hiding his true identity, he served Thengel of Rohan and Ecthelion II of Gondor, where he was known as Thorongil after the star that the Rangers wore. During this period he defeated the corsairs of Umbar in a surprise attack on the port with a handful of Gondorean ships. On his return, he travelled to the east and south, 'exploring the hearts of me, both evil and good, and uncovering the plots and devices of the servants of Sauron', wearing the plain green and brown of a Ranger. These experiences were said to have made him the hardiest and wisest of men, possessing both the foresight of the Dúnedain and the wisdom he picked up from being around elves. He was also a skilled healer, depending almost exclusively on a plant known as athelas, or kingsfoil.

In TA2956, Aragorn met Gandalf and their friendship began. Then in TA2978, Aragorn visited Lórien where he met Arwen again. This time he gave her the ring of Barahir as a token of their betrothal. Elrond gave his permission for the match if Aragorn became the king of both Arnor and Gondor – only then would he be worthy of his daughter's hand.

By TA3001, Gandalf was on the trail of Gollum and asked for Aragorn's help, but it was not until TA3017 that Aragorn managed to capture Gollum in the Dead Marshes and take him to Mirkwood to be held by the Elvenking Thranduil. He then learned from Gandalf that Frodo was about to leave the Shire with the ring and went to meet him at The Prancing Pony under the name Strider. At this time he was said to be lean, dark and tall, with shaggy dark hair 'flecked with grey', grey eyes, and a stern pale face. Later, during their travails, he said to be 'somewhat grim to look upon, unless he chanced to smile'.

After guiding Frodo, Sam, Merry and Pippin to Rivendell, Aragorn joined the Fellowship of the Ring and the shards of Narsil were re-forged by elven-smiths to make Aragorn's new sword, which he named Andúril. He is said to be the tallest of the company, though Boromir was only a little shorter. Tolkien said that Aragorn was at least six foot six (two metres) tall.

After Gandalf was slain by the Balrog in the Mines of Moria, Aragorn led the Fellowship until they parted near the Falls of Rauros. Despite his acknowledged wisdom, Aragorn was given to moments of self-doubt and blamed himself for the Fellowship's subsequent misfortunes.

In Lórien, Galadriel gave him an elfstone as a wedding gift, foretelling his marriage to Arwen. Aragorn showed his steel at the Battle of Hornburg, then had a series of victories, first over the corsairs of Umbar, then at the Battle of Pelennor Fields and finally at the battle before the Black Gate of Mordor. As a result he became the king of the reunited kingdoms of Arnor and Gondor, allowing him to marry Arwen. He ruled as King Elessar, which means elfstone, taking the surname Teclontar, which means 'Strider'. He reigned for 120 years, dying at the age of 210, and was succeeded by his only son Eldarion.

Elrond

Born in the year 532 of the First Age, Elrond was said to be 'as strong as a warrior, as wise as a wizard, as venerable as a king of dwarves, and as kind as summer'. Though he was clearly immortal, he was said to be only half elven, though when you study his lineage he is only five-sixteenths human. But following the War of Wrath at the end of the First Age, he was given the choice to be counted among the elves or the men. He chose to be an elf, while his brother Elros opted to be a mortal.

During the Second Age, when the elves were pitted against Sauron, Elrond established the sanctuary of Imladris, also known as Rivendell in Common Speech. During the War of the Last Alliance, when Isildur cut the ruling ring from Sauron's hand, Elrond and Círdan advised him to destroy the ring. Sadly, he did not follow their advice. After the war, Elrond returned to Rivendell, where he became keeper of Vilya, the ring of air, which was given to him for safekeeping by Gil-galad. With Gil-galad dead, Elrond was in line to become high king of the Noldor, but he did not take up the title, possibly because there were few Noldor left.

When Isildur died, Elrond also became the keeper of the shards of Narsil and fostered Isildur's surviving son Valandil. Later, when Arnor fell, Elrond also took charge of the ring of Barahir and the Sceptre of Annúminas.

Elrond married Celebrían, daughter of Celeborn and Galadriel, in TA109. Their sons Elladan and Elrohir were born in 130, their daughter Arwen in 241. He then fostered Aragorn in TA2933. Elrond played host to Gandalf, Bilbo, Thorin and his company of dwarves on their way to Lonely Mountain, authenticating the elven swords they had found in the trolls' cave. He also recognized the 'moon letters' on Thorin's map.

Along with Gandalf, Elrond was a member of the White Council that planned an assault on Dol Guldur in TA2941 in an attempt to oust the Necromancer – that is, Sauron. Consequently, when Frodo left the Shire with the ring, he headed for Rivendell to consult Elrond. Despite his great age 'the face of Elrond was ageless, neither old nor young, though in it was written the memory of many things both glad and sorrowful'. His hair was dark and he wore a discreet silver crown. He had grey, twinkling eyes. Yet he had the authority of a king who had ruled for many years, and was respected by both elves and men. And having lived so long he was in a position to tell the Fellowship about the history of the ring.

When Frodo volunteered to take the ring to Mount Doom, Elrond confirmed he had made the right decision. In his roundabout way, he seemed to have picked the rest of the Fellowship. Despite his distinguished military career, Elrond did not join the battle against Sauron and Mordor. Instead he sent his sons. Elrohir, particularly, conveyed Elrond's advice to Aragorn – first to take the shortcut down the Paths of Death, then to attack Mordor as a diversionary tactic to allow Frodo to reach Mount Doom with the ring.

When Sauron was defeated, Elrond departed for the west with the other ring bearers. It was Elrond's departure that marked the end of the Third Age and the beginning of the Fourth Age – the age of men.

Boromir

The eldest son of the steward of Gondor Denethor II, Boromir was ten when his mother Finduilas died. Though he was forty when the War of the Ring began, he was not married. His main interest was war. A man of strength and valour, he led the company that drove back the orcs when Sauron attacked Osgiliath, defending the last bridge until it could be destroyed.

He came to the Council of Elrond because of a dream that both he and his brother had. It told of Isildur's bane, a broken sword and a halfling. At the meeting Boromir is introduced as 'a tall man with a fair and noble face, dark-haired and grey-eyed, proud and stern of glance'. His hair was shoulder-length and he wore expensive clothes. His cloak was lined with fur and he had a silver collar with a single white stone set in it. And he carried a great horn tipped with silver on a baldric over his shoulder.

He tried to persuade the council to let him take the ring to Gondor which was the bulwark against the hordes of Mordor, but Elrond explained that the ring could not be used for good as it would inevitably twist the intentions of whoever possessed it.

As he intended to go back to Gondor, he decided to ride along with the Fellowship of the Ring as they were going the same way. When crossing the Misty Mountains, he persuaded the company to carry wood, which saved their lives when they were hit by a blizzard. Forced to turn back, he was against going through the Mines of Moria, but was outvoted. He showed his mettle in the fighting there, blocking the west door and hacking off the arm of a cave-troll. And the sound of his great horn gave them pause.

Boromir was also dubious about entering Lórien, but Aragorn said that only those who were evil or did evil had to fear Lórien. There Galadriel read their minds and gave them each a gift. Boromir was reluctant to admit that she gave him a gold belt, though he was inordinately interested in what she discovered from Frodo.

As they travelled down river, Boromir became increasingly obsessed with the ring. Eventually, when they camped before crossing the Anduin, he followed Frodo out into the wood and tried to take it. Afterwards he was overcome with guilt and when the orcs attacked, he sounded his horn, but was killed.

Faramir

Born in TA2983, Faramir was five years younger than his brother Boromir. They had been close since childhood and Faramir looked up to Boromir as his protector. While his older brother distinguished himself fighting against Mordor, Faramir was sent as a Gondorian ranger to fight the Haradrim in Ithilien. Frodo and Sam found themselves spectators at one such action, and Faramir's men captured them, thinking them spies.

During their interrogation Frodo discovered that Boromir was dead. Faramir had been sitting by the banks of the Anduin when he heard Boromir's horn sounding. He then saw Boromir's body in a boat floating by, but his horn was missing. Later the two halves of the horn were washed up and returned to Denethor, showing him that his son was dead.

Faramir is said to be 'bold, more bold than many deem . . . Less reckless and eager than Boromir, but not less resolute'. He was also hardy and showed swift judgement in the field. However, unlike Boromir he was well read, studying both the scrolls of lore and song. Nor was he obsessed with war like his older brother, saying: 'I do not love the bright sword for its sharpness . . . I love only that which they defend.'

He wore the traditional Rangers outfit of green and brown with green gauntlets, and a green hood and mask. Tolkien describes him as 'modest, fair-minded and scrupulously just, and very merciful'.

Talking of the ring, Faramir says: 'I would not take this thing, if it lay by the highway. Not were Minas Tirith falling in ruin and I alone could save her . . .' However, when he realized that Frodo did have the ring, he was momentarily tempted and knew that his audacious brother could hardly resist it. However, he realized the folly of that course and gave Frodo and Sam provisions to continue on their way. He also had the good sense not to kill Gollum, which he was duty-bound to do when he caught Sméagol fishing in the Forbidden Pool. Gollum was then released with Frodo and Sam to act as their guide.

After encountering the hobbits, Faramir returned to Osgiliath to lead the strategic withdrawal across the Pelennor Fields. He was almost killed by Nazgûls, but was rescued by Gandalf, an old friend. Indeed, his friendship with Gandalf had long upset his father. However, as part of the rearguard, Faramir was injured by a Southron arrow and rendered unconscious by the 'black breath'.

Seeing his stricken son, Denethon wanted him burnt on his funeral pyre. Faramir was rescued by Gandalf again. He was taken to the House of Healing where he was cured by Aragorn. It was there that he met Éowyn, who was also recovering. She got over her love for Aragorn and agreed to marry Faramir.

As hereditary steward of Gondor, Faramir organized Aragorn's coronation. He was then made Prince of Ithilien so he could guard Gondor's eastern border with Mordor. Faramir and Éowyn settled on the Emyn Arnen hills on the east bank of the Anduin and had at least one son who was named Elboron. Faramir died in FA82 at the age of 120.

Samwise Gamgee

Born on 6 April TA2980 (1380 Shire Reckoning), Sam was the gardener at Bag End, before overhearing the conversation between Gandalf and Frodo concerning the ring. His father was Hamfast Gamgee, better known as 'The Gaffer', and his mother was Bell Goodchild, a childhood playmate of Bilbo's. They lived at Bag Row, near to Bag End, where Sam had five brothers and sisters, namely, Hamson, Halfred, Daisy, May and Marigold.

As Sam's eavesdropping means that he was privy to the secrets of the ring, he was sent with Frodo on the first leg of his journey, to Rivendell. He was a useful companion as he was literate, having been taught by both Bilbo and Frodo. This meant he knows about elves and the other legends he was about to get mixed up in. He also wrote poetry, often recited it at inappropriate moments, and he could cook. He was loyal despite the trying circumstances. Tolkien said: 'My Sam Gamgee is indeed a reflection of the English soldier, of the privates and batmen I knew in the 1914 war, and recognized as so far superior to myself.'

At the Council of Elrond Sam volunteered to accompany Frodo to Mount Doom, even though he was not supposed to be present. He was an invaluable companion, giving his support whenever Frodo felt that the task was too much for him. Frodo affectionately dubbed him 'Samwise the stouthearted'.

After Shelob had seeming killed Frodo, Sam was prepared to take over the quest and see it through to the end, despite his mistrust of Gollum.

After returning to the Shire, he married Rose 'Rosie' Cotton and they had thirteen children: Elanor the Fair, Frodo, Rose, Merry, Pippin, Goldilocks, Hamfast, Daisy, Primrose, Bilbo, Ruby, Robin and Tolman In FA7 he became Mayor of Michel Delving, and Sam was elected Mayor of the Shire for seven consecutive seven-year terms. He was ninety-nine when Frodo sailed to the west, entrusting him with the *Red Book of Westmarch*. When Rosie died in FA62, he entrusted the book to his firstborn Elanor and followed Frodo to the Undying Lands.

Meriadoc Brandybuck

Son of Saradoc Brandybuck, heir to Brandy Hall, Meriadoc Brandybuck, aka Merry, was gloriously unprepared for the task that befell him. He was armed only with a small pocket knife until he was waylaid by the barrow-wights. Then he armed himself with one of the Dúnedain daggers that he found among the barrow-wight's treasures. He used this to good effect in the Battle of Pelennor Fields, stabbing the Witch-king in the back of the leg. For his bravery in battle, the new king of Rohan Éomer honoured him with the title 'Holdwine of the Mark'. Back in the Shire, he was known as Meriadoc the Magnificent.

Born in TA2982, Merry had a love of boats, ponies and old maps of Middle-earth. He was also interested in calendars and botany – at least as far as pipe-weed was concerned. Guarding Bag End after Bilbo's party and organizing the transportation of their gear, Merry was key to the quest. His mother Esmeralda Took was the younger sister of Paladin Took, making his sidekick Pippin his first cousin. Merry was also a second cousin to Frodo. He was irrepressible and adventurous, perhaps due to Fallohide blood. He pledged his service to the king of Rohan and rode with them to Gondor.

Merry goes through several changes of outfit during the course of the book. When we first meet him, he is dressed as a typical hobbit with knee breeches, a jacket, a waistcoat and a short cloak. After the encounter with the barrow-wights, he lost his light-weight summer clothes and donned a burial shift. He was forced to wear heavier woollen clothing the rest of the way to Rivendell. In Lórien, he was presented with an elven cloak to help him blend into his surroundings. When he offered his services to Théoden, King of Rohan, he was then equipped with a coat of mail, a light leather helmet and a small green shield with Rohan's white horse emblem on it. Éowyn also gave him the horn of Rohan. Returning to the Shire, Merry wore chain-mail and carried a new sword of Gondor or Rohan origin. Later, he and Pippin rode about the Shire showing off their Lórien cloaks with distinctive leaf-shaped clasps. They were then seen as the tallest of the hobbits – taller even than the legendary Bandobras 'Bullroarer' Took – due to their supping of ent-draughts.

Another educated hobbit, Merry can make out some words of Rohirrim and, after returning from the War of the Ring, wrote *Herblore of the Shire*, *The Reckoning of the Years* and a short treatise called *Old Words and Names in the Shire*, which was no doubt of considerable interest to Professor Tolkien. He became Master of Buckland in FA11 and was made counsellor of the north, alongside Pippin and Sam, by King Elessar in 1434 Shire Reckoning. Merry married Estella Bolger and they had at least one son. At the age of 102, he returned to Rohan and Gondor with Pippin, dying there around the year FA64. It was said that he was buried in the House of the Kings.

Peregrin Took

Born in Tuckborough in TA2990, Peregrin 'Pippin' Took was the youngest of the company. When they set out, he was still in his tweens – that is, the irresponsible period between childhood and a hobbit's coming of age at the age of thirty-three. His great-great-grandfather was the patriarch of the clan Gerontius Took. His father was Paladin Took, his mother Eglantine Banks and he had three older sisters, Pearl, Pimpernel and Pervinca. He was also a cousin to Merry, Frodo and Bilbo, only later becoming related to Sam when his son Faramir married Sam's daughter Goldilocks.

Pippin was unusual for a hobbit, having almost golden hair. Thanks to ent-draughts he became four foot six tall – along with Merry one of the tallest hobbits that had ever lived. He was cheerful and resourceful. When he and Merry were captured by orcs, he dropped his elven broach to alert Aragorn who was tracking them. He also retrieved the palantír of Orthanc when Gríma Wormtongue dropped it and slew a troll at the last battle before Morannon, saving the life of Baranor, son of Beregond. However, Elrond doubted his suitability for the quest. True, he was a little reckless. He pinched the palantír from a sleeping Gandalf and looked into it, causing Gandalf to call him: 'Fool of a Took.' He also spoke in familiar turns to the Steward of Gondor when Gandalf had told him not to. Nevertheless, Aragorn named him a Knight of Gondor.

His name appeared alongside that of Merry on the top of The Roll, the battle honours of the hobbits following the Battle of Bywater, as captains in the uprising of the Shire. In SR1427, Pippin married Diamond of Long Cleeve. Their son Faramir was born three years later. In SR1434, he became thirty-second Thain of the Shire, a position he held for fifty years, and a counsellor of the north. Then in FA63, he went with Merry to Rohan and Gondor, where he died some time after FA70. He is thought to lie alongside Merry in the House of the Kings on the Rath Dínen in Minas Tirith.

Gimli

The dwarf Gimli the Noldo was one of Durin's Folk, a direct descendant of Durin the Deathless, through Náin II's son Borin. Born in the Blue Mountains 109 years after the sacking of Erebor by Smaug, he was judged too young to join Thorin and Company on their quest to the Lonely

Mountain, as he was a mere stripling of six-two at the time. His father Glóin was on the expedition though, distinguishing himself at the Battle of the Five Armies. Both father and son attended the Council of Elrond. This time Gimli got his chance.

An axe-wielding warrior he becomes hopelessly enamoured of Lady Galadriel, asking as his parting gift only for a single strand of her golden hair. She gave him three and, after that, called him 'lockbearer'.

Approaching the Misty Mountains, he said that he needed no map, though he had only seen them once. Presumably he was relying on ancestral memory. Initially there was friction between Gimli and Legolas, due to an old grudge between dwarves and elves over the fate of the Necklace of the Dwarves and the destruction of Doriath in the First Age. More recently Legolas' father Thranduil had imprisoned Gimli's father. But after their visit to the elven kingdom of Lórien, they became mates and Gimli was honoured as an 'Elf-friend'.

After the coronation of Aragorn, Gimli led a large number of Durin's folk south to establish a new dwarf-realm at Aglarond behind Helm's Deep in Rohan. There he became the first Lord of the Glittering Caves. Thanks to their industry much of the damage incurred during the war was repaired. Notably, Gimli's dwarves replaced the ruined Great Gate of Minas Tirith with a new one made of *mithril* and steel.

In FA120, Gimli sailed with his friend Legolas, bound for the Undying Lands, the only dwarf ever to do so.

Legolas

A Silvan Elf, Legolas first appears as a messenger from his father Thranduil, come to warn the Council of Elrond that Gollum had escaped from captivity in Mirkwood. This had not happened out of incompetence, he explained, but rather out of kindness.

Like other Sindarin Elves, he had superior sight and hearing, and he was so light-footed that he could walk on top of the snow while they were crossing the Misty Mountains, while the others had to trudge through it. He mocked Boromir and the other 'strong men' who almost got buried in a snow-drift.

A great archer, he was also armed with a long white knife, and was dressed in green and brown, like a Ranger. This, Tolkien remarks, makes him a 'strange elf'. Elsewhere, Tolkien says that Legolas was as 'tall as a young tree, lithe, immensely strong, able swiftly to draw a great war-bow and shoot down a Nazgûl'. He was also 'endowed with the tremendous vitality of Elvish bodies, so hard and resistant to hurt that he went only in light shoes over rock or through snow'. And he was the most tireless of the Fellowship.

He was also relentlessly cheerful, often bursting into song along the way. He never baulked at passing through the Mines of Moria or following the Paths of the Dead. Like the rest of his race, he was captivated by beauty and, in *The Lord of the Rings*, proved a loyal friend to Gimli, once they had put aside their initial quarrel. On one occasion, challenged by Éomer, they joined in a drinking game where Legolas proved he can hold his liquor, while Gimli passed out.

His name meant 'Green-leaf' and, although Legolas appeared young, he was immensely old, far older than Gimli and Aragron. The others, to him, were children, he said, boasting that he had seen 'many an oak grow from acorn to ruinous age'.

After visiting Gimli in the Glittering Caves and travelling to Fangorn, he settled with other elves in Ithilien, helping to restore the devastated forests of the war-ravaged lands there. After the death of King Elessar, Legolas left Middle-earth to go to the Undying Lands, inviting Gimli to join him.

Gollum

Originally a Stoorish hobbit named Sméagol, Gollum was born about TA2430. This was during the so-called Watchful Peace when Sauron was hiding in the east. On Sméagol's birthday in TA2463, he went fishing near Gladden Fields with his relative Déagol. After being pulled into the water by a large fish, Déagol spotted a ring on the river bed. But when Sméagol saw it, he wanted it. Déagol would not give it to him, so Sméagol murdered him and took it.

Soon realizing that the ring made him invisible, he took to stealing and blackmail. As a result, he was alienated from his family and began talking to himself. His relatives then called him Gollum after the strange gurgling sound that issued from his throat. His grandmother turned him out of their *smial*. He found refuge in the caves in the mountains, eating raw fish he caught in the underground pools there, hiding from the sun. Fearing both the moon and the sun, he called them 'white face' and 'yellow face'.

Alone and friendless, the only thing he cared about was the ring – or 'my precious' as he called it. His life was all the more unbearable because of the longevity that the possession of the ring gave him. He was some 511 years old when he met Bilbo under the Misty Mountains where Gollum was living on a small island in the middle of a subterranean lake. Rather than wanting company, Gollum craved hobbit meat, as a refreshing change to his fish diet. But he lost the riddle game – and the ring. According to Gandalf, this was because the ring was trying to find its way back to Sauron.

By then, he had become a slimy creature with long fingers and big feet, which were webbed like a swan's. His face was thin and he had two large, pale, lamp-like eyes, presumably adapted for underground living. His skin was variously described as 'dark as darkness', bone-white or sallow, like the orcs. This confusion may be explained by Tolkien who said elsewhere that Gollum had pale skin, but wore dark clothing and was often seen in poor light. During the riddle game, Gollum thought of all the things he kept in his pockets. These included 'fish-bones, goblins' teeth, wet shells, a bit of bat-wing, a sharp stone to sharpen his fangs on, and other nasty things'. By then, he only had six teeth left.

His speech was sibilant, hissing his 'S's. This was emphasized later by his use of 'handses' for hands and 'hobbitses' for hobbits. He also made a horrible swallowing sound when he said 'Gollum'. Bilbo was referred to as 'it', which was appropriate as Gollum considered him an item on the menu. And when Bilbo made off with the ring, Gollum began to refer to himself in the plural, saying: 'Thief, thief, thief! Baggins! We hates it, we hates it, we hates it forever!'

By the time we meet Gollum again in *The Lord of the Rings* over fifty years later, he has become clearly more deranged. Reminded of his own name, he began to refer to himself as Sméagol. He was clearly schizophrenic, priding himself on being a good servant to his master Frodo, while plotting to kill him to get his hands on the ring. Sam identified his good and bad sides as Slinker and Stinker. Gollum was also happy to adopt the epithet after Sam called him a 'sneak'.

Once tamed, Gollum became more amenable. There was less hissing and whining, and he spoke directly to Frodo and Sam, rather than to himself. Avoiding the touch of their elven cloaks, he would flinch and cringe when they came near. He was even friendly and pathetically anxious to please. If Sam or Frodo made a joke, he would cackle and dance around. And when Frodo was kind to him, he was pitifully grateful. But when Frodo reproached him, he would cry. But he was not pitiful. According to Aragorn, 'his malice gives him a strength hardly to be imagined'.

By then he had become starved and haggard, with his skin drawn tightly over his bony frame. Seen from a distance in Mirkwood, the men of Ithilien mistook him for a large squirrel. He was seen as a dark crawling shape at night. Now emaciated, he had a big head, long neck and thin lank hair, and his large protruding eyes seemed to glow in the dark.

But then, Gollum had been through hard times since he lost the ring. He left his cave and spent a few years looking for Bilbo. Then on the borders of Mordor he met the spider Shelob, providing her with other food than her regular diet of orcs – prisoners of war, say. The orcs of Cirith Ungol called him Shelob's 'sneak . . . little black fellow; like a spider himself, or perhaps more like a starved frog'.

Gollum was then captured by Sauron's men and tortured until he revealed the names 'Baggins' and 'the Shire'. Gandalf and Aragorn then tracked him down. After a prolonged interrogation, Gollum was imprisoned in Mirkwood by the wood elves, before he managed to escape.

He sought a new underground refuge in Moria, where he found himself in close proximity to the ring again and began following Frodo. Forced to act as Frodo's guide, Gollum appeared ambivalent in that role. Without his help, Frodo and Sam would not have found their way into Mordor, but Gollum only helped so that he could be close to the ring and, at every opportunity, tried to repossess it.

Eventually he succeeded, biting off Frodo's finger on the brink of Mount Doom. But then, in his joy, he danced and slipped over the edge into the crack, thereby inadvertently fulfilling Frodo's quest. According to Tolkien, God – Eru – had intervened at this point, pushing him over.

Despite everything Gollum had gone through, he remained recognizably human – well, hobbitish at least – enough for Frodo to feel pity for him. By the time he died, he was some 589 years old.

Saruman

The wizard Saruman the White was the head of Gandalf's order of Istari. Like Gandalf, he came to Middle-earth in TA1000 to fight Sauron. Head of the White Council, his Sindarin name was Curunír, which meant 'man of skill'.

Like the other Istari, he took the form of an old man. Initially he had black hair, but towards the end of the Third Age, the hair only remained black around his ears and in the beard around his lips. The rest was white. He was tall, with a long face and dark, deep-set eyes. Known for the depth of his knowledge, he was also said to have hands that were 'marvellously skilled'.

At first he travelled to the east with the two blue wizards, obtaining new skills and collecting arcane knowledge. Then after 1,500 years he returned to the west, just as Sauron was establishing himself in Dol Guldur. Already when the White Council reformed in TA2463, Saruman sensed the resurgence of Sauron's power and began to envy it. Nevertheless, Beren, the nineteenth steward of Gondor, thought that Saruman might prove a useful ally and allowed him to take up residence in the Tower of Orthanc at the ring of Isengard. It was there that he found a palantír – the lost seeing stone of Gondor – which would allow him to communicate directly with Sauron.

At the meeting of the White Council in TA2850, Saruman overruled Gandalf's plan to attack Sauron at Dol Guldur. It was then that Gandalf began to suspect that, like Sauron, Saruman had ambitions to possess the ruling ring.

Having studied the techniques of the Noldor of Eregion, Saruman tried to create his own ring, boasting that he was 'Saruman the Ring-maker'. But his true power lay in his voice. According to Aragorn: 'The wise he could persuade, and the smaller folk he could daunt.'

But it was the ruling ring that he craved and he secretly searched the shallows of the Gladden for it. It was then that he learnt that Sauron was also searching for the ring. So then, in TA2941, Saruman agreed to an attack on Dol Guldur, but Sauron found refuge in Mordor. He also became convinced that Gandalf the Grey was closer to finding the ring and spied on him.

By communicating with Sauron via the palantír, Saruman inadvertently became a slave of the dark lord, while simultaneously running an arms race against him. Saruman had 'blasting fire' which he used to breach the walls at Helm's Deep, though there is little other indication of gunpowder in Middle-earth – except in Gandalf's fireworks, of course. He also cross-bred men and orcs and genetically engineered Uruk-hai, orcs that did not shrivel in sunlight. And he was able to communicate with the birds, who acted as his spies. This ability was also attributed to fellow wizard Radagast the Brown.

Saruman used his henchman Gríma Wormtongue to blunt the military might of Rohan. Confronted by Gandalf, he imprisoned him in Isengard, though he was rescued by

Gwaihir, the 'wind-lord' of the eagles. Now exposed, Saruman swapped his white cloak for one that changed colour when he moved.

Saruman sent out his Uruk-hai to capture Frodo and get the ring, but they took Merry and Pippin instead. Misjudging the situation, he had already alienated the ents by sending orcs out to cut down the trees in the forest of Fangorn.

'He has a mind of metal and wheels,' says Treebeard, 'and he does not care for growing things, except as far as they serve him for the moment. And now it is clear that he is a black traitor.'

Saruman was then overcome by the ents and Gandalf broke his staff, expelling him from the order of wizards. But even in defeat Saruman was dangerous as he still had mastery over words.

'There are not many in Middle-earth that I should say were safe, if they were left alone to talk with him,' says Aragorn. 'Gandalf, Elrond, Galadriel, perhaps, now his wickedness has been laid bare, but very few others.'

While Gandalf, Aragorn and the rest of Middle-earth were involved in the final confrontation with Sauron, the silver-tongued Saruman managed to persuade the ents who were guarding him to let him go. He escaped to the Shire with Wormtongue where he masqueraded as the mysterious Sharkey, introducing villainy and ruining the rural way of life. But his plans were foiled by the return of the four hobbits. He was killed by Wormtongue who himself perished.

Saruman's body then became a grey mist that rose in the air and was blown away by a cold wind from the west.

Sauron the Great

By far the biggest villain in *The Lord of the Rings* is Sauron the Great, though the reader never gets to meet him. He is far away in the distance, watching from his dark tower. Even in earlier incarnations, we rarely catch a glimpse of him. He was a shape-shifter, taking many forms, including those of a serpent, a vampire and a great wolf. He even appeared in a fair form as Annatar, 'the Lord of Gifts', to fool the elves in *The Silmarillion*. It was a trick he repeated on Númenor, but after its destruction he was never able to do it again.

According to Tolkien's letters, Sauron took the form of a man, though of larger than human stature. Apparently he gave off great heat. Gil-Galad was burned to death by his touch. Isildur described him as burning like fire. He was blackened, as from fire and heat. Gollum, one of the few characters who had actually seen Sauron, said he had four fingers on his blackened hand. Presumably the missing finger was the ring finger, which Isildur cut off. In *The Silmarillion* he was a 'dreadful presence', the manifestation of hatred and malice that would drive the soundest mind to madness.

Like the other villains, he did not start out bad. Originally, he was one of the Maiar, created by Ilúvatar before the beginning of time. Initially known as Mairon, meaning 'the Admirable', he was a servant of the Vala Aulë, the Smith, but then transferred his allegiance to Melkor. Only later was he called Sauron, 'the Abhorred', by the High-elves, while the Grey-elves called him Gorthaur, 'the Cruel'.

Even before the elves were first awoken, Sauron was a spy, reporting to Melkor on the doings of the other Valar. He also spread discord.

'Sauron was not a beginner of discord; and he probably knew more of the music than did Melkor, whose mind had always been filled with his own plans and devices,' said Tolkien.

When Melkor established a stronghold in Arda, Sauron joined him there. Then when Melkor was captured, Sauron escaped into Middle-earth where be began breeding orcs, so the fortress of Angband was already fully manned when Melkor returned as Morgoth the Black Enemy. Sauron then became his lieutenant. Though he was master of werewolves and vampires, Sauron was defeated by Lúthien and Huan the wolfhound of Valinor.

When Morgoth was defeated, Sauron hid again in Middle-earth. By SA1000, he began to establish himself in Mordor, building the dark tower of Barad-dûr near Mount Doom. Disguising himself as Annatar, he befriended the elves of Eregion, helping them forge the rings of power, while forging his own ruling ring in secret. It carried that famous inscription in the language Westron: *'Ash nazg durbatulûk, ash nazg gimbatul, ash nazg thrakatulûk, agh burzum-ishi krimpatul'* – which translates as: 'One Ring to Rule Them All, One Ring to Find Them, One Ring to Bring Them All, and in the Darkness Bind Them.'

Three rings were given to the elves of Eregion, seven to the dwarf lords and nine to the kings of men. But the elves sensed Sauron's treachery, removed their rings and hid them. Sauron also failed to force the dwarves into submission. However, the nine kings of men were susceptible and became his Nazgûl. The Númenóreans were safely out of the way over the sea on the island of Númenor at the time.

Sauron declared war on the elves. By SA1699, he had conquered all of Eriador and set fire to the forest there to drive off the elves and their allies, Númenórean colonists known as the Edain. However, a huge army arrived from

Númenor the following year and Sauron was forced to retreat back into Mordor.

Unable to succeed by force of arms, Sauron persuaded the king of Númenor to break the Ban of Valar and sail for the Undying Lands. As a result, Númenor was destroyed, but Elendil and his son escaped to found Arnor and Gondor. Returning to his stronghold in Mordor, Sauron attacked Gondor. Taking Minas Ithil, he burnt the white tree. But the men and elves then formed an alliance. Sauron was defeated. In the last battle, Isildur cut the ring from Sauron's finger. He quit his body and his spirit went into hiding. Soon after Isildur lost the ring following the Battle of Gladden Field.

For the first thousand years of the Third Age, Sauron remained a disembodied evil. Around the year TA1050, the shadow of fear fell on Greenwood and it became Mirkwood. Centuries passed as his power grew. The presence of a dark power there was only noticed at around the time of the quest for Erebor in TA2941 when the inhabitants of the Vale of Anduin began talking about a mysterious figure they called the Necromancer who lived at Dol Guldur.

Gandalf was already aware of his presence, having been there in TA2063, but Sauron had retreated to the east. He returned some 400 years later, around the time Déagol and Sméagol found the ruling ring. In TA2850, Gandalf went back to Dol Guldur and confirmed that Sauron was the evil presence there, but Saruman prevented a pre-emptive strike against him. Sauron had even managed to corrupt the leader of the Istari sent from Valinor to oppose him.

When the White Council did move on Dol Guldur in TA2941, Sauron fled back to Mordor where he rebuilt Barad-dûr. From there, using his palantír, the great Eye of Sauron – a lidless eye, rimmed with fire – he could see out over Middle-earth. He built a mighty army of orcs, trolls and men. Under normal circumstances they would have been impossible to defeat. However, he was outsmarted by a couple of small hobbits.

After the ring's destruction, the power of Sauron was broken and his physical form in Middle-earth was destroyed. His departing spirit rose over Mordor like a black cloud, but was blown away by a powerful wind from the West, presumably originating in the Blessed Realm of the Valar. Leaderless his armies lost heart and were easily defeated. His empire of evil collapsed. The Nazgûl were consumed in a vast hail of fire erupting from Mount Doom and the dark tower of Barad-dûr crumbled. And on 25 March Third Age 3019, the long reign of terror of the second dark lord finally came to its end.

Gandalf had already described what the destruction of the ring would mean to Sauron.

'If it is destroyed, then he will fall; and his fall will be so low that none can foresee his arising ever again,' he told Aragorn, Théoden, Éomer, Prince Imrahil and the sons of Elrond before the final battle. 'For he will lose the best part of the strength that was native to him in his beginning, and all that was made or begun with that power will crumble, and he will be maimed for ever, becoming a mere spirit of malice that gnaws itself in the shadows, but cannot again grow or take shape. And so a great evil of this world will be removed.'

But how could he be so sure?

9

THE LANGUAGES OF
MIDDLE-EARTH

Tolkien was a life-long student of languages. From an early age, he learnt Latin and Greek. While a student he added to his repertoire French, Spanish, German, Anglo-Saxon or Old English, Middle English, Old Norse or Icelandic, Gothic, Welsh, and a bit of Finnish. He also made up a profusion of invented languages that underpinned his stories. These were not just a few random nonsense words. Tolkien spent years developing a proper vocabulary and grammar for his fictional tongues.

He was also scrupulous about names. They needed to make sense and have some reasonable derivation no matter how obscure. He was always critical of earlier fantasy writers, such as Edward Plunkett, Lord Dunsany, who seemed to pick names at random. For Tolkien names had to be fashioned by sound linguistic rules. Not only that, Tolkien also developed an alphabet for his various languages and wrote an 'Outline of Phonology', showing how they should be pronounced. Tolkien became so proficient at some of the languages he invented that he wrote poems and songs in them.

Elvish

Tolkien spent much of his professional life studying how languages relate to one another and how one develops from an earlier form. And he began work on the elvish tongue in 1910, developing at least fifteen elvish languages and dialects that are all interrelated.

For Tolkien, the language the elves speak begins with the ancient language of Primitive Quendian. This is the proto-language that they began to fashion after their awakening. According to the 'Cuivienyarna', the story of the awakening in *The War of the Jewels*, when the first three elves awoke, the first thing they saw was the stars and they exclaimed '*Ele!*', which means 'Lo! Behold.' This gave the elvish language the root 'el'. The next thing they saw laying on the grass beside them was their wives and they began to think up words to describe their beauty in prose and song. They named themselves Quendi, which also gave a name to their language.

From Primitive Quendian – known as Quenderin in Quenya, the later language of the high elves – Common Eldarin was developed by the Eldar, or Western Elves, who made the journey to Valinor. Those who had refused the call and stayed behind developed the Avarian languages. The tongue of the western Avari was related to the Eldarin languages. The Nandor elves who stopped at the Misty

Mountains spoke Nandorin, which became the language of the Silvan Elves of Mirkwood and Lothlórien.

The formal language of Quenya was developed by the elves that had gone to Aman. It seems to have been inspired by Finnish. Quenya had a vernacular – Parmaquesta, used for the lore and ceremonies, and Tarquesta, for everyday use. The Noldor and Vanyar developed their own dialects – Noldorin and Vanyarin. Later Noldorin Quenya became Exilic Quenya, when most of the Noldorin Elves followed Prince Fëanor back to Middle-earth, while Vanyarin, the Vanya dialect of Tarquesta Quenya, incorporated words of Valarin, the language of the Valar. The Noldor also developed another language called Goldogrin, or Gnomish. Tolkien created this around 1915 and it drew its inspiration from the Celtic languages. But around 1925, he dropped it in favour of Noldorin, a Welsh-style language developed from the Old Noldorian spoken in Valinor. Old Noldorian itself had been developed from Koreldarin, the language of elves who lived in the Kór hills in Valinor, and Old Noldorian only developed into Noldorin when the Noldor returned to Middle-earth. In the early 1930s, Tolkien wrote a new grammar of Noldorin.

Alongside Quenya, another elvish language grew up among the Teleri who arrived in Eldamar, the elvish colony in Aman, later. This was sometimes seen as a dialect of Quenya, though it developed alongside it. Later the men of Númenor and their descendants in Arnor and Gondor learnt Quenya to communicate with the elves. Aragorn spoke it. During the Third Age, Quenya occupied the same role in Middle-earth that Latin had in medieval Europe. Indeed, Tolkien called it elven-latin. Drawing its inspiration from Brythonic Celtic, including Welsh, it remained the language of the Undying Lands and was also known as Lindalambë – that is, the language of the Lindar.

From what became known as Common Telerin, Sindarin and Nandorin developed. Tolkien created Sindarin, the language of the Grey-elves, around 1944. It is a mixture of Noldorin and the Doriathin dialect of Ilkorin, the distinctly non-Welsh language developed by the elves who had remained in Beleriand.

Mannish

Tolkien also worked on various languages for the human inhabitants of Middle-earth to speak. He developed the grammar and vocabulary for three.

Taliska was based on Gothic and was the language of the Edain when they first entered Beleriand during the First Age. Its dialects developed into Adûnaic, the language spoken by the men of Númenor during the Second Age. It was influenced by the dwarfish language Khuzdul as well as Sindarin, Avarin, Quenya and possibly even Valarin. It spread throughout Eriador. However, after the destruction of Númenor, the inhabitants of Arnor and Gondor shunned Adûnaic in favour of Sindarin.

However, Adûniac did form the basis of Sôval Pharë, or Common Speech, called Westron in English. This was the language spoken by both hobbits and men during the Third Age. It replaced Quenya as the lingua franca of Middle-earth. Tolkien meticulously translated speech and names from Westron into English in his works. But other mannish languages were still spoken.

The men of Rohan spoke Rohanese or Rohirric, which is represented by Anglo-Saxon in *The Lord of the Rings*. Tolkien called the language of the Rohirrim just plain Rohan.

The men of Dale had their own variation, Dalish, while the men of Rhovanion spoke their own language which was represented by Gothic. Other languages were spoken by the Haladin, Dunlending, Easterlings, Drûg and Haradrim. Although Tolkien did not spend a great deal of time detailing their separate languages, he did work on the etymology of their names.

Dwarfish

The dwarves spoke a secret language called Khuzdul. Tolkien gave it Semitic roots. It is not related to the Oromëan languages of the elves of Middle-earth. Instead it was devised by Aulë the Smith, before the elven awakening. The dwarves preserved their language in its original form and kept it secret out of respect for their maker. However they could hardly keep their battle cry *'Baruk Khazâd! Khazâd ai-mênu!'* – 'Axes of the Dwarves! The Dwarves are upon you!' – secret. Balin's tomb in Moria also has the legend *'Balin Fundinul Uzbad Khazad-Dûma'* – 'Balin, son of Fundin, Lord of Mora' – inscribed upon it in Khuzdul.

Nevertheless, to preserve the secrecy of their language, dwarves took names in other languages. Even so, Eöl the Dark Elf was one of the few outsiders who could speak the language of the dwarves. Khuzdul is written in the same Cirth script at Quenya and Sindarin.

Because of the dwarves' reverence for its origin, Khuzdul remained 'astonishingly uniform and unchanged both in time and in locality'. The same could not be said of *iglishmêk*, the sign language the dwarves learnt alongside the *aglâb* or spoken language.

Entish

The elves were naturally loquacious and taught the trees in the primordial forest to speak. The ents developed what they learnt into their own language. However, being slow creatures everything was extended until the name included the entire history of the object being discussed. Just part of Treebeard's name in Old Entish was *a-lalla-lalla-rumba-kamanda-lindor-burúmë*. He could not tell them the rest of it because he did not know the words in other languages. Besides, the greatest sin in Entland was haste. According to Tolkien, the ents had made their language unlike all others: 'slow, sonorous, agglomerated, repetitive, indeed long-winded; formed of a multiplicity of vowel-shades and distinctions of tone and quantity which even the loremasters of the Eldar had not attempted to represent in writing'. However, the ents had an ear for language and learnt various elf languages, favouring particularly Quenya.

Black Speech

Tolkien invented a distorted, corrupt form of elvish for Sauron and the orcs to speak. It was called Black Speech. He wrote: 'The Black Speech was not intentionally modelled on any style, but was meant to be self consistent, very different from elvish, yet organized and expressive, as would be expected of a device of Sauron before his complete corruption. It was evidently an agglutinative language ... I have tried to play fair linguistically, and it is meant to have a meaning not be a mere casual group of nasty noises, though an accurate transcription would even nowadays only be printable in the higher and artistically more advanced form of literature. According to my taste such things are best left to orcs, ancient and modern.'

The purest example of Black Speech is the inscription inside the ruling ring: '*Ash nazg durbatulûk, ash nazg gimbatul, ash nazg thrakatulûk agh burzum-ishi krimpatul*' – 'One ring to rule them all, one ring to find them, one ring to bring them all and in the darkness bind them.'

Other examples are *Lugbúrz*, which means 'dark tower', or Barad-dûr in Sindarin; *snaga*, meaning 'slave'; and *ghâsh* meaning 'fire'. The name Nazgûl is in Black Speech, combining '*nazg*' meaning 'ring' and '*gûl*' meaning 'wraith' or 'wraiths'.

A number of orcish dialects derive from Black Speech. In *The Two Towers*, where Mordor's Grishnákh curses Isengard's Uruk Uglúk, he says: '*Uglúk u bagronk sha pushdug Saruman-glob búbhosh skai!*' Christopher Tolkien translates this as: 'Uglúk to the cesspool, sha! the dungfilth; the great Saruman-fool, skai!' Elsewhere it is rendered: 'Uglúk to the dung-pit with stinking Saruman-filth, pig-guts, gah!'

10

FILMING TOLKIEN

From the beginning, *The Lord of the Rings* attracted the interest of Hollywood. Of course, Tolkien should have been against the idea from the beginning. In his lecture 'On Fairy-Stories' given at the University of St Andrews in 1939 and published in 1947, he says that fantasy is best left in words as drama is naturally hostile to fantasy. However in 1957, writer Forrest J. Ackerman, screenwriter Morton Grady Zimmerman and producer Al Brodax approached Tolkien with a movie proposal. He was impressed by Ackerman, who produced some visuals that owed more to the English book illustrator Arthur Rackman than to Walt Disney, who Tolkien despised.

Tolkien and Urwin made a simple agreement – art or cash. Either a movie deal should bring them both a good deal of money, or Tolkien should have an absolute veto on the content. Given the climate of the time, Tolkien was adamant that the orcs should not be portrayed as Communists. However, when he read Zimmerman's treatment, he was far from happy. It seemed to Tolkien that Zimmerman had only skim-read *The Lord of the Rings* and had made some elementary mistakes. He also complained of Zimmerman's 'extreme silliness and incompetence'.

The proposed film – a mix of animation, miniature work and live action – was to be three hours long with two intermissions. Eventually, Tolkien wrote a two-thousand-word critique of the proposal, which was almost as long as the proposal itself. He was particularly annoyed that the movie treatment seems to set the action in 'fairy-land', while Tolkien was adamant that the events in the book take place in the real world. Tolkien combed through the first two parts of the treatment, picking up details. He objects to 'incantations, blue lights, and some irrelevant magic', with Gandalf dispatching attacking wolves with a few well-aimed lightning bolts, opening a chasm to swallow marauding orcs, levitating Faramir from Denethor's funeral pyre and miraculously turning the Ringwraiths into stone, one by one, at the Battle of the Black Gate while their armies look on in silence. He also disliked Zimmerman's 'preference for fights', though there is enough violence in *The Lord of the Rings*. And when he reached part three, he simply wrote in exasperation: 'Part Three . . . is totally unacceptable to me, as a whole and in detail.'

However, Tolkien did not dismiss the project out of hand. He conceded that, if the ents and the Battle of Hornburg could not be treated at sufficient length, they should be left out. And he did think that the script could be rewritten in a way that he would find acceptable. But the cash was not forthcoming and the project ended there.

In 1966, the animator Gene Deitch, who worked on the 'Tom and Jerry' and 'Popeye' cartoon series, made a twelve-minute film of *The Hobbit* with Czech illustrator Adolf Born. In the mid-1960s, The Beatles contemplated making a cartoon version of *The Lord of the Rings*, possibly at the suggestion of Al Brodax who produced their animated film *Yellow Submarine*. John Lennon wanted to play Gollum, with Paul McCartney as Frodo, Ringo Starr as Sam and George Harrison as Gandalf. Four mop-top lads from Liverpool were hardly Tolkien's cup of tea and he vetoed it.

In 1969 Tolkien sold the film rights of *The Lord of the Rings* to United Artists for £104,602 ($250,000). John Boorman, who went on to make *Deliverance*, was employed to write a script in exchange for a seven-figure sum. However, the producers wanted the entire story condensed into one two-and-a-half-hour script. Boorman was convinced that he could make a live-action version. But by the time he had finished the treatment, there had been changes at the top of United Artists. The new management were unfamiliar with the book and could not make head nor tail of the script. As a result, the movie was dropped. Boorman tried to hawk the script around Hollywood. He even tried Disney, with no luck. But his efforts did not go entirely to waste. Some of the locations and special effects developed for the project were used in his film *Excalibur*.

What Tolkien would have made of Boorman's script it is hard to say. It featured sex between Frodo and Galadriel, gratuitous nudity and rebirthing rituals. Well, it was the 1970s.

A TV version of *The Hobbit* by Jules Bass and Arthur Rankin aired on NBC in 1977. Tolkien's songs from the book were used to give the programme some musical content and the stars turned out for the production. Bilbo Baggins was voiced by Orson Bean, Gandalf by John Huston and the Elvenking, with a German accent, by Otto Preminger. The animation was done by a Japanese production company. Reviews were mixed.

Then in 1978, director Ralph Bakshi produced an animated version of *The Lord of the Rings* using a technique called 'rotoscoping', a way of combining animation with live action before modern computer-generated imagery was available. The movie is reviled by Tolkien fans, though it stuck closer to the original than Boorman did, and it was slated by the critics for stopping abruptly part way through the story. Like the later version, Bakshi planned his movie as the first part in a series telling the entire saga. But the money dried up and the project was shelved.

As Bakshi's *The Lord of the Rings* was based on *The Fellowship of the Ring* and *The Twin Towers*, Bass and Rankin returned with their animated version of *The Return of the King* in 1980, with Roddy McDowall voicing Sam. It aired on ABC before appearing as a Warner Bros DVD.

In New Zealand, would-be filmmaker Peter Jackson saw Ralph Bakshi's *The Lord of the Rings* when he was seventeen. Then he sat down to read the books. Nine years later, his home-made cult movie *Bad Taste* was shown at the Cannes Film Festival. Five years after that, he made his first professional movie *Braindead*.

In 1995, he had just finished making *The Frighteners* with Michael J. Fox, when his thoughts returned to *The Lord of the Rings*. It seemed to him that, with the computer-generated imagery used in *Jurassic Park*, it was now possible to make a live-action version of the story. By then the rights belonged to Saul Zaentz, who had produced *Amadeus* and

The English Patient. A complex deal was worked out with Harvey Weinstein of Miramax, and Jackson and his partner Fran Walsh sat down to write a treatment. It was clear from the outset that there was too much material in the books to fit into one movie, so the treatment for a first instalment picked its way through *The Fellowship of the Ring*, *The Two Towers* and the beginning of *The Return of the King* up to the death of Saruman, and Gandalf and Pippin going to Minas Tirith. Bob and Harvey Weinstein then agreed to make two movies with a budget of $75 million.

Jackson sat down with a scriptwriting team and produced two scripts. He planned to shoot the films in New Zealand. But when costings were done, it became clear that it was not going to be possible to bring the two movies in at under $150 million. Miramax did not have that sort of money. But they had already spent $15 million on development, so they decided to cut corners and condense *The Lord of the Rings* into one movie. But when Bob Weinstein produced a treatment for one two-hour film, Jackson protested that he had left most of the good stuff out.

Jackson then began to hawk his version around Holly-wood. Mark Ordesky of New Line Cinema, the company that had produced *A Nightmare on Elm Street*, now a subsidiary of Warner Bros, liked what he saw, but producer Robert Shaye wanted to know why Jackson only wanted to make two movies when the book had come in three volumes. So Jackson and his team began working on three scripts.

Although the film trilogy borrows the titles of the three volumes of *The Lord of the Rings*, it does not divide the story up the same way. Some things still had to be left out, such as the meeting with Tom Bombadil and the Scouring of the Shire. Other adjustments had to be made. For example,

Saruman and Gríma Wormtongue have to be killed at the Othanc Tower at Isengard.

In August 1997 Jackson began storyboarding the three films while work began on designing the prosthetics and make-up needed to create the orcs and other creatures, the armour and weapons, sets and the various miniatures that were going to be needed. Locations had to be scouted and the village of Hobbiton had to be built well in advance so that the plants could grow realistically in situ. Overall, 19,000 costumes had to be made, along with 48,000 pieces of armour, 500 bows and 10,000 arrows. Some 1,800 pairs of hobbits' feet had to be made, along with countless false ears.

Jackson shot all three movies in one go. Principal photography lasted from 11 October 1999 to 22 December 2000, with pick-up shots being made over the next four years. Over 150 locations were used, as well as 350 purpose-built sets and sound stages at Wellington and Queenstown. Seven different units were used in the shooting, with Jackson reviewing the results via satellite feed.

Some 2,730 special effects were used in the cinema cut of the trilogy; 3,420 in the extended DVD version. Over 500 people worked on the visual effects on *The Two Towers* alone. Each film then went into post-production for a year, with Jackson sitting in the Dorchester Hotel on London's Park Lane, with an editing feed piped in from Pinewood Studios in Buckinghamshire, some sixteen miles away. There were some six million feet (over 1,100 miles) of film to edit down to the eleven hours and twenty-two minutes of the extended version of the trilogy and nine hours eighteen minutes of the cinema cut.

The Lord of the Rings: The Fellowship of the Ring was released on 19 December 2001 and grossed $47 million in its opening weekend in the US, making around $871 million worldwide. *The Lord of the Rings: The Two Towers* was released 18 December 2002. It grossed $62 million in its first US weekend and made $926 million worldwide. *The Lord of the Rings: The Return of the King* was released 17 December 2003, grossing $72 million in its first US weekend. It made some $1,120 million worldwide, making it the second film, after *Titanic*, to gross over $1 billion. Between them the *Lord of the Rings* films earned seventeen Oscars and made some $3 billion at the box office.

As well as the extended DVD edition, there is a specially extended Blu-ray edition that runs to 123 hours and six minutes. There is also a series of *The Lord of the Rings* computer games and it is possible to take 'Lord of the Rings' tours in New Zealand. Perhaps Professor Tolkien was wrong and fantasy can work in a dramatic medium.

Despite the evidence of the box office, some hold fast to the Professor's dictum. Christopher Tolkien said: 'My own position is that *The Lord of the Rings* is peculiarly unsuitable to transformation into visual dramatic form.'

Other Tolkien scholars have condemned the movie, complaining that, while it was pretty faithful to the original in the basic plot, the characterization of the protagonists was altered and much of the subtlety and depth of the book has been lost. However, it has been pointed out that to make a film that could meet all the detractors' criticisms it would have to be forty hours long. Some fans of the book have taken matters into their own hands and produced their own eight-hour edit, called *The Lord of the Rings: The Purist Edition*.

But the power of cinema is undeniable. Although readers regularly voted *The Lord of the Rings* their favourite novel of the last century, it took forty-eight years to sell 100 million copies. The first film was seen by 150 million people in its first year, boosting sales of the book sixfold.

There seems to be an insatiable hunger for Tolkien's fantasy. A low-budget movie called *The Hunt for Gollum*, based on the appendices of *The Lord of the Rings*, was shown at the Sci-Fi-London film festival in May 2009. It had a budget of just £3,000 ($5,000) and was filmed in North Wales, Epping Forest and Hampstead Heath. But since it was released on the internet it has been seen by over fifteen million people. Another fan film, *Born of Hope: The Ring of Barahir*, has also gone online on the Daily Motion's website.

And the story does not end there. Or rather, *The Lord of the Rings* is having a new beginning. Peter Jackson is releasing two more Tolkien films – *The Hobbit: The Unexpected Journey* and *The Hobbit: There and Back Again*. Undoubtedly, the movies will again boost book sales. That means millions more people will enter Middle-earth and journey through the extraordinary fantasy world that existed within the mind of J.R.R. Tolkien.

BIBLIOGRAPHY

Works by J.R.R. Tolkien

The Adventures of Tom Bombadil and other verses from The Red Book, Allen & Unwin, London, 1962.

The Annotated Hobbit (annotated by Douglas A. Anderson), HarperCollins, London, 2003.

The Book of Lost Tales: Part One, Allen & Unwin, London, 1983.

The Book of Lost Tales: Part Two, Allen & Unwin, London, 1984.

The Children of Húrin, HarperCollins, London, 2007.

Farmer Giles of Ham: Aegidii Erortus, or in the vulgar tongue, the rise of the Little Kingdom, HarperCollins, London, 1999.

Father Christmas Letters, Allen & Unwin, London, 1976.

The Fellowship of the Ring, George Allen & Unwin, London, 1954.

Finn and Hengest: the fragment and the episode, Allen & Unwin, London, 1982.

The Hobbit, HarperCollins, London, 1991.

The Lays of Beleriand, Allen & Unwin, London, 1984.

The Legend of Sigurd and Gudrún, HarperCollins, London, 2009.

The Letters of J.R.R. Tolkien (edited by Humphrey Carpenter), George Allen & Unwin, London, 1981.

The Lord of the Rings, HarperCollins, London, 2005.

The Lost Road and Other Writings, Allen & Unwin, London, 1987.

The Monsters and the Critics: and other essays, Allen & Unwin, 1983.

Morgoth's Ring: The Later Silmarillion, Part One: The Legends of Aman, HarperCollins, London, 1993.

The Peoples of Middle-earth, HarperCollins, London, 1996.

The Return of the King, George Allen & Unwin, London, 1955.

The Return of the Shadow: The History of the Lord of the Rings, Part One, Unwin Hyman, London, 1988.

Roverandom, HarperCollins, London, 2002.

Sauron Defeated: The History of the Lord of the Rings, Part Four by J.R.R. Tolkien, HarperCollins, London, 1992.

The Shaping of Middle-earth, Allen & Unwin, London, 1986.

The Silmarillion, HarperCollins, London, 1998.

Sir Gawain and the Green Knight, Pearl and Sir Orfeo (translated by J.R.R. Tolkien), Unwin, London, 1979.

Smith of Wootton Major, HarperCollins, London, 2005.

Tales from the Perilous Realm, HarperCollins, London, 1997.

The Tolkien Reader, Ballantine Books, London, 1966.

The Treason of Isengard. The History of the Lord of the Rings, Part Two, Unwin Hyman, London, 1989.

Tree and Leaf, George Allen & Unwin, London, 1964.

The Two Towers, George Allen & Unwin, London, 1954.

Unfinished Tales of Númenor and Middle-earth, Allen & Unwin, London, 1980.

The War of the Jewels: The Later Silmarillion; Part Two: The Legends of Beleriand, HarperCollins, London, 1994.

The War of the Ring: The History of the Lord of the Rings, Part Three, Unwin Hyman, London, 1990.

Works about J.R.R. Tolkien

Bored of the Rings: A Parody of J.R.R. Tolkien's The Lord of the Rings by Henry N. Beard and Douglas C. Kenney, New American Library, New York, 1969.

The Complete Guide to Middle-Earth: From The Hobbit to The Silmarillion by Robert Foster, Unwin, 1971.

The Complete Tolkien Companion by J.E.A. Tyler, Pan, London, 2002.

Essays Presented to Charles Williams edited by C.S. Lewis, Oxford Unversity Press, London, 1947.

The Evolution of Tolkien's Mythology: A Study of the History of Middle-earth by Elizabeth A. Whittingham, McFarland & Company, Jefferson, North Carolina, 2008.

J.R.R. Tolkien: A Biography by Humphrey Carpenter, Unwin, London, 1977.

J.R.R. Tolkien: A Biography by Leslie Ellen Jones, Greenwood Press, Westport, Connecticut, 2003.

J.R.R. Tolkien: Architect of the Middle Earth by Daniel Grotta-Kurska, Running Press, Philadelphia, 1976.

J.R.R. Tolkien: Artist and Illustrator by Wayne G. Hammond, HarperCollins, London, 1995.

J.R.R. Tolkien Companion and Guide by Christina Scull and Wayne G. Hammond, HarperCollins, London, 2006.

The Lord of the Rings: A Reader's Companion by Wayne G. Hammond and Christina Scull, HarperCollins, London, 2005.

The Lord of the Rings: The Making of the Movie Trilogy by Brian Sibley, HarperCollins, 2002.

The Mythology of Tolkien's Middle-earth by Ruth S. Noel, Granada, London, 1979.

Out of the Silent Planet by C.S. Lewis, HarperCollins, London, 2001.

Peter Jackson: A Filmmaker's Journey by Brian Sibley, Harper-Collins, London, 2006.

The Plants of Middle-earth: Botany and Sub-creations by Dinah Hazell, Kent State University Press, Kent, Ohio, 2006.

A Reader's Guide to the Silmarillion by Paul H. Kocher, Thames & Hudson, London, 1980.

Tolkien: A Biography by Michael White, Abacus, London, 2001.

Tolkien: A Look behind 'The Lord of the Rings' by Lin Carter, Gollancz, London, 1969.

Tolkien and The Lord of the Rings: A Guide to Middle-earth by Colin Duriez, Azure, London, 2001.

Tolkien and The Silmarillion by Clyde S. Kilby, Harold Shaw Publishers, Wheaton, Illinois, 1976.

Tolkien: Man and Myth by Joseph Pearce, HarperCollins, London, 1998.

Tolkien's Modern Middle Ages edited by Jane Chance and Alfred K. Siewers.

Tolkien on Fairy-stories edited by Verlyn Flieger and Douglas A. Anderson, HarperCollins, London, 2008.

Understanding Tolkien and the Lord of the Rings by William Ready, Warner Books, New York, 1968.

Watching the Lord of the Rings edited by Martin Baker and Ernest Mathijs, Peter Lang, New York, 2008.

INDEX